WEALTH
HAPPENS
ONE DAY
AT A TIME

WEALTH HAPPENS ONE DAY AT A TIME

365 Days to a Brighter Financial Future

Brooke M. Stephens

HarperBusiness
A Division of HarperCollins*Publishers*

This book is designed to provide readers with a general introduction to the concepts of financial planning and investing. It is not designed to be a definitive investment guide or to take the place of advice from a qualified financial planner or other professional. Given the risk involved in investing of almost any kind, there is no guarantee that the investment methods suggested in this book will be profitable. Thus, neither the publisher nor the author assume liability of any kind for any losses that may be sustained as a result of applying the methods suggested in this book, and any such liability is hereby expressly disclaimed.

Designed by Interrobang Design Studio

Library of Congress Cataloging-in-Publication Data
Stephens, Brooke M.
    Wealth happens one day at a time : 365 days to a brighter financial future / Brooke Stephens.
    p. cm.
    ISBN 0-88-730982-8
    1. Finance, Personal. 2. Investments. I. Title.
    HG179.S8346 1999
    332.024'01—dc21   99–17723

99 00 01 02 03 ❖/RRD 10 9 8 7 6 5 4 3

CONTENTS

INTRODUCTION

A FEW YEARS AGO, I BEGAN THE HABIT OF MEETING WEEKLY WITH A friend for lunch and good conversation. We would often move on to a couple of hours of "boutique browsing." To me, browsing is one step removed from window shopping: you look, feel, try on, play with, fantasize, and then put it back. Not for my friend. Invariably, she had to buy something. A scarf. A hat. Shoes. A dress. I rarely bought anything, which annoyed her greatly. One Sunday afternoon, in an antique jewelry shop, my friend insisted that I had to buy the onyx and silver earrings that I admired. For $75.00. I laughed and explained that I lose too many earrings and had much better things to do with $75.00. With a determined look in her eye, she wouldn't let me get away with that and solicited the interest of the salesclerk to pressure me.

"Name something you can do with $75.00 that would be better than treating yourself to something you obviously enjoy?" my friend smirked with an intense, challenging gaze. Now was my chance to make an unforgettable point that I hoped would help her confront her own fragile financial life. "What you see is a pair of earrings for $75.00," I said. "I see the cost of three shares of a utility stock I've been studying, which is now selling for $25.00 a share and which will pay me a 7% dividend. The stock will go up and the dividends will keep paying me income long after I've lost those earrings." My friend and the saleswoman looked at me in stunned silence.

"How did you ever do that to your mind?" she whispered. "I could never learn to think like that!"

"Yes, you can, if you want to."

Over the next few months when we met for lunch, I gave my friend little anecdotes, news clips, affirmations, stories, and examples of how to become more financially aware of the way money worked in her life. She labeled me her "money coach." A quick two- or three-minute explanation of a financial idea was all she could handle—especially on a topic that stirred up in her so many feelings of insecurity, uncertainty, and intimidation. After a few weeks, she began asking questions and looking forward to her "wealth notes," as she called them, that I would give her at each meeting. Eventually she began to act on them. She started to watch her spending, she planned a budget, organized her records, read some financial news, and bought health insurance. She had clarified her goals and started making a schedule for herself to conquer her debts and slowly examine her fears and resistance to investing. As she became more comfortable with the world of money, she started investing in mutual funds, and now she considers herself a pro at following the news on CNBC. She subscribes to several personal finance publications and has gotten a group of friends to start an investment club!

This book is the compilation of many of the short notes and examples I used to begin making her aware of how she could become financially comfortable even with a few dollars a month and the right attitude. Consider these daily pages to be little kernels of financial wisdom to be planted in your thinking process in order to point you in the right direction. This is the same "three-minute-money-message" approach that I used years later as a personal finance spokesperson on FX's *Breakfast Time* show. Three minutes a day is all it takes to read a day's entry here. Guidance, simple directives and down-to-earth, cut-to-the-chase types of information for busy people who need to know what to do but who don't have a whole lot of time to devote to finding the answers.

The book is divided into five sections.

Part One, "Wealth Consciousness," addresses how you think, feel, and behave with money. The money messages from your childhood and your social environment color all your choices. Resistance, avoidance, and self-sabotage are all learned behaviors that can be changed with effort. Once you get in touch with some of these feelings and deal with them properly, this book guides you through several steps that help you begin to reshape your thinking about money and to create a financial plan. Simple guidelines are offered for laying out goals and setting a timetable for getting what matters to you with the money you have. The process of opening an investment account, filling out the forms, signing the checks, and putting money into a mutual fund account takes about fifteen minutes. Yet when you're stuck in some of the old fears, habits, and self-defeating patterns that keep getting in your way, it can take fifteen years to get past them—if you ever do. This book is designed to help you break through the old patterns, sweep them out like the life-cluttering debris that they are, and move on to a brighter financial future. You won't know you're happy unless you define what it will take to make you happy. Setting goals is how you define some of the steps you want to take to know you have arrived there. First you have to believe that it's possible for you to get there.

Part Two, "Wealth Foundation," addresses the nuts and bolts of getting started: doing a budget or a spending plan, dealing with issues of credit and debt—cleaning up mistakes and making clear choices in the future—and finding out where to get help with financial problems. In short, this chapter deals with saving money, teaching you how to do it, and where in your life to turn in order to begin. Building a cushion for financial emergencies is the foundation that has to be established before taking on the bigger choices of risking money in the world of investing.

Part Three, "Wealth Creation," is the longest section of the book and requires the most time. It focuses on learning about building long-term assets, such as a home, and opening investment accounts to reach those goals. Investment recommendations of mutual funds are based on research provided from various financial publications, investment literature, and sources on the Internet. All fall into the $1,000-or-less category for the small investor who is totally new to the idea and doesn't want to take a great deal of risk. Individual stocks and brokerage firms are discussed and suggested as a means for guiding the average new investor through the maze of investment choices. Simple definitions are offered that avoid the jargon that frequently confuses and intimidates novice investors. The largest and most important investment choice, buying a home, is covered in detail in this section.

Part Four, "Wealth Protection," offers a basic introduction to what you should know about buying all forms of insurance and protecting the assets you are accumulating in the wealth-building process. After the sweat and effort that goes into accumulating assets, the wisest move for a financially savvy person is to protect what you have from possible loss wherever it's reasonable to do so. These simple suggestions will cut to the bottom line of how it should be done, with the least amount of aggravation if you choose to buy insurance on your own, or with the confidence of a knowledgeable buyer if you choose to work with an insurance agent.

Part Five, "Wealth Preservation," covers the issues of retirement and estate planning. Who said that retirement was the end of life? It's the next phase when you get to enjoy all you have earned and accumulated from investments. This is also the time of life when you think about whether you want to spend your children's inheritance on the beach house in the Bahamas or leave an intact estate to your grandchildren.

How to use this book is up to you.

Whether it's a New Year's resolution, a milestone birthday, a new job, or a new life situation like marriage, divorce, or the birth of a child, you know that you could be doing a better job or managing your money—but you don't have the time!

You can follow the 365-day format by reading a page a day, or you can open it at random whenever you have a moment and are curious about a specific financial topic. You can race through it in one night if you wish—how you handle it is up to you. The short entries are meant to give you the most basic information necessary to begin building your knowledge base about money. The 800 numbers, Web sites, and recommended readings will lead you to more information when you are ready to explore a topic further.

If you commit the time to reading each page, after a year, money will no longer be frightening and foreign to you. The "Review and Reassess" entries are there every fourteen to fifteen days as milestones: to show you what can be accomplished if you follow the process day by day.

Take your time! Give it a full year. Don't try to do it all at once. If you do, you'll be emotionally exhausted by your own unrealistic expectations before the end of the week and find yourself next New Year's Eve or on your next birthday in the same financial situation that you had hoped to change. To find out how simple it is, turn the page and lace on your track shoes to become a long-distance runner training for a financial marathon.

If you come away from this book with a new attitude and a comfortable grasp of the right tools for creating a practical approach to having a prosperous life, I have accomplished my goal!

Peace and prosperity,
Brooke Stephens

ONE

WEALTH
CONSCIOUSNESS

INTRODUCTION

BELIEFS AND BEHAVIOR: YES, YOU CAN!

They can conquer who believe they can.

—Virgil

Money may seem complex, confusing, boring, or impossible to understand when you read *Barron's*, *Forbes*, or *Worth* magazines. Turn off CNBC, CNN-FN, *Wall Street Week*, and *Bloomberg's Business Channel* and give yourself a break from the mind-scrambling stream of symbols at the bottom of the screen. Don't subscribe to the *Wall Street Journal* or *Investors' Business Daily* yet—one day you will, but not yet. Start with yourself. Get in touch with your outlook, your dreams, your wishes. You still have them somewhere inside you, so find them! Take a look at your pay stubs, your checkbook, your tax return. Make a list of your questions and concepts about how money works and examine the ideas you have about building wealth. Reawaken that vision of how you want your financial life to be and start making it happen. You can do this! Not overnight—not after a two-hour seminar, a crash course over a long weekend, or an afternoon reading a personal finance magazine. Like any educational process, absorbing new concepts take time. Three steps forward, two back. If you were going to run a marathon, you would give yourself at least a year of training and work at it every day. Each morning you would begin by stretching your muscles, warming up your body, and getting out on the track to build your strength and stamina for the long-haul run. You would prepare yourself for that moment when you have to test your ability and push yourself the extra distance to make the goal. It's the same with money. Building wealth begins in your head. You are going to dedicate a year to learning new concepts, testing your attitudes, exploring new ideas, and engaging in a change in your beliefs and behavior about the various aspects of money. Sit and let the new ideas work their way into your consciousness. You also have to get honest with yourself about the mistakes you've made with credit cards and irrational spending, but don't spend all your time focusing on the financial mess you may have created. Give yourself time to learn how to turn it around and start over. You can't rewrite the past, so accept it and move on. Think about each new idea for a few minutes a day, and little by little, step by step, with the right attitude you will discover that money isn't a foreign or frightening substance or an obstacle to achieving the balance and completeness you yearn for. Money is a tool that can be used in whatever way you desire and plan for. You have taken the first step toward financial empowerment by picking up this book. Congratulate yourself on being open to a new perspective and the possibility of making it work for you. Turn the page and read on to a wealthier life!

Day 1

MONEY IS . . . WHAT?

Money Is Something!

—Victor Bloc

You're going to spend an awful lot of your lifetime involved in getting, managing, using, or worrying about money, so it would be a great idea to define what it represents to you. Do you go by Webster's traditional definition of money as "a medium of exchange for goods, services, and the necessities of life?" Does it represent the power to impress, embarrass, or get even with your enemies? Would endless money mean that you could shop till you drop and never worry about bills at the end of the month? Do you see money as the measure of your daily energy output in the workplace? However you may define money, it is a fact of life that is dangerous to deny or ignore. Money must be reckoned with.

Before you go any further you must create your own definition of money and how you want it to work in your life—whether it's for spiritual, economic, material, or social uses. To your mother, it may mean a mortgage-free home. To your father, it may mean a comfortable retirement and the chance to go fishing every day without having to take on a part-time job. Your best friend may think of money as a means to start a business or enjoy unlimited travel. Your spouse may want to live on a houseboat in the Caribbean. How do you see money? Is it an enemy to be attacked and conquered or to be feared and avoided? A personal definition of money also means you understand its power and have begun to take the mystery out of how it operates in your life. Defining money is also the first step toward financial empowerment where you set the terms and conditions for having money in your life. Perhaps you see money as the path to a life of prosperity and unlimited luxury. Or you can use money to strengthen the social and financial well-being of your family; educating your children or helping a relative start a business. It may give you the political clout to make a difference in your community or do meaningful volunteer work, comfort an elderly person whom you love, or help a sick child. The meaning and purpose of money in your life must come from inside you.

Affirmation:

I have the courage to find the answers inside myself.

Action Step:

Make some notes on how you define money for yourself. This can be your working definition of money as you begin to examine your financial concepts.

Day 2

FOCUS ON THE INVISIBLES

Only poor people put on a show.

—Ashanti Proverb

Now that you have thought about what money is, consider the difference between money and wealth. One relates to your income, the other is defined by what assets you collect and how you use them. True wealth has nothing to do with an obvious display through the clothes you wear, the car you drive, or the bulge in your wallet, particularly if that bulge is a stack of credit cards that finance that conspicuous display of your power to consume material goods. True wealth comes from the self-assurance and sense of well-being that comes from knowing you have money and you have used it well. There is a certain peace of mind that comes from those aspects of having money that the rest of the world cannot see. They cannot see that your bills are paid; that your life and health insurance is sufficient to care for your family in comfort; that you tithe a portion of your income in gratitude for the blessings you have received; that you have a portfolio of comfortable investments which are growing with your income, that your retirement plan is going to reach the $1 million you will probably need to live 30 years beyond age 65. The instruments of true wealth do not need to be seen by anyone but you; the rest of the world only needs to see the confidence you project as you go about your life and the self-esteem that arises from inside you when you are comfortable and in charge of your financial life.

Affirmation:

I create a sense of wealth within myself by managing my money better.

Action Step:

Start a discussion among some friends or coworkers about how they define money and the difference between money and wealth. See how many are willing to even talk about it.

Day 3

MONEY AND YOU

Money is a terrible master but an excellent servant.

—P. T. Barnum

Every relationship takes effort, and it's no different with money. Perhaps you see money as an employee you have hired to perform a service that you require; maybe you view it as an associate who works with you to accomplish a task, or a servant waiting to do your bidding. One thing is for sure, you have to take charge and decide who is boss. As in any relationship, you must be clear about what you expect from the alliance and what you are willing to do to make it work to your benefit. The key to making any relationship successful is to be willing to grow, learn, compromise, experiment occasionally with a new point of view and even a change of attitude and behavior. It's no different with money. The best relationship is based on defining money as a tool to attain material goods as well as a means to achieve fulfillment and pleasure for yourself and others. Clarifying your relationship with money also puts you fully in charge of pursuing your life goals. Spelling out your financial expectations gives you the power to grow to be in control of your time and your life. Will your relationship with money be stressful and tense, hostile and silent, or calm and in control? You and you alone determine how much work you're willing to do to create a positive, healthy, and profitable interaction with the money that comes through your life.

Affirmation:

Wealth is worth the effort.

Action Step:

Review your daily schedule and set aside ten minutes at lunchtime or before going to sleep each night to write out the money issues you wrestle with and how they limit your growth.

Day 4

ATTITUDE ADJUSTMENT

Making my first million was easy. Convincing myself that I could do it was the hard part!

—Les Brown

Les Brown and his twin brother were born on the linoleum floor of a deserted shack in a Miami ghetto and abandoned by their mother. Because of his slow learning processes as a child, Les was deemed retarded and uneducable, and he quietly accepted those labels. Then one teacher looked at his hyperactivity and told him that if he believed he could do better and worked at it, he could make something of himself. He changed how he saw himself and has become one of the highest-paid motivational speakers in the country. If you see yourself as always being financially insecure and struggling from paycheck to paycheck, then it's pretty likely that that's all you'll ever attain in life. It pays to examine your underlying beliefs about money, wealth, and prosperity. If, somewhere inside yourself, you have come to believe that you are unlovable, undeserving, unworthy, or unable to attain any of the creature comforts that would make your life more pleasurable, then no matter how hard you work or how quickly you accomplish some of your financial goals, this negative belief system will find a way to destroy them. Attitude is the most important ingredient in changing your financial life. No amount of information, professional advice, or group support can overcome a cynical attitude about prosperity. The possibility of wealth begins in your head. Affirmations help conquer conflicting ideas that keep you at war with yourself. They change the direction of your energy to make your dreams a reality. You may not believe yourself the first time you hear yourself say or write, "I can achieve financial well-being," but cognitive therapists have proven that it takes 21 days for a new habit or thought to become a normal part of your daily consciousness. Twenty-one days isn't such a long time to change your mind when you realize that you are breaking down a life-time of concepts and habits. The thought/habit gradually takes hold and begins to influence your actions each day. What do you have to gain? A new view of yourself and your possibilities. It's only a thought—but a powerful one. Try it.

Affirmation:

I can achieve financial well-being!

Action Step:

Write this affirmation ten times a day on a page in your appointment book, your calendar, or a personal journal for twenty-one days.

Day 5

MONEY AND VALUES

Since money has as much to do with values as with Value, should some future archeologist want to get a lead on our priorities, even our character, all he or she will have to do is read our check stubs.

—F. Forrester Church, Ph.D.,
Minister, Unitarian Church of All Souls

Our values are based on our past experiences and our future expectations. The best evidence of them is in the daily paper trail created by our mail, checks, sales receipts, and cash vouchers. What would a stranger learn about you by looking through your wallet, your mailbox, and your checkbook? Cash receipts for lots of takeout meals? Movie stubs and torn-up lottery tickets? Frequent cash withdrawals from the ATM for purchases you don't remember? Does the mail carrier deliver several late payment notices to you each month? Reminders of past-due bills? What evidence of your money habits would someone who peeked in your checkbook find? Fees for bounced checks? Minimum payments to creditors? More payments for loans and bills than for savings and investments? Frequent contributions to churches and social causes or frequent purchases of shoes, clothes, and entertainment? Well, you're not alone in this behavior. Most people whose spending is out of control don't keep track of what they are doing with their money. Think about it. If you want to be proud of the evidence of your spending you have to develop new habits for handling money. You can get help to break the cycle of excess spending, but first you must pay attention to what you're doing with your money. Starting today.

Affirmation:

I respect myself enough to be honest and fair with myself.

Action Step:

Put an old shoebox on your desk or dresser and for the next three months empty your wallet/pockets/briefcase of the receipts, charge card slips, coupons, credit card receipts, debit card vouchers, traveler's checks, ATM slips, invoices, and records of bill payments by phone. Start keeping a financial journal or make notes in your daily appointment book of the ways you spend money that don't require cash. It adds up!

Day 6

GETTING STARTED

Just Do It!

—Nike slogan

You don't need a Ph.D. in Boolean algebra, an MBA from Wharton, or a mind-numbing software program to keep track of your money. You need about $5 for a calculator, 89 cents for a pocket notebook, and $1.39 for a decent ball point pen. Write down your expenses each day—in ink so you can't lie to yourself about the double cappuccino at Starbucks that pushed you $7.50 over your budget for the week! Become a "dollar detective" in your own life for a few days, only you're the sleuth *and* the subject under surveillance. Don't be judgmental with yourself yet. This exercise is about getting to know yourself and your financial values. How many trips do you make to the ATM? How much do you take out? $50? $100? What do you do with that cash? Eat out? Order pizza for dinner? Go grocery shopping? Pay for a car repair? How did you spend the cash? Magazines? Coffee and Danish? Haircuts? Newspapers? Gum? Snacks? Dry cleaning? Write it in your notebook or jot it down on your appointment calendar. Just make sure you have a system for keeping track of it all. Knowing where your money goes is a huge step toward taking control. This also becomes an ongoing process that will keep you aware of what you're doing with your money. By the way, don't start this on a Monday morning. Too many resolutions that begin on Monday usually crash by Thursday. Try starting it on Thursday or Friday, the two paycheck days.

Affirmation:

I will analyze my money habits and learn from them.

Action Step:

Stop at any drugstore or stationery store to buy what you need to get started. Devote at least two weeks to recording all your cash activities, then ask yourself what you could do differently.

Day 7

GETTING PAST THE FEAR

It's a kind of spiritual snobbery that makes people think they can be happy without money.

—Albert Camus

All of us have hated money at one time or another. We cursed and condemned its power, wished we could function without it, and swore the world would be a better place if money didn't exist. Some people become "money monks," declaring that money is evil and poverty is noble and they are "morally and spiritually superior" since their life goals have nothing to do with "filthy lucre." They believe they will "gain their reward in heaven" but constantly ask for loans, handouts, or donations to support their noble causes. A truly spiritual person is quite aware of the power of money. Mother Teresa was well aware of how many children and dying patients she could feed and care for with the $1 million Nobel Peace Prize.

Behind all the posturing and well-crafted reasons not to take money seriously often lurks deep-seated fears. Fear of success. Fear of failure. Fear of being responsible for oneself. The fear that surrounds money, like any taboo subject, paralyzes us from becoming financially responsible beings. As long as we cling to fear, we reject prosperity. Fear can be eliminated by developing a different view of money.

Affirmation:

I accept money into my life without fear or shame.

Action Step:

Make a list of charities that you admire and donate $10 a month to them. Contact http://www.guidestar.org for a free copy of *The Guide for the Responsible Donor.*

Day 8

MONEY MESSAGES

By taking stock of all the past influences on your money life, you will become more and more detached from their powerful voices. This will enable you to relate to money as you alone would choose to do, in a way that reflects your fundamental values.

—Olivia Mellan

Rosemary G. is a 42-year-old bookkeeper in a construction company in Indianapolis, Indiana, and she is being badgered by her accountant to open a Roth IRA, add money to the company SEP plan, and take out a tax-deferred annuity because she has no retirement savings. She resists his input and is thinking of finding another tax preparer to avoid listening to his lecture again. Now the nine women in her book club are talking about becoming an investment club, and Rosemary is the only one who has voted against the idea. All the "money talk" makes her anxious, nervous, and uncomfortable, yet she doesn't understand why. Money messages are so deeply ingrained in us from childhood and frequently trigger painful emotional reactions. What did your parents tell you about money? Did they talk openly about it at all? How many negative statements did you hear as a child, when you asked for an extra dollar or two?

"Money doesn't grow on trees!" or "Do you think I'm made of money?" These stress-inducing aphorisms have become encoded in our heads and control our daily behavior, yet we are barely aware of their influence. We may earn more and be more educated than our parents, but many of us are still replaying their disapproving messages. It's time to stop the old tapes and record a different message for your financial well-being. Maybe your parents didn't invest in mutual funds, but how do you know they wouldn't have if they had known about them? Getting unstuck takes time. You can turn your financial life around, but it means being willing to explore ideas and concepts that your parents may never have heard of. That doesn't make them wrong or impossible. You may not attain wealth beyond your dreams within the next year, but you'll be much closer to it if you get past being stuck in the same old nonproductive, financially unpromising place that you were in before. New financial ideas and new behavior that will encourage wealth begin in your head.

Affirmation:

I am not trapped or limited by the money attitudes of others.

Action Step:

Sit for a moment and write down all the negative comments you heard about money while growing up. Ask yourself how many of these concepts and attitudes you still share today. Then rewrite each negative comment as a positive statement.

Day 9

BELIEFS BECOME BEHAVIOR

We are what we think. All that we are arises with our thoughts.
And with our thoughts, we make our world.

—Gautama Buddha

If you grew up thinking that money was sinful and dirty, that people who wanted it were spiritually unhealthy, that talking about money was a social taboo, then your adult behavior will exhibit these beliefs. You probably deal with your finances by denying your debts, shoving aside the 401(k) brochures in your desk and never reading them, and assuming that all the financial talk shows and stock market news reports don't apply to you. You also probably don't think about the terms of your health and life insurance or any other form of financial obligation until it becomes a crisis. You can continue to live successfully in today's world with those attitudes for a while, but sooner or later, something's going to happen and you won't be able to use the excuse, "Gee, I didn't know." If talking about 401(k) plans, writing wills, or setting up an investment plan gives you an anxiety attack, then you will need to put some effort into working through your feelings if you want your life to develop financially over the next decade. Even the vaguest dream of taking a new path in your life—be it relocating to another city, going back to graduate school, or implementing a career change—has a financial reality connected to it.

Affirmation:

I can change my financial attitude and perception of how money can be used for my well-being and for others.

Action Step:

Make a list of everything you own. On the left side of a sheet of paper write out all of it, from cash and savings in the bank, to IRAs, insurance policies, and stocks or bonds. Include your car, clothes, hobby equipment, furniture, real estate—all of it. These are your assets. Put a financial value next to each item and total it up. Now on the right side of the page, make a list of debts, your liabilities, and see what the total is. Which list is larger? If your asset list is higher in value, congratulate yourself! If your debts are greater, think about how you want to change them. This is your net worth statement. Your long-term, consistent goal in life is to always increase the total on the left side of the page and decrease the amount of debt on the right side of the page.

EXCUSES, FEARS, AND WORRY

He [she] who is good at excuses is seldom good at anything else.

—Sallie Adams Brooks

It can be quite a big psychological challenge to confront all the preconceptions, feelings, and passionate reactions that we have to money, but guess what? These emotional anxieties are all in your head. Above all else, you must remember one thing: Money is totally innocent. It's not out to get you. Money does not create enmity and jealousy, petty hostilities, and shallow values. It may be comforting for a moment to blame money but, bottom line, we are the real enemy. Money brings no emotional baggage to the daily process of earning, spending, saving, and investing. Have you ever heard someone say, "I'm not into money?" That's like saying, "I'm not into breathing, bathing, eating, or working." You can't have a life without these actions, nor can you get through life without money. Money is simply another way of keeping score of how well you're doing with your life's activities. Accepting money for what it can offer is the first step toward being a financially responsible adult.

Affirmation:

I develop mastery over money and how I use it by learning more each day about how to use it better.

Action Step:

List your daily activities that don't have a money-related component. Then list the ones that do and see which list is longer. Be honest with yourself and try to explain how important money is to you for accomplishing your goals.

Day 11

THE ROAD TO WEALTH IS PAVED WITH KNOWLEDGE

Only fools despise wisdom and discipline.

—Proverbs 1:7

With today's information resources, your first stop should be the nearest library. Most public libraries provide free access to the Internet, scads of personal finance magazines, investment newsletters, and books at every level of interest. Newsletters on money matters fill the shelves. Free brochures from the federal government on insurance, investing, taxes, and retirement fill the file cabinets. You can tackle a *Morningstar* report on a blue chip mutual fund you heard about on CNBC, or look for a Standard and Poor's report on your snack or beverage company, like Pepsi or McDonald's. In addition to absorbing all those calories, you could also be earning quarterly dividends if you owned a few shares of that stock. When you had to write term papers in school you spent a lot of time in the library: Why not apply those same research skills to learning about money? Watch your mind and your world begin to open up to a new vision of stretching your dollars and your paycheck. Your questions about your financial situation won't get answered if you don't make the effort to find another way to face them.

Affirmation:

I learn information that empowers me to change my financial reality.

Action Step:

Spend an hour in the personal finance section of the public library looking at the books available to help you learn to manage your money.

Day 12

MONEY AND EMOTIONS

Money is a topic that activates shame for everyone. When you are ashamed about money, no amount seems right . . . money is a whole lot more subjective and emotional than is commonly believed.

—Phil Laut

Adam Hochschild, cofounder of *Mother Jones* magazine, grew up in the proverbial lap of luxury and was the heir to a huge estate and a tremendous fortune earned in mining and minerals over several decades. During the sixties, Adam discovered that the source of his fortune was the exploitation of Third World workers in Africa and Asia. He was so humiliated that he rejected his family and wealth and created a completely different life for himself as a journalist. After the death of his parents, Adam gave away most of the money to social causes. Based on what we have learned from our family, friends, peers, society, school, or church, we see money as either a blessing or a stigma; something to use for empowerment or to be secretly coveted and hated at the same time. Emotional reactions to money are often very negative and very powerful, and can include shame, fear, jealousy, greed, worry, anger, and anxiety. Yet in the heat of our emotions, we forget two major things: (1) Money doesn't have any feelings—people do. We approach buying insurance, signing a mortgage, and investing in the stock market with the attitudes and beliefs we learned about money as children—usually with dread, anxiety, and misgivings. Filling out the application and signing the check takes about ten minutes, but dealing effectively with the emotions attached to facing the facts, the math, the heavy-duty legal documents and big decisions, can take ten years. (2) Money is a tool. It can be used to attain specific goals for you and for people that you touch. Adam Hochschild decided not to avoid his fortune and feel guilty about it, but to make positive and altruistic use of it that fit his ideals for social change. He created a foundation for political and environmental change. The family's country estate has been converted into an artists' colony for writers and painters, and a retreat center where social and political activists can conduct planning conferences.

Affirmation:

I know that I can use money for many good purposes in my life.

Action Step:

Find one charity that you want to support and begin sending regular contributions of $10 a month to it.

Day 13

WATCH YOURSELF

We are what we repeatedly do. Excellence then is not an act but a habit.

—Aristotle

Jennifer D. uses her monthly commuter card to take the train to work each morning. She stops at the ATM to make a funds transfer to pay her mortgage. At work she logs on to her computer and orders a new thriller at Amazon.com. During lunch, she picks up a prescription at the pharmacy and makes her copayment with her Visa card. On the way home, she writes a check at the grocery store and gives her son a book of vouchers for his school lunch, which she pays for as a part of his quarterly tuition bill. She fills the tank in her car and pays with her gas card, picks up her daughter at the babysitters' play group and gives the woman a money order for next week's activities. If you asked Jennifer how much money she spent that day, she would only remember the $1.75 cash for a newspaper and cup of coffee on her way into the office, and the $5 for a tuna sandwich and soda at lunch. Money flows through your life in several ways but you often don't notice it. Before you can change a habit you have to know what it is! Sure, you can recite the rent or mortgage payment in your sleep. Not to mention the car loan, the student loan, and the monthly cost of health insurance. But these expenses are usually less than half your monthly income (or they should be!). You have an idea what the telephone and utility bills usually are (or you should!), but the rest is a mystery. In the computerized world of electronic money, credit cards, checks, and noncash payments, we spend without thinking because we don't see cash going through our fingers. A recent merchandising study proved that people who shop with credit cards spend 25 percent more than people who use only cash. Stop. Watch yourself.

Affirmation:

Watching my spending is the first step toward empowering myself financially.

Action Step:

Pay all your daily expenses for one week with cash. Make a mental list of how many times you change your mind about buying something.

Day 14

SPIRITUAL MATERIALISM

Money can't buy happiness but then, happiness can't buy money either.

—Sir Joseph Goldsmith

God never intended that we had to be poor to be faithful, yet we delude ourselves into thinking that money isn't important and we would all be happier without it—but don't try to convince a beggar or a hungry child with that argument. A truly spiritual person sees that money can be used for good or ill. Hospitals and hungry children require cash, not platitudes about the evils of money. The confusion of how money should be used as an example of our commitment to faith and charity comes from within us; it is not created by money itself. Churches, temples, synagogues, and other holy places all require lots of money to build and maintain. Stained glass windows, velvet throne chairs, golden candelabra, marble altars, and jewel-encrusted robes all come with a price tag. However, imagine how many children could be fed, clothed, sheltered, and educated with the cost of one stained glass window. Money constantly offers these choices. It's within your own power to make a positive use of money and direct it toward a good purpose in the world around you.

Action Step:

If you want to investigate a charity call the National Charities Information Bureau at 212–929–6300.

Day 15

WORRY, WONDER, OR PLAN?

My life seems like one long obstacle course, with me as the chief obstacle.

—Jack Paar

When you were a kid, I'm sure you learned to sing the Jiminy Cricket song, "When You Wish upon a Star" from *Pinocchio*. In the world of money, wishing alone will not make your dreams come true. Yet that's how most people choose to address their financial lives. (1) They worry about what will happen, (2) look for someone to blame because nothing is happening, or (3) like the ostrich, keep their heads in the sand and hope the problem is gone when they look up again. None of these choices leads to anything but frustration, and lack of financial growth. The only choice that works is planning.

Creating prosperity and abundance in your life starts with believing that a change in your behavior and your perspective can make something different happen for you. Half the effort goes into getting up and doing something new and different from how you've been handling things until now. Remember, the definition of insanity is "doing the same thing and expecting different results." The choice is always in your hands and in your head. Which one do you want to do? Worry, wonder, or plan?

Affirmation:

I can make something positive happen today.

Action Step:

Identify one daily habit related to money that you can change.

Day 16

FIND THE TIME!

Procrastination is the thief of time.

—Edward Young

When dealing with money we often look for any excuse to avoid the issue. But aren't you worth fifteen minutes a week to gain a better understanding of new financial opportunities that await you? Make an appointment with yourself just as you would for a haircut, a manicure, a trip to the gym, or a deadline at work. Put it on your calendar as a separate time from "bill paying." Be firm with yourself and stick to it. What time is good for you? Thursday night before your favorite hospital or cop show? Saturday morning while doing the laundry? Ignore the crossword puzzle and look at the personal finance column in the newspaper you brought along. Set aside an evening, perhaps Sunday night; put on some relaxing music and turn off the phone. Read that article you clipped from the newspaper. Watch a personal finance show on CNBC or CNN-FN, all of which have hourly five-minute segments on topics from credit cards to car leasing. One of them will relate to some aspect of your life. Each week as you become more comfortable with new financial concepts, you will expand the time and look forward to it.

Affirmation:

I deserve to take a moment out of each week to get my financial life in order.

Action Step:

Look in your appointment book and block out at least fifteen minutes a week to browse through a personal finance magazine, read a news article, or brochure about investing.

Day 17

CREATING MORE MONEY IN YOUR LIFE

I'd like to live like a poor man with lots of money.

—Pablo Picasso

Maybe one of the reasons you avoid the topic of money is that you earn so little! Whatever your current income, it can always be better. If you're not earning enough to support your lifestyle and plan a financial future, maybe you need to do a personal reassessment of your potential career and income prospects. Check with a career counselor to determine your worth. Think about the last time you got a raise or had a salary review. It isn't being disloyal to your boss or your company to go out into the job market and shop around. With all the corporate mergers that have occurred, what usually follows are downsizing, layoffs, cutbacks that can leave you wondering about your future paycheck. Your first loyalty should be to working for yourself—even if you're on someone else's payroll for now. Changes in job prospects and starting a part-time business on the side for greater income are possible for everyone. Consider it your duty to yourself to make the most of your income prospects. Doesn't your company always explore expanding into new markets?

Affirmation:

I will focus on having a job or being self-employed in a way that pays well and provides daily satisfaction.

Action Step:

Read the classified ads in the Sunday paper, the *National Business Weekly,* and any professional publications that list job openings to get an idea what you're worth. Make an appointment with a career counselor or explore options for a part-time job or small business opportunity.

Day 18

"TO HAVE SOMETHING"

The trick to money is having some!

—Stuart Wilde

Like most 20-somethings, Bridgette T., a 28-year-old freelance graphics designer from Austin, Texas, struggled to keep her business afloat and barely managed to hold on from month to month. "Financial planning" couldn't possibly apply to her life. She was talented but had no savings and long-term goals like retirement. One afternoon, she found herself listening to a financial radio talk show that talked about "The Rule of 72" (see Day 203) and how long it took for money to grow. That two-hour discussion made her think about how the pressure of debt and money worries got in the way of her creativity. Each afternoon, she tuned in again, eagerly listening to questions and stories from callers—many expressed her own doubts and uncertainty about investing. After a month, Bridgette realized that investing wasn't as frightening as she thought, and she would have to redirect her focus if she wanted to "have something" one day. An old car, her small apartment, her college wardrobe, and credit card debt were all she had, but each afternoon people talked about investing small amounts in mutual funds. She scribbled the names of books that were mentioned and began reading. It took two years to get the courage to meet with a financial consultant and convince herself that she could get into the rhythm of adding investing to her daily life.

Affirmation:

Wherever I am in my life, I can begin learning about saving and investing.

Find a local financial radio talk show or visit the Web site for *Sound Money,* an excellent nationally syndicated financial talk show on National Public Radio stations, at http://www.money.npr.org.

Day 19

PRIORITIES

Life is what happens to you while you're busy making other plans.

—John Lennon

Financial planning is life planning. You can't separate finances from your daily activities, whether you are focused on short-term needs or long-term fantasies. You can deal with your financial life in two ways: you can *react* or you can *initiate.* Suppose your car is about to fall apart and you need a new one. Do you wait for the old one to end up in the junkyard before you think about getting another or wait until it's towed away for good? Doing some homework can save 20–30 percent and lots of aggravation and get you an affordable deal. If you opt not to take the initiative and plan for the inevitable—and "plan" is the operative word here—you'll be surprised at how much aggravation you avoid and how much you'll save. It doesn't matter if you're a teenager or in middle age—you always need to plan how to use your money. When Alice fell down the rabbit hole in Wonderland the Mad Hatter asked her where she wanted to go, her reply was "I have no idea." The Mad Hatter said, then it didn't matter where she ended up. The lesson is clear: When you have no plan for your life, chances are you'll end up in a place you never wanted to be. Financial awareness is necessary for making sensible plans, but it takes more. A spiritual and moral commitment to yourself and the people who matter to you is vital. Planning is about allocating and designating funds for specific goals and objectives—until you do, you're sailing in uncharted waters.

Affirmation:

I will learn to put order to my long-term financial responsibilities.

Action Step:

Write it down—where you are, and what you want in life.

Day 20

"POOR ME"

Your financial health is a function of the attitudes you have learned and taught yourself about money over the years.

—Albert Ellis, Ph.D.

At 68, Christine B. is a widowed grandmother who recently retired after 38 years of clerical work in a real estate office. She spends most of her $412 pension check and her $463 Social Security check on gifts for her grandchildren. Christine has no savings, and assumes that her children and grandchildren will take care of her. Her actions are understandable when you look at who she is. Women, particularly, have been conditioned to believe that thinking of themselves is self-centered and insensitive to the people around them. And despite women's growing earning power, the issue of unequal pay for working women is evident now as the average retired woman has a monthly pension income of $452, 57 percent of the $785 collected by the average retired man. Women live about seven years longer than men, so they need to pay closer attention to wealth building. If Christine had known more about money and retirement planning, she would have made better choices and not become a financial burden to her family.

Affirmation:

I can learn how to take care of myself financially.

Action Step:

Use your financial journal and chart of your current living expenses to determine what your fixed expenses are, such as rent/ mortgage, insurance premiums, and loan payments. Make a comparison of how much these have increased over the last two or three years. Imagine how much they will be in ten years if they increase 2 percent a year and your income stays the same. Make an appointment with the benefits counselor to discuss the company retirement plan.

Day 21

MONEY IS A LIFETIME ISSUE

Youth is the time of getting, middle age of improving, and old age of spending.

—Anne Bradstreet

You are a financial being from the day you were born but you don't become fully conscious of it until you reach adulthood. There is never a time in your adult life when money doesn't affect your plans and decisions about how to accumulate wealth. At 22, you need to establish credit, begin developing a good career, open a savings account, put a few dollars in the 401(k) plan, and save to buy a house or apartment. If you get married and babies come, you must get life insurance. When the next baby comes, you'll need more insurance, and when that baby is walking you have to think about buying a bigger house and how you'll pay for your children to go to college. If one parent drops out of the work force to care for the children, you need to make up for that lost income. Divorce or health crises will eat up money faster than you can imagine, but let's say you've managed to stay healthy, married, and relatively free of financial worries. You're not off the hook, because it's time to think about retirement. At a time when more and more Americans are living past 80, you've got to plan for the future, and the only realistic way to do it is through savings and investments. You don't just want to live a long time without leaving money to your children or charities, do you? From the moment you're an adult you will be facing the next stage in life, and eventually beyond life, so it's never too early to plan and make yourself financial responsible.

Action Step:

Pick up a copy of *Live Long and Profit: Wealth-building Strategies for Every Stage of Your Life* (Dearborn, 1997) by Kay R. Shirley. It is an excellent guide to understanding the financial stages of life and what should happen for each group from age 22 to age 82. The Web site at http://www.iVillage/com/money also has financial planning recommendations by age group.

Day 22

REVIEW AND REASSESS

Go back and review your spending diary/financial journal for the past few weeks. By now you should have kept all your receipts for at least a week and you are more aware of your spending habits than you were last month. Use the record you have so far to start making a chart of your spending priorities. How many times did you change your mind about making a purchase when you only had cash available? If you still haven't gotten past square one, then go back and reread the first seven days here. If you are doing more than just turning the pages, you have moved forward; congratulate yourself and

turn the page to the next new money insight that will help you build
your own path to financial freedom and well-being. Remember, if
you do nothing, then nothing will happen.

Day 23

VISION

If you can conceive it, you can achieve it.

—Jesse Jackson

Talk to any successful person from Rosie O'Donnell to Tiger
Woods or former President Jimmy Carter, and they will tell you that
long before they became famous, they could visualize their goal in
their mind's eye, long before they knew how they would get there.
It's the same with money. If your financial image of yourself is one of
spending the rest of your life living from paycheck to paycheck,
strung out on credit card debt, robbing Peter to pay Paul, never having any savings, and believing that investing isn't for you, then
you're predicting your lifelong relationship with money. Before you
begin learning the nuts and bolts of stocks and bonds, life insurance,
your 401(k) plan and adjustable vs. fixed mortgages, you need a "gut
feeling" that it is possible for you to overcome your current financial
problems. The old-fashioned gut feeling is a signal from inside that
wealth can work for you, too—if you allow it. Your thoughts are a
form of your life energy that directs your actions each day. If you can
picture yourself acquiring the abundance that you seek, then that
vision will begin to direct your actions, regardless of what obstacles
may appear in your life. It doesn't matter that you don't know the
details of how to make it happen. The means to that end will appear
once you commit yourself to the possibility. Have you read or heard
any news stories about people who started like you did, without a
clue about money or investing, but were able to achieve remarkable

success? Then you know that it's possible to reach the goal with a clear vision. Success and financial security begin in your head.

Affirmation:

Today I will begin seeing myself as a financially secure person.

Action Step:

Go to the library or bookstore and start reading at least one biography of someone you admire who has achieved the kind of success you are seeking: Helen Keller, Donald Trump, Oprah Winfrey, Famous Amos, Thomas Edison, or John D. Rockefeller—anyone you admire.

Day 24

CHANGE YOUR THOUGHTS AND CHANGE YOUR WEALTH

Change your focus, you'll change your future.

—Oprah Winfrey

Brian L., the youngest of three brothers from Seattle, was born just when his parents' small business had begun to fail. His older brothers recalled a childhood full of material possessions, prosperous parents, and generous allowances. Brian only remembers hand-me-down clothes and bag lunches at school. When he complained, his mother told him it wasn't right to think of himself first—"You mustn't be selfish" was her mantra—so Brian grew up thinking he didn't deserve to have money. He worked low-level jobs, even though he was intelligent and far from lazy, and his employers encouraged him to spread his wings. He spent every penny he earned, scoffing at the idea of saving even a part of his salary, because what good would it do? "I'm not cut out to succeed in life, I come from poor people" was his self-denigrating little joke, along with his comments about not getting caught up in the money race. His poor-but-happy line forced him to borrow constantly from friends before payday rolled around, or when a wisdom tooth became impacted and—surprise!—he had no insurance for dental care. It is never selfish to want to have enough money to care for yourself. As an adult, if you don't put yourself first, who will? By feeling that he didn't deserve to have money, Brian cast himself right back into a childlike dependency. If you approach money with the belief that you don't deserve to have it or you're selfish to want it, you'll be poor and bewildered forever. Wanting money is neither selfish nor greedy. It is simply the only realistic approach to living in the world like a grown-up.

Affirmation:

I am not my parents. I have more opportunities and a brighter future than they did.

Action Step:

Ask three friends if they own stocks, bonds, or mutual funds. Begin investigating how you would go about opening a brokerage account.

Day 25

PUT IT ON PAPER

Anytime you see someone more successful that you are, they are doing something you aren't.

—Malcolm X

Ask some people what their goal is and they'll say, "I want to be rich!" This is not a goal but a fantasy, like winning the lottery or having the Easter Bunny slip you a fortune. Money by itself is no goal—you have to know what you want to do with it. Do you postpone the idea of money management because it sounds so dull and boring? Do you secretly think a "white knight" will rescue you from the financial doldrums, or your Uncle Charlie will remember you in the will? (Something to think about: If you are financially irresponsible, Uncle Charlie might not want to leave his hard-earned cash to someone who'll just squander it.) Your goal should be to become financially independent. Examples of your short-term goals should be to pay off your credit cards, buy a decent used car (paying in cash!), and attend a jazz festival on vacation, which you also pay for with cash. Whatever the goal, write it down. Then write down your medium-term goals——going back to school, buying a condo in two to five years, getting a better job. Finally, make a list of long-term goals to be accomplished in ten years' time, whether it's buying a vacation home or starting a greeting card business. Writing it all down makes it more real and give you an idea of what you could accomplish if you took money management more seriously. It doesn't seem so boring if you can visualize the rewards you'll earn.

Action Step:

Write down a long-term goal you've never mentioned to anyone for fear of seeming unrealistic.

Day 26

FEARING PROSPERITY

Without money this world is not fit to live in.

—Talmud

In the western states of India, the Hindu New Year, called Diwali, comes in the fall and honors Lakshmi, the goddess of prosperity and abundance. The event is celebrated by cleaning the house, buying new clothes, and preparing a scrumptious meal. In the evening, each family lights lots of candles, rings prayer bells, and chants special mantras to attract the spirit of Lakshmi. Everyone who attends the celebration is expected to bring a gift of fruit, flowers, or a pot-luck dish to be shared among the group. The lights are lit and a special tray offering some of the gifts is brought forward by the youngest female member of the family. The special "Lakshmi Puja" prayer is repeated three times by everyone in unison. The first prayer is for the goddess to take away all your sins; the second repetition asks the goddess to bless you and your loved ones with material wealth and abundance for the coming year; the third is for the attainment of spiritual grace and fulfillment in this life. After the prayers, each person is allowed to make one wish for health, wealth, and grace, invoking Lakshmi to bless them with a prosperous future and asking her to come and live in their homes and hearts for the coming year. This ritual belongs to a heritage and tradition that is honest and open to the idea of having wealth—unlike Western religious practice. According to Hindu thinking, wealth is attracted to those who appreciate it and what it can offer. Too often, we go through the motions of asking, praying, and begging for abundance without being clear or sincere about what we are seeking. What is the abundance we pray for? An abundance of poverty? An abundance of fear? Too often our behavior is out of line with our prayers. Having wealth might also mean a change in lifestyle and outlook that many of us are not yet ready to embrace. The first step is to open your mind and your heart before you open your wallet. How open is your heart to the concept of prosperity?

Affirmation:

I welcome money into my life with open arms and an open heart.

Action Step:

Write your own prayer for abundance and use it every day.

Day 27

A PUBLIC EDUCATION

If a man [or woman] empties his purse into his head, no man can take that away from him. An investment in knowledge always pays the best interest.

—Ben Franklin

Learning about money has never been easier. There are television talk shows that tell you how to get a mortgage or pick a mutual fund. Radio call-in shows discuss retirement plans and credit card problems. Check out your local newspaper or the corner magazine stand—they are all full of financial publications, with numerous commentators, articles, and advice columns that have mushroomed in popularity in the last twenty years. The public air waves and the public library now offer the chance to learn anything and everything you could ever hope to about mutual funds, Roth IRAs, variable annuities, types of stockbrokers, the hidden costs of cash advances on credit cards, mortgage rates, interest rates on CDs and savings accounts, where to find the best money market funds for a short-term savings account, and why the stock market is moving the way it is. The only way to avoid becoming financially literate in today's information age is to avoid paying attention. Just turn on your radio or television. Or start with your daily newspaper.

Action Step:

Pick up your daily newspaper and scan through the business section every day for the next month. Clip and save any articles on money issues that apply to you and your special financial interests.

Day 28

CARNEGIE'S ZEAL

Watch the costs, and the profits will take care of themselves.

—Andrew Carnegie

If you think that you need an MBA degree to become wealthy and powerful, think again. Visit any small town in America that was established before 1910 and you will notice that all the public libraries look alike. Each of these structures was the gift of one man who had a passion for reading and was quite disappointed in his lack of education. Andrew Carnegie firmly believed that if people could read they could learn anything they wanted to learn. He started in a cotton factory for $1.20 a week and worked at night for Western Union delivering telegrams in Pittsburgh until he got a job on the railroad and used the time on the long trips to read. Railroads were the most successful transportation business at that time, so Carnegie invested his savings in iron, which was needed to build railroad bridges. He soon learned that steel was superior to iron and went to work for a steel manufacturer. He eventually created his own company, which became U.S. Steel, near his hometown of Pittsburgh. U.S. Steel soon outstripped Great Britain in supplying steel to the world. In 1901, Carnegie sold U.S. Steel to J. P. Morgan for $400 million. Carnegie was unique as a magnate because he remembered his days as a struggling laborer and plowed $5 million a year back into a pension fund and health benefits for his workers, which was unheard of at that time. Carnegie firmly believed that wealth should be used for public good. After the sale of U.S. Steel he set up Carnegie-Mellon University and created the Carnegie Institute with an endowment of $350 million. Carnegie single-handedly created more than 2,800 public libraries in the United States and the United Kingdom before his death in 1919.

Affirmation:

I am becoming more positive about having money as I increase my knowledge about my wealth potential.

Action Step:

Pick up a copy of *Nine Steps to Financial Freedom* by Suze Orman the next time you're in the library.

Day 29

REALITY CHECK!

With money in your pocket, you are wise and you are handsome and you sing well, too.

—Yiddish Proverb

Isn't it amazing how we get caught up in the commercialism fantasies of our culture and start believing the crazy things about what money can do for us? Consider the toothpaste commercial that implies that we will get a better job if we buy that brand; or the sports car ad that makes every man believe that the cute blond sprawled across the hood comes with the car if he buys it in red! We must learn to laugh at ourselves when we become too serious or irrational about money. It's wonderful to dream about new possibilities and visualize new strategies but it also helps to stay grounded in reality. No matter how much money you have, you can't buy Michael Jordan's hook shot, sing like Barbra Streisand, or dance like Fred and Ginger. Having a few million dollars won't guarantee a seat in heaven or make up for the pain and rejection you felt after not getting invited to a classmate's birthday party when you were in sixth grade, but it will give you the flexibility to make choices that can add more comfort and freedom to your lifestyle as you become older. It will make it possible to quit a lousy job, buy that beach condo in Martinique, or give your daughter a wonderful wedding. Money choices must be grounded in your own version of reality—not what Madison Avenue wants you to believe are the trappings of a good life.

Affirmation:

I will keep a balanced perspective on money and how to use it wisely in my life.

Action Step:

Make a list of the unrealistic fantasies that get in the way of facing your true financial situation. After you review it, burn it!

Day 30

FINANCIAL STEWARDSHIP

It is easier for a camel to go through the eye of a needle, than for a rich man to enter into the kingdom of God.

—Matthew 19:24

This Bible verse has often been cited to justify a negative attitude toward the idea of building wealth. But where in the Bible does it say anything about God wanting us to be poor and deprived? Perhaps if you begin to look upon the money that comes through your hands as a God-given responsibility, you will be more careful about how you use it and more committed to learning about tithing, saving, investing, and long-term planning. The blessings of wealth and abundance begin when we demonstrate to God that we can handle the money that comes to us with gratitude, respect, and appreciation for each and every penny. If we cannot show that we understand the power of money then perhaps God has decided that we aren't yet ready to have more. Imagine how you would parent a child who wastes the allowance that you give her. Would you continue to provide more and more cash to support such irresponsibility? Probably not. We must display a humble respect for the money that we have with the understanding that it is on temporary loan to us from a Higher Power.

Affirmation:

I will fulfill my commitment to God by accepting the money that passes through my life as a blessing, and by managing it with care and respect.

Day 31

THE "LUCK" MYTH

I got rich because I always made my own lucky breaks.

—Uncle Scrooge McDuck

Luck doesn't usually happen by accident. Like the actress or rock star who struggles for ten years and suddenly becomes an "overnight sensation," building wealth requires years of commitment on the path to prosperity. Building a fortune requires constant studying, asking questions, learning, exploring opportunities, and the basic discipline to put away a few dollars every day or every week. "Lucky" people are always exploring new options, measuring risks, planning strategies, and studying and working for new opportunities to make something happen. When the "big break" suddenly appears for lucky people, they are ready to roll.

Affirmation:

I will prepare myself for my "lucky break" with hard work and discipline.

Action Step:

Pick up a copy of *Money* magazine from the newsstand for your commuter reading next week. Mark all the articles that offer information that you can immediately apply to your life. Find the "Yields and Rates" page that gives a list of money market funds that will pay higher interest on your savings.

Day 32

THE INFORMATION GOLD MINE

You pays your money and you takes your choice.

—Punch magazine

You've already made an important investment in your financial education, and you did it with your tax dollars. It's your library card. A trip to the library can be enlightening and profitable when you discover how many different kinds of books, magazines, newspapers, and newsletters it has devoted to money. Libraries offer free access to the Internet for learning about everything from mortgages to money market funds. Want to find out who makes the best refrigerator in your price range? Look in *Consumer Reports*. Heard about a stock or a mutual fund that sounds interesting? Ask the librarian to show you how to use *Morningstar Mutual Fund Reports* or *Value Line*. You want to know about mortgage rates in another city where you may be relocating? Check out http://www.homeshark.com on the Internet. Not sure how the new Roth IRA works? Pick up the recent copy of *Fortune* magazine entirely devoted to retirement planning. Wondering about the cost of college and how to get a scholarship? Check out a copy of the *College Costs and Financial Aid Handbook* published each year by the College Board Guidance Publishing Company. Every library has one, along with oodles of other directories that can enlighten you about every aspect of money that you can imagine. Most libraries have free access to the Internet, so if you don't have a computer available to you, the reference department of most libraries, large and small, can introduce you to the information superhighway.

Action Step:

Make a list of ten questions you have about money—no matter how small or silly you may think they are—and go to the library and ask for help on how to look up the answers.

Day 33

THE MATH HANG-UP

Nothing has changed but my attitude, therefore, everything has changed.

—Anthony DeMello

If you're turned off by the thought of dealing with all those numbers, let's take a simple look at what you really need to know to play the wealth-building game. Can you tell if 12 is a larger number than 8? How much is 5 times 9? What is 48 divided by 6? What is 5 percent of 50? All the steps you need to know to do money management are the same basic arithmetic skills that you learned by the time you reached fifth grade—adding, subtracting, multiplying, and dividing, with a few fractions thrown in, and percentages that look more complicated than they are. No complicated formulas or spreadsheets. Just simple arithmetic.

Action Step:

If you don't already have one, spend $5 and get a calculator, then order a copy of an excellent booklet published by the Federal Reserve of New York, "The Arithmetic of Interest Rates," which explains how compound interest is computed. Order free copies from: Public Information Office, Federal Reserve Bank, 33 Liberty Street, New York, NY 10045.

Day 34

50 CENTS A DAY

You can make the best investment in your financial education Monday through Friday at your newsstand. It's the green "Money" section of the *USA Today* newspaper. It has some of the best weekly columnists and information, and is written for the true novice to the world of money and investing. Each Friday, the "Money" section has a special column devoted to personal finance issues, from getting out of debt and clearing up credit problems to managing your 401(k) plan and refinancing your mortgage. It's the cheapest, best written financial textbook that's out there—next to the public library.

Action Step:

Spend 50 cents a day for a copy of *USA Today* and read the "Money" section thoroughly for two weeks.

Day 35

GIVING BACK THE GIFT

The gains of education are never really lost.

—Franklin D. Roosevelt

Thayer Brown and his wife, Dorothy, found that their ticket to success was a library card. Before getting married during the Great

Depression, they didn't have the money to buy a 25-cent movie ticket, so their dates were at the public library for free readings and book discussion groups. Dorothy was fascinated with *Forbes* magazine and read it religiously, even after she and Thayer were married and had a son. The year that Thayer got a $1,500 bonus from his sales job, Dorothy decided to start investing in the companies she read about in *Forbes*. Over the years, the couple stuck to their quiet lifestyle, indulging in a few luxuries—extended winter vacations in Florida and a small vacation house in upstate New York. Dorothy never held a job but did quite well with her "investing hobby" and treated herself to a pink Thunderbird one year as a birthday gift—purchased with cash from some of the dividend checks she received from her investments. When Dorothy died in 1989 of Alzheimer's disease, Thayer continued managing their portfolio with the same deftness and old-fashioned, long-term investing style as his wife. When he died seven years later, 91-year-old Brown left the Teaneck library the largest single gift in its history, $56,000. In fact he filled the coffers of many other charities with total donations of $1.3 million. Most of the recipients of his generosity—The Salvation Army, the Boy Scouts of America, the American Red Cross, the American Heart Association, Fairleigh Dickinson University, and his alma mater, Syracuse University—were shaking their heads when they found out. They didn't have a clue who Thayer Brown was or why he was leaving them money. In the end, Thayer and Dorothy Brown left behind a wonderful legacy to the art of saving and investing money wisely.

Action Step:

Get that library card today and use it!

Day 36

LIGHTEN UP!

Charity begins at home.

—Anonymous

There is a special cultural tradition among Native Americans known as the "Great Give-Away." Tribal chiefs and prominent families sponsor these charitable celebrations as a means of showing their dedication to the community and their concern for the welfare of their people. The gifts are not secondhand clothes, run-down shoes, used cars, or cast-off toys. The "Give-Away" isn't created for passing along old clothes, used books, and broken lamps to friends, neighbors, and relatives. It is a carefully planned event for which invitations are sent out and new gifts are purchased, with sacred spiritual meaning for each person who receives them. The gifts are accepted as love offerings, tokens of appreciation and respect. Each person who shares the experience comes away with much more than a new gift. The gifts and the event symbolize the ebb and flow of prosperity between people who care about one another as fellow human beings. The celebration lasts for several days and begins and ends with prayers, dancing, and a huge feast.

Affirmation:

When I give to others, I give to myself.

Action Step:

Go through your closet and find at least three items that you have not worn or used in the last three years. Call Goodwill, the Salvation Army, Volunteers of America, or St. Vincent DePaul Society and donate them to someone who needs them. They will give you a tax-deductible receipt for the donation.

Day 37

TITHING

God gave me my money. I believe the power to make money is a gift from God. . . . I believe it is my duty to make money and still more money and to use the money I make for the good of my fellow-man according to the dictates of my conscience.

—John D. Rockefeller

If you have mixed feelings about the religious practice of tithing, giving 10 percent of your earnings to the church or charity, study the biography of John D. Rockefeller, once dubbed "the richest man in the world." He was born on a farm in Hartford Mills, New York, in 1839 into a struggling family with a father who was the classic carnival huckster peddling phony cancer cures and having flagrant affairs with other women. John Davison Rockefeller's faith was the backbone of his belief that he would be wealthy one day. No matter how little he earned—60 cents a day as errand boy for a shipping company—he never failed to tithe 10 percent of his income. Rockefeller went from clerk to bookkeeper to junior partner in a hay and grain company and started in oil as a sideline. Through iron-willed bargaining, Rockefeller eventually controlled 95 percent of the nation's oil production by 1880. The Sherman Antitrust Act of 1890 broke his oil monopoly into 34 separate companies known today as Amoco, Exxon, Chevron, and Mobil. In 1905, his annual tithe was close to $100 million! In 1897, giving away money was his full-time occupation, beginning with creating the University of Chicago, expanding Spelman College for Women, and establishing the Rockefeller Institute for Medical Research, and the Rockefeller Foundation followed in 1913. Rockefeller's net worth was estimated at more than $1.4 billion when he died in 1937 at 98 years of age.

Action Step:

Make another donation to the charity you chose to support. Consider it a gesture of gratitude for wealth you already have that you can share, and also get a tax deduction.

Day 38

MUTUAL MISERY INDEX

Wherever you are it is your own friends who make your world.

—William James

How many friends do you have who live from paycheck to paycheck and treat shopping as the all-American social sport? How many of them laugh at the idea of saving and investing? Do you join in the conversation out of nervousness and a desire to fit in? Do they joke about their debts and the mistakes they've made with money? Sometimes this mutual misery can be the basis for friendship. But as you change your attitude and outlook, your relationship with some of these friends will change. They may feel threatened by your desire to rise above the financial distress that you share. That doesn't mean that they are bad people; you have simply outgrown them. Achieving prosperity will probably mean loosening your bonds with those who do not want to change and grow. Don't worry. As you begin to change your perspective on money, you will meet other like-minded people who will support and share your goals and concepts for wealth building. Make sure there is room for them in your life. They are out there.

Affirmation:

I open my mind and my eyes to new friends who will encourage me.

Action Step:

Visit the Web site for the Investor Education Alliance at http://www.investoreducation.org to find out more about where and when events for investors and other financial conferences are scheduled. Plan to attend one so that you can get a better idea of the people in your community.

Day 39

CASH UNDER YOUR NOSE

Do you want to spend years at a job or in a relationship you hate just for financial security, or would you rather write your own game plan and do it your way? Look around your house or apartment. Are there a lot of doodads and knickknacks, dust collectors that are there just as space fillers? How many of these "things" in your living space do you really want to keep and maintain? If you don't need them, get rid of them. Have a garage sale. Discard unnecessary tchotchkes, or sell them and use the cash for a much-needed evening out. A garage sale won't finance your retirement, but it could be a first step toward realizing your priorities and stripping the dead wood from your life.

Action Step:

Sell, donate, or swap any household items you haven't used in a long time. You'll be amazed at how much waste and clutter has been filling your life—and emptying your wallet. Use the cash to make an extra payment on a debt or add it to your savings account for a specific goal.

Day 40

WHERE AM I?

All virtue lies in individual action, in inward energy, in self-determination. There is no moral worth in being swept away by a crowd even toward the best objective.

—William Channing

Before you set a goal, you must take a close look at your current position. The real work begins in your head, with instilling in yourself the habit of watching what you spend and how you spend it on a daily basis. The first step is to take a close look at how money is operating in your life. Take a pen and paper and go over your pay stubs. List your income in one column. List your living expenses in the next column. List your monthly payments for loans, credit cards, and other debts in another column. Go through your canceled checks and credit card bills from the last six months and find out how much you've been spending in each of these categories before you go any further. Suppose your income is $3,000 a month and your debts are $750 a month. $750 divided by $3,000 is 25 percent of your monthly income. That's how large your debt payments are and how much you will have to pay down before you can consider borrowing any more money for major commitments such as mortgage debts. Bankers have a strong interest in looking at the debt-to-income ratio. If a loan applicant has a high debt load, with monthly payments eating up 30 percent or more of his or her income, the application for borrowing additional funds will be rejected. Now that you have a picture of how cash is flowing through your life, you can decide if there are any patterns that you want to change.

Action Step:

Look at your monthly spending to see how you can reduce the amount of debt. Visit the "Debt to Income" worksheet at http://www.educaid.com/debt2inc.html.

Day 41

THE "MONEY" RULES

The rules of money are probably Ben Franklin-type rules, such as never squander it, don't be a spendthrift, be very careful, you have to account for what you're doing, you must keep track of it, and you can never ignore what happens to money.

—Michael Phillips, *The Seven Laws of Money*

Sheldon C., an editor at a small publishing house in New York, could not understand why he was always broke. He paid his rent, utilities, and the minimum on his credit cards, but there was never any money left over to plan. "I don't understand it, I'm not extravagant. Why can't I afford to have some extras?" You don't have to wear Armani suits and Hermes ties to overspend. Sheldon used his credit card for business lunches, rationalizing that with an expense account it would be taken care of by the company. He forgot the many lunches that were not covered by the expense account, and he never went to reasonably priced restaurants. Sheldon thought of his credit cards as "found" money. If one card was maxed out, another was arriving in the mail. There's no such thing as "found" money— if you use your card to buy groceries, that meal will cost you twice as much in the long run, and it won't taste any better. In the end, a financial counselor helped Sheldon plan his expenditures and rely less on credit, showing him just how much he paid in interest every month.

Affirmation:

I will keep track of where my money is going and avoid impulse spending.

Action Step:

Review your financial journal and your see where you have been impulsive with your spending.

Day 42

WHAT SHOULD I DO WITH MY MONEY?

Earn, spend, save, share. This is what you should do with a dollar.

—Neale Godfrey

There are basically only four things that you can do with your money after you earn it: spend, save, lend, and invest it. The smart money manager does all four things well at the same time.

Spending. You already know how to do this part and, unfortunately, this function often gets in the way of the other ones.

Saving. This is the slipperiest part of the money management process because it's easy to find a thousand excuses a day not to do it.

Lending. Most people assume that a loan is not an investment. But you are lending money whether you put it in a passbook account or a CD at the bank, open a tax-free money market fund, buy U.S. Savings Bonds, or loan it to your brother Fred.

Investing. This is the scariest option because there are no guarantees about what will happen to your money. You need to learn some guidelines for handling this aspect of your long-term planning for a comfortable future. You want your money to work as hard after you get it as you did in order to go to it.

Action Step:

Review your goals and attach a dollar value and a date for attaining each one of them.

Day 43

WHAT'S ENOUGH?

To have enough is good luck, to have more than enough is harmful. This is true of all things, but especially of money.

—Chuang-tse

How much money do you need to earn each year to live comfortably and be happy? Take a guess and write down that number before you read any further, and put it aside. The answer to this question seems to vary over the years. A poll done by the Roper Center at the University of Connecticut shows that the average American adjusts his or her ideas about how much money is adequate for a comfortable lifestyle as the economy changes. Take a look at the following lineup over the last few years and see where your estimate fits.

How Much Is Enough?

Year	Median Response
1987	$50,000
1989	$75,000
1991	$83,800
1994	$102,000
1996	$90,000

Action Step:

Compare your current salary with what you think you should be earning at this point in your life. Write down how much you think you want to be earning when you retire. Final salary levels often determine pension income and Social Security benefits.

Day 44

REVIEW AND REASSESS

Your attitude about your financial situation should be changing toward what is possible for you as you understand your habits and behavior with money. And the first step toward changing those attitudes is identifying what your current feelings are. What have you learned about your idea of what money is and what it can do for you? What have you learned about your attitudes that are harder to articulate about money? It's a good idea to put some of your thoughts in writing: It will help clarify your thinking and give you something to look back to as you progress. List five new ideas you have learned about your spending habits and how you can change them. Review your financial journal and your records of the past month and congratulate yourself on coming this far.

Day 45

GOALS—DREAMS WITH DEADLINES

If you don't know where you want to go, then it doesn't matter where you end up.

—Will Rogers

Do you pack for your vacation, go to the airport, and *then* decide where you want to go? Of course not! When you buy a computer, a car, or anything that costs more than $50, don't you do a bit of research before you lay out the cash or whip out the plastic? You can do the same thing with the broader aspects of your life. Start with a calendar and a deadline. Write down at least one thing you would like to do to improve your financial situation. Putting it on paper forces you to become clear and realistic about what you really want.

Any "dream" can be broken down into daily, weekly, and monthly steps. You want to go to Martinique in October? Call a travel agent in January and find out that it will cost $800. Put aside $80 a month for ten months to pay for the trip with cash. It's more fun to work on your tan, shop for souvenirs, and sample the local cuisine without a hefty credit card bill waiting when you get home. Apply this method to everything you want to do. Make a list of future events that are important to you and find out the price tag for each. Planning to get a new apartment? What's the real estate agent's fee? How much is a moving truck? The phone deposit? Thinking ahead saves headaches and disappointments on moving day.

Affirmation:

Each of my financial dreams can be translated into a workable daily plan for my prosperity—one day at a time.

Action Step:

Write down one of your important dreams that can be measured in dollars. Set a date on your calendar for when you want to get there. Look at your paycheck and estimate how much you have to set aside. You will soon discover that the $40 a week you spend on lunches is the same money that could pay for a vacation, buy a car, or pay off a credit card earlier than you expected. Brown-bagging it begins to make sense now, doesn't it?

Day 46

"$2.74 A DAY"

When schemes are laid in advance, it is surprising how often circumstances fit in with them.

—Sir William Osler

If you saved $2.74 every day for a year, you'd have $1,000. For less than the cost of a Big Mac or a large coffee at Starbucks every day you would be able to pay for a nice five-day vacation for two in Cancun at a comfortable hotel resort—in cash. Once you decide what your goals are they can be put to a timetable and divided into attainable dollar amounts. Bigger goals can mean saving bigger amounts, but if you begin with what matters to you, you will find the money to match the motivation. It's up to you to make that decision, starting today!

Action Step:

Get out your calculator, your piggy bank, and your calendar. Then review your "wish list" and choose one item that seems within reach within the next six months. Do a little research to find out what it will cost you. Calculate how much you will have to put aside each month to save for it. Circle a date on your calendar and begin putting aside your pennies and dollars each day to make your wish come true.

Day 47

CREATE YOUR OWN DREAM

Consider the postage stamp; it's usefulness consists in the ability to stick to one thing 'til it gets there.

—Josh Billings

When 22-year-old Lisa Wax left Detroit eight years ago, her only clear goal was to get away from the suburbs and live closer to nature. The Wayne State graduate fulfilled the first phase of her dream by heading West for a three-year assignment as a paralegal for an environmental law firm. In Alaska. She pocketed most of her $36,000 a year since her "office" and "living space" were either a tent or ice cave as she conducted interviews about environmental abuse in remote villages. An added incentive from her employer was a double bonus if she completed the project ahead of schedule. At the end of her second year, Lisa discovered Tsaina Lodge, an abandoned property scheduled for foreclosure. This would fulfill the second part of her dream: to own a vacation lodge in the Great White North. The buildings needed renovation, so Lisa began studying Alaskan building codes along with real estate laws and the hotel business. A year later, when the auction was finally scheduled, Lisa worried that her $106,000 she had saved wouldn't be enough to compete against experienced real estate developers. When she arrived at that auction, she was the only person there! Lisa recently celebrated her 30th birthday in the dining room of Tsaina Lodge with her eight-person staff, who help manage the cabins for the nine months that she is open for business. Due to recent publicity, Tsaina Lodge (http://www.alaskan.com/tsainalodge.index.htm) is booked through 2000 by skiers and outdoor enthusiasts who appreciate the luxury and four-star restaurant she has created in such a remote location as Valdez, Alaska.

Affirmation:

I can create my own dream!

Day 48

"AFTER I PAY MY BILLS . . ."

Can anyone remember when the times were not hard and money not scarce?

—Ralph Waldo Emerson

If you wait until you've paid your bills to set aside some savings, it will never happen! Bills are a constant fact of life, along with laundry, unmade beds, and dirty dishes, so don't even think about them disappearing before you can save money. When your weekly paycheck barely seems to stretch from one weekend to another, the idea of putting some of it into savings may sound like absolute insanity, but you have to force yourself to do it so that something will be left over for the special goals and important events in your life. Quick, look in your wallet. If you're like the average American, you carry about $1.87 in change in your pocket everyday. Those nickels, pennies, dimes, and quarters are a heavy lump in your pocket that gets tedious after a few days, so put it into a piggy bank. That $1.87 a day adds up to $56.10 a month—you could be using it to buy groceries, reduce your credit card bill, pay for the dry cleaning, or treat yourselves to dinner and a movie without using credit or stopping at the ATM. Or that money could go into a vacation savings account to pay for next summer's vacation. In cash.

Affirmation:

I can balance saving and bill paying at the same time.

Action Step:

Find an old milk carton, a bread box, a piggy bank, a tin can, or whatever you like. Call it your "dream jar." Put it in a convenient place, such as the bedroom dresser, and start putting all your spare change into it each night. Tape a label to the jar to remind yourself of what the savings goal is. The spare nickels, dimes, and pennies that become a weighty nuisance in your pocket can add up very quickly to about $50 a month. That's painless saving!

Day 49

FLEXIBILITY

When Jeff K. got a football scholarship to the University of Alabama and was tagged for a minor league team, his dreams of being an NFL running back loomed large, with visions of a Super Bowl ring and a seven-figure contract for product endorsements spurring him on. His dreams crumbled on the gridiron in the final game of the season when a knee injury created irreparable harm to his right leg. That fall, Jeff began working on a bridge-building construction job as his teammates headed for training practice. His resentment was great, but with help from his boss, another former jock, Jeff kept working at changing his expectations and business opportunities. Ten years later, as his former fellow jocks are limping off the field and looking for second careers, Jeff is hiring a few of them to help him build profits for himself and his 28 employees as he grosses $3.6 million a year building golf courses around the country with a client roster of major sports celebrities and real estate developers. His winning attitude often attracts new business because he is always open and flexible in his expectations and willingness to "go with the flow," but still get the job done.

Affirmation:

I keep my mind open and flexible in my financial opportunities.

Day 50

HOW DO YOU KNOW
IF YOU DON'T TRY?

Go for the moon. If you don't get it, you'll still be heading for a star.

—Willis Reed

Every successful venture started as a dream in someone's head. Look at the wealthy families of any country and you will consistently find one person in an earlier generation whose vision and discipline was the foundation for building a fortune. Someone had to take an initial financial risk or make a sacrifice and follow up with a strategy for accumulating wealth to pass it on to the next generation. In each of the Rockefeller, DuPont, Ford, Mellon, and Busch families, at least one ancestor saw the money to be made from railroads, oil, or bottled beer or many other things we take for granted today, and then acted on that vision. Wealth didn't come to seek them out—it never does. Haven't you known people who had great ideas for money-making schemes, who talked about them all the time but never did anything to get the ball rolling? Uncle Fred, who just knew there was money to be made from computers, but never followed through on it? Or your Cousin Louise, who swears she knew that IBM would be a big winner but never invested for herself? You have to be prepared to take a risk and discipline yourself for the long haul. Even if you don't succeed on a grand scale, it's better than never having tried.

Affirmation:

I will not let my life be an exercise in regrets.

Action Step:

Pick one stock that you feel good about and go to the library and do some research on it.

Day 51

PLAN YOUR WORK AND WORK YOUR PLAN

Pennies do not come from heaven, they must be earned right here on earth.

—Margaret Thatcher

Wealth doesn't happen by accident except to the one person in 60 million who guesses the right numbers on the lottery ticket. Studies have shown that without a plan for managing that newfound wealth, many "instant millionaires" find themselves in financial chaos that leads to unhappiness, lawsuits, and, ultimately, despair and loss. Having money and knowing what to do with it aren't the same thing. Look at the Newark bus driver who won $4 million. He spent $100,000 on a wedding to his new girlfriend and maxed out on ten credit cards within three months. His six weeks of nonstop shopping put him in debt for the next two years, which meant he couldn't quit his job right away. His former wife and other girlfriends sued him for unpaid alimony, child support, and a share of the lottery money. He failed to pay his taxes, so the IRS attached his lottery check for two years. Fortunately, he found a good accountant, lawyer, and financial adviser to teach him how to turn his impending nightmare into financial common sense. He now runs a business that provides day care services, tutoring support, and job training opportunities to the youth of the neighborhood. Now his sudden wealth has built a nest egg for himself and his children with a solid plan and sound advice.

Affirmation:

I approach financial planning for prosperity with a positive attitude for myself and my future generations.

Action Step:

Look for a copy of *It's Never Too Late to Get Rich* by James Jorgensen or visit his Web site at http://www.itsyourmoney.com to get some ideas and guidance on long-term goals. Sign up for a free copy of his financial newsletter.

Day 52

THE R&R OF MONEY

Financial management is 80 percent behavior and 20 percent know-how.

—Dave Ramsey

There are two ways to approach financial decisions: with respect and responsibility or with remorse and regret. We've all heard the "if only I had . . ." story from people talking about stock they should have purchased, property they should have bought, or a business opportunity that they ignored. If you don't want to wake up one day with those same words on your lips, you'll have to start studying, planning, discussing, and deciding how to handle your money today. Logical behavior with money today will make a mountain of difference in your financial future tomorrow. Wishing doesn't open the investment account and get the check written each month. One step at a time. One day at a time.

Affirmation:

I'm quite comfortable with the idea of being wealthy!

Action Step:

Spend 20 minutes reviewing your goals list and adjusting your expectations.

Day 53

MAGAZINES

In the last twenty years, talking about money has become not only fashionable but downright obsessive. Newsstands offer ample evidence of our new preoccupation with wealth. Whatever your level of interest, one of the titles should appeal to you.

FOR THE NOVICE

Consumer's Digest. Offers information in its "Money Watch" department. Six issues, $15.97.

Consumer Reports. The "bible" of unbiased advice on buying anything from cars to soap. Good personal finance data in "Your Money" section. $24 a year.

Your Money. Simple language, down-to-earth profiles, and practical tips on saving and investing. 12 issues, $15.97.

FOR THE SOMEWHAT KNOWLEDGEABLE

Black Enterprise. "MoneyWise" column on personal finance. Special money management issues each February and October. $12.97 a year.

Kiplinger's Personal Finance. Columns on "Smart Shopping," "Career Changing," "Mutual Funds," "Yields and Rates," and "Health and Fitness" address personal finance topics. Good writing and excellent recommendations for $19.95 a year.

Money. The granddaddy of personal finance magazines. "Family Finance," "Money Trends," and "Investing" are just a few of the useful columns. $29.95 a year but worth it.

Smart Money. Produced by the publishers of the *Wall Street Journal* to focus on personal finance issues for the upscale investor. $14.97 a year.

FOR THE SOPHISTICATED INVESTOR

Business Week. "Smart Money" section offers advice on personal finance. 30 issues for $27.95.

Forbes. Advice from five columnists in "Money and Investments." The first issue of each September offers the magazine's rating of the best mutual funds of the year. 17 issues for $23.95.

Fortune. "Portfolio Talk," "Smart Spending," and "Investment Strategy" are regularly featured. 20 issues for $43.80.

Mutual Fund. In-depth data on how funds operate, who the managers are, and new funds. Monthly recommendations on what to buy, sell and hold. One year, $14.97, or get a free issue from the publisher at 800–443–9000 or at the Web site: http://www.mfmag.com/abk.

Worth. Published by the Fidelity Fund network, advice on taxes, banking, and family finance. Also reports on mutual funds and global markets. One year, $14.97.

Day 54

ENDLESS DECISIONS, ENDLESS CHOICES

Money is never out of season.

—Anonymous

Should you go out for that $20 box lunch to make yourself feel better about not getting the promotion? Can you afford to contribute to the retirement party pool for your boss? Do you really need a cellular phone, or should you add that $30 to your monthly check to pay off your student loan sooner? Is this the right time to think about getting another car, or can you do some repairs on the old one and keep it another year or two? Money questions like these will crop up throughout your life so you should become comfortable with them. They are where you begin to set priorities. You probably won't be able to make any sensible financial decisions until you get a better idea of what you're doing with your money each day, with each paycheck. By now you should have several days' worth of experience recorded in your money diary. Review those pages. Have you made any notes about your spending patterns? Imagine how much more cash you would have had in your pocket this week if you hadn't ordered takeout dinners every night last week. The impact on your bottom line is evident with each choice that you make.

Affirmation:

I will change my focus so I can change my future.

Action Step:

Review your daily spending habits and add at least one new thrift habit to your daily behavior. For example, make yourself a meal for lunch or dinner when you might otherwise have eaten out. Focus on this as a positive action for wealth building.

Day 55

CHANGE YOUR GLASSES

The world is as you see it.

—Swami Muktananda

Money has always been important since the day you were born and you became a tax deduction and an expense item in the family budget. At age two, you giggled at the sound of coins in your father's pocket. At three, you questioned why a nickel is bigger than a dime, why a penny is brown, and why a dollar is green. At four, you began to understand the connection between food, shopping, and money as you followed your mother around the grocery store. By six, you learned to count pennies, nickels, dimes, quarters, and dollars. At eight, you wanted your "own money" to buy Christmas gifts and birthday cards and discovered how to get the "reward for good behavior" by being quiet for a dollar an hour. By ten, you were telling Mom what clothes, videos, or shoes were "really kewl" and how you'd just die if you didn't have them because all your friends did. By age 14, you wanted to borrow Mom's credit card, cash in the savings bonds Grandma sent for your birthday, and negotiate for cash or additional allowance for the big-ticket items like bikes, Nintendo games, and clothes. At sixteen, you had a part-time job at minimum wage to finance your "little extras." At 22 you discovered credit cards as a way to replace the allowance your parents no longer gave you! You grew up reacting to other people's rules about money. Now you have the choice of creating your own money style. Your goal should be to learn how to make money work for you instead of you working so hard for it. The process begins with your perception of money. You may need to change the prescription of your glasses, at least metaphorically, taking a fresh look at yourself and how you view money. Can you see the possibility for wealth in your life?

Affirmation:

I take control of my money and my life by creating a new viewpoint on money.

Action Step:

Review your childhood habits with money. Think about the allowance you received, how you spent it, and what jobs you had to earn money then and what you did with the money. Make notes to yourself about how your concepts of money have changed over the years.

Day 56

MARRIAGE AND MONEY

Home life ceases to be free and beautiful as soon as it is founded on borrowing and debt.

—Henrik Ibsen

Karen F. inherited some money from her father two years ago and gave it to her husband, Frank, to invest. She has seen a few brokerage statements, but Frank never discussed them with her, so she has no idea what happened to her money. Karen also pools her paychecks with Frank's, but feels that it is a matter of trust and respect to rely on how he handles their finances as long as the bills get paid and they have a comfortable lifestyle. She doesn't know where the life insurance policies and the savings passbooks are, or how to contact the accountant about their taxes if a question comes up.

The number one cause of fights in most marriages is a lack of communication about money. Couples may love each other, but don't seem to be able to stop shouting and accusing each other of mistakes or sulking in corners in angry silence. Forty-eight percent of all marriages end in divorce because couples never talk enough about their financial expectations before marriage. Marriage counselors have also noted that it is usually the partner who earns the most who makes the financial rules in the family. Too many wives surrender their involvement in the family finances because they feel intimidated by their husbands' higher earning power or because they assume that men have all the answers about handling money. This can lead to disagreements and power struggles between partners. Husbands and wives need to realize that building a comfortable financial life is a joint effort.

Action Step:

Set aside a time once a week to go over "checkbook" issues with your spouse. Make a list of the questions you should ask each other about how you are spending and saving. Determine if you have mutual goals for your future income. Outline the areas of disagreement and discuss how you can compromise to meet them. Set a timetable for doing research and learning about money and investment options together. Sharing information and responsibility about money creates a much closer, trusting and honest relationship.

Day 57

REVIEW AND REASSESS

Reread Day 15. Do you accept that financial planning requires a spiritual and moral commitment to yourself and the people who matter to you? Repeat the affirmations for Days 17 and 19. Compare the unrealistic fantasies you've had about wealth with the long-term goal you identified. A real goal, however grand, will help keep you on the path of education, savings, and investment. Have you kept a 15-minute appointment with yourself to look at a new financial idea? Go back through your calendar, your spending diary, and the list of financial questions that you have written out. Cross off the ones that have been answered.

Day 58

ADULTS ONLY

There's some relief in actually feeling like a grown-up.

—Colette Dowling

Remember when you were 17 and couldn't wait to get out from under your parents' watchful eye so you could "live your life your own way"? Go to bed when you want to, eat whatever you want to, leave the bed unmade if you feel like it? Now that you're independent, you get to decide for yourself how to set those spending/shopping/saving priorities for yourself, and *voilà*, you discover that some of those rules your parents talked about, especially about money, make sense! Putting aside a few dollars each month, being careful about what you're spending, looking for sales and bargains—these habits don't seem so "adult" anymore, do they? Despite all the outward trappings of adulthood, there are inevitably times when many of us resent growing up, especially when it comes to money. Like any new experience, dealing with money can be sobering, scary, and somewhat uncomfortable, but not fatal. If you make a few mistakes, welcome to the club, it means that you're human. But making the commitment to managing your money is the final step toward true adulthood. Learning from your mistakes, forgiving yourself, and growing beyond them—that's being a financially sensible adult. How you handle your money is a reflection of how you feel about yourself. The first step is deciding that you like the idea of doing this for yourself.

Affirmation:

Day by day, I grow more comfortable with becoming a financial success on my own.

Action Step:

Write a letter to yourself offering congratulations and good wishes on how well you are doing with accepting the new responsibility of creating your own financial life.

Day 59

MONEY GAMES

Remember the fun (and fights!) you had as a kid whenever you played Monopoly? Throw the dice, count off your moves, get your $200 as you pass Go, buy property, charge rent to anyone who lands on your space, and build up your nest egg. Believe it or not, this simple childhood board game was the only lesson John Shmilenko needed to start investing in real estate in his hometown of Portland, Oregon. With his skill as a carpenter and a roofer, John took every extra dime he made and followed the principles of Monopoly: Buy small properties that no one else wants in good neighborhoods, like Baltic Avenue or Mediterranean, fix them up, rent them out, and resell at a profit a few years later when real estate values increase. Although he never went to college, John can't complain about his $60,000 a year income as a landlord, and is quite happy with his net worth of more than $1 million. Today John calls himself a semi-retired roofer who spends his free time fishing on the Columbia River when everyone else is heading off to an office on Monday morning.

Action Step:

Go to the attic, the cellar, or the closet where you stored the Monopoly game and dig it out. Spend a few evening playing the game again, but this time look at it as a financial awakening process and a learning experience.

Day 60

PERSONAL FINANCE COLUMNS

Nearly every newspaper around the country has a daily or weekly column on personal money issues. If you look closely, most of them are written by one person: Jane Bryant Quinn. She is the most respected personal finance columnist in the United States, and her articles are syndicated in more than 200 newspapers around the county. Her advice also appears every other week in *Woman's Day* magazine and *Newsweek* magazine. She writes about any and every money and investing issue in a down-to-earth style that's readable and simple to understand. Her two books, *Making the Most of Your Money* and *Jane Bryant Quinn's Money Book* are best-sellers that can easily explain every aspect of any money issue with common sense, a sense of humor, and objective honesty that is rare in the business of financial journalism. Browse through either of her books the next time you're in the library.

Leaf through one of the magazines that features a column by Jane Bryant Quinn next time you're in a bookstore or at a newsstand. Find at least one issue you like and purchase it.

Day 61

INVEST IN YOURSELF!

That year-end bonus from your boss, the raise you finally got, or the $2,000 you got as a cash gift from your Great Aunt Sybil or an inheritance of $5,000 or $20,000 from your Uncle Lou that you haven't seen or heard from since you were in fourth grade should be seen as the seed money for starting an investment program if you don't have the available cash now. Divide any "windfall" money between paying off debt, creating a savings plan, and starting an automatic investment program in an equity mutual fund. The last thing you need to do is go shopping!

Affirmation:

I will make wise use of all gifts.

Action Step:

Review your goals and decide how to apply any "found money" wisely to an investment program.

Day 62

GROUND ZERO GOALS

I want to be rich enough to buy new soap when the letters wear off.

—Andy Rooney

Sure, Andy, and each of us would like a purple Lamborghini reserved just for the five-mile drive past our private airstrip and personal jet on the way to the mailbox on our country estate. There's nothing wrong with dreaming about living like the rich and famous, or with being ambitious, but sometimes we hurt ourselves by not being realistic about what we're aiming for. You know you're never going to wake up tomorrow and be Madonna or Michael Jordan, so why focus on that fantasy? Give your time, attention, and life's energy to something attainable and joyful.

Affirmation:

I constantly weigh my options and alternatives on the road to financial well-being.

Action Step:

Review your goals and decide if you are aiming for ones that are realistic and possible with hard work, effort and discipline.

Day 63

SOMEDAY . . .

First, have a definite, clear, practical ideal—a goal, an objective. Second, have the necessary means to achieve your ends—wisdom, money, materials, and methods. Third, adjust all your means to that end.

—Aristotle

How long are you going to wait for someday to come along? How often have you told yourself, "Someday I'll get out of debt." Or, "I'll think about retirement someday, but not now." Or even, "Someday I'll have time to read the mutual fund brochures and investment literature I've ordered." "Someday" is a weak answer to give yourself when you talk about setting goals. It isn't a specific enough timetable for achieving a goal. Study the lives of millionaires, and you'll see that they didn't wait for "someday." Some of your friends, family, and coworkers may tell you you're crazy, but you know that success starts with a plan, an attitude, a timetable, and persistence. "Someday" can become today with a game plan.

Affirmation:

I will open my mind to achieving wealth for myself and my descendants.

Action Step:

Pick up a copy of *The Wealthy 100* by Michael Klepper and Robert Gunther at your library. Read up on the lives of the richest people in America and how they got there.

Day 64

THE PAST IS OVER!

But the bravest are surely those who have the clearest vision of what is before them, glory and risk alike, and yet not withstanding, go out to meet it.

—Thucydides

Sure, you've made some unwise money moves in the past, but who hasn't? You can sit and have a pity party and really do a browbeating head trip on yourself over your losses, foolish mistakes, or missed opportunities, but that won't turn back the clock or recover anything. What's done is done. Accept the fact that your financial practices haven't been working for you. The next step is to forgive yourself for your mistakes, making allowances for not always knowing what to do. Make some notes for yourself on the lessons and insights you want to remember. Then prepare to move on. Be grateful that you have awakened from your state of misunderstanding. Think of how fortunate you are to be able to learn from your mistakes and think clearly as you move forward. Tomorrow is truly another day.

Affirmation:

I let go of bad feelings about past mistakes and look forward to learning about how to use money wisely in my life.

Day 65

CONGRATULATIONS, YOU'RE A MILLIONAIRE!

No, the Prize Patrol from American Family Publishers didn't stop at your house while you were out shopping, but the truth is that if you add up your yearly salary over a lifetime, you will earn over $1 million. Here's how it works. Suppose you start a job at age 22, earning $20,000. If you remained in that same job for the next 40 years (perish the thought!), received no raises other than an annual 3 percent cost-of-living raise, and decided to take early retirement at age 62, your total lifetime income would be $1,508,035. The difference between you and the wealthy is they got theirs in a lump sum and you have to work for yours over a period of time. But the real question is, how much of your $1.5 million are you going to keep? Most of us will make career changes and, we hope, have an ever increasing salary over a lifetime. If you take just 1 percent of each raise, or a modest $200 per year for the next 40 years, and invest it in a growth and income fund earning an average total return of 10 percent, your $8,000 will grow into $32,000. If you apply the same principle of disciplined investing to at least 1 percent of your lifetime earnings, you could retire as a millionaire and have the money when you truly need it.

Action Step:

Call the Social Security Administration at: 800–772–1213 and request a copy of your Pension Earnings and Benefits Estimate Statement. This will tell you how much money you have earned so far in your working life.

Day 66

THE RICH TEACHERS

Everybody knows that teachers are not millionaires. But the exceptions are Barbara and Dennis Dailey, two science and chemistry teachers from San Jose, California. Long before the advent of Apple computers, Microsoft, and Intel, Barbara and Dennis decided that the commonsense approach to investing was to buy stock in all the companies that appealed to their two children—from toys to clothes to snack foods. Although their incomes did not allow for extravagant investing, they committed $100 a month to buying four or five shares of Gerber, Kellogg, Vanity Fair (they own Lee Jeans and Carter's baby clothing), Oshkosh B'Gosh, Toys "R" Us, The Gap, Nintendo, Nike, and Schwinn through dividend reinvestment plans. When their son, Kevin, got excited about computers in the early eighties, the Daileys shifted their stock picks to focusing on Silicon Valley and purchased stock in Apple since it was user-friendly and simple for the family to use. After 23 years of following this "home-grown" formula, the Daileys, now in their mid-50s, have decided to go for the ultimate freedom since both children have finished college and left home. They will not need their pension checks or their Social Security checks. They will be funding their "early retirement" with the quarterly dividend checks they received from their $3.6 million investment portfolio.

Affirmation:

I know why I want money and the freedom it can give me.

Action Step:

Investigate at least three products that appeal to children and ado-
lescents, such as Nintendo, The Gap, and Handleman, distributors
of Teletubbies.

Day 67

BLAMING SOMEONE ELSE

If it is to be, it is up to me.

—Paul Harvey

Is someone else the cause of your current financial situation? Of
course! Grandma gave you $50 each Christmas and told you it was
"fun money." Dad never discussed money except to complain
about his struggle to pay the bills. Mom gave you an allowance but
didn't tell you how to spend it. When you ran short, you gritted
your teeth through the lecture your parents gave you before they
bailed you out with an extra $20. The school system didn't give
you the vaguest clue about how the word "budget" was supposed
to fit into your life. These reasons worked at 12, but now that
you're a grown-up, those days are over. Your boss isn't going to ask
if your salary is enough. Your landlord won't adjust the rent to fit
your paycheck. The phone company won't excuse you for too many
calls to your college roommate who moved to Phoenix last year.
Your parents probably didn't know any more than you do about
managing money, but banking and financial choices are quite different today. If you learned to ride a bike, drive a car, and operate a
computer, you can learn to manage your money. It isn't a special
gift like red hair or brown eyes. It's a skill that can be learned, with
effort, if you care.

Affirmation:

Others may have taught me bad financial habits but I now have the power to learn and improve my beliefs and behavior about money.

Action Step:

Call the National Center for Financial Education at 610–232–8811, write them at P.O. Box 34070, San Diego, CA 92163, or check out their Web site at http://www.ncfe.org. Their online catalog offers the best personal finance books available in all price ranges and at all education levels. Choose one that fits your interest.

Day 68

NATIONAL NEWSPAPER RESOURCES

New York Times. Each Sunday edition has a "Consumer Rates" column, giving a national average of current interest rates on mortgages, passbook savings, money market funds, personal loans, and tax-exempt bonds. Another regular Sunday feature is the "Fund Watch," a column that offers an "up-close" examination of a particular mutual fund, its manager, and its problems or successes. "My Money" is a first-person personal finance essay written by various readers.

USA Today. The green "Money" section has features on "Business Travel," "The Economy," "Personal Finance," and "Mutual Funds" that appear throughout the week in the business section of this national daily paper. The columns are also archived for one month on the newspaper's Web site at http://www.USAToday.com. On Fridays the "Managing Your

Money" page tackles major issues of personal finance such as consumer debt, refinancing mortgages, the cost of college, and 401(k) plans.

Wall Street Journal. "Your Money Matters," which focuses on personal finance issues, is a daily column on the front page of section three, "Money and Investing."

New York Daily News. Andrew Leckey writes two columns a week on personal finance issues. The Sunday edition often has a pull-out section on investing published by the Bloomberg financial group (http://www.bloomberg.com).

Action Step:

Buy one copy of each publication once a week for the next month.

Day 69

REVIEW AND REASSESS

Have you found or obtained a library card? Spent an afternoon browsing through the financial magazines at a newsstand? Bought a calculator? Read the "Money" section of *USA Today* at least three times in the past month? Congratulate yourself if you have. If you haven't, ask yourself why you're resisting the opportunities the develop some new ideas about prosperity and wealth-building.

Day 70

SWIMMING AGAINST THE TIDE

Success seems to be largely a matter of hanging on after others have let go.

—William Feather

Each spring the salmon along the Columbia River in Oregon make the arduous journey upstream to lay their eggs, while all the other fish in the river are going the other way. Taking control of your financial destiny can sometimes make you feel like those salmon who swim against the tide to create the next generation. When you begin to change your habits and financial behavior you must be prepared to get strange looks and perhaps even some criticism from your friends, family, and relatives. When it comes to showing a new attitude, especially about money, friends, family, and coworkers may not support you and could even make fun of your effort to "get rich." Don't worry about it. Stay focused on your goal. There's no need to drag the critics and "nay-sayers" along the road to prosperity if they aren't ready. Developing a "money consciousness" is a personal process. The only mind and spirit you are in control of is your own. Think of how much further along you'll be after six months or a year when your debt statements have turned into dividend statements and you have something more exciting to read in the mail than late-payment notices. It doesn't take an extraordinary effort like that of the salmon to begin saving and investing; it takes a simple will to do it.

Affirmation:

I have a new sense of prosperity that is not determined by others.

Day 71

THE COMPANY YOU KEEP

Keep away from people who try to belittle your ambition. Small people always do that, but the really great make you feel that you, too, can become great.

—Mark Twain

When you begin to change your financial behavior—by eating out less, refusing to shop till you drop every weekend, reading financial magazines—some of your friends may laugh and make jokes about how you're trying to be Donald Trump. Are these people your true friends, or are they jealous of your effort to get ahead? In all fairness to yourself, you deserve the opportunity to expand your horizons and broaden your experiences of financial well-being. If your old friends are not interested in your new ideas about prosperity and abundance, then you must accept that you cannot change them. It's time to let go, move on, and make space in your life for new people who share your goals. Meanwhile, explore new options, like setting up an automatic monthly investment account with a payroll savings plan through your employer, a money market account with your bank, or a mutual fund for long-term investing. One of the few funds left that allows you to begin with $50 a month is the Strong Opportunity Fund, which you can call anytime for free literature explaining how the company works. The average investment growth over ten years for this mutual fund has been 16.5 percent.

Action Step:

Spend an evening exploring the Strong Opportunity Fund Web site at http://www.strong-funds.com or call one of its 24-hour investment advisers (800–368–1030), who can talk you through filling out the application.

Day 72

SET GOALS THAT SATISFY YOU!

Don't let other people tell you what you want.

—Pat Riley

Are you a person who has to consult 16 other people for advice before making a decision? Your Aunt Sadie tells you to cut your hair; your girlfriend thinks it's fine the way it is. Your Uncle Andrew thinks you should buy a five-year-old used car; your brother Michael wants you to get a new red Bronco (but how much will he contribute to that down payment and monthly note?). Your mechanic tells you about a mutual fund he invested in, but his expertise is in oil changes and carburetors, not growth stocks. Your hairdresser mentions an annuity she bought, but, think about it, did you go to her for a wash and set or investment advice? How many of these opinion givers share the responsibility for your happiness and prosperity? None? Then why do you ask them what they think? When you follow someone else's idea of what to do with your time, your life, or your money, you're giving away the power to shape your own financial well-being. Only professional advisers can give you objective answers and point you in the right direction. They should educate you about options and alternatives you may not be aware of, but the final decision should be yours because in the long run, you and you alone live with the results. The only opinion that matters in life decisions about money, health, career, or anything with a price tag on it is your own!

Affirmation:

It's my life and my money so I can learn how to make my own decisions.

Action Step:

Make your own decisions but take advantage of the 30-minute free consultation offered by most fee-only financial planners. Call 800–242–PLAN, the Institute for Certified Financial Planners, and ask for a referral to two or three financial professionals in your area.

Day 73

SHORTCUTS

Inch by inch, anything's a cinch.

—Dr. Robert Schuller

There are no shortcuts to learning about money or to changing your financial situation. It happens day by day, week by week, month my month, year by year. In the same way that you age and become an adult, your knowledge of and experience with money grows and changes as you watch how you use it and how it works in the world, and learn to make better choices about getting the most out of each dollar that comes through your hands.

Affirmation:

I recognize when patience is required to make financial changes in my life.

Action Step:

Review the ten money questions you wrote down in your first week. How many of them have you answered? Look how far you've come already!

Day 74

NAIC REGIONAL WORKSHOPS

The National Association of Investors Corporation, based in Madison Heights, Michigan, has regional investment clubs in each of the 50 states. Each regional chapter offers regular classes and workshops on the basics of personal financial planning, from doing the math, analyzing investments, and choosing stocks, to becoming your own broker and putting together an investment portfolio, to setting up an investment club.

Action Step:

Call NAIC at 248–583–6242 and get on the mailing list of a chapter in your region. Plan to attend one of the events so that you can meet like-minded people in your community. Check the calendar of events for the upcoming year at www.better-investing.org.

Day 75

THE "MONEY" SHOW

From Seattle to San Francisco, Las Vegas to Lake Buena Vista, money is a topic about which everyone has questions and curiosity. Enter the investment information expo! These one-, two- and three-day conferences have become a popular method for potential investors to meet, greet, and learn from financial professionals in a comfortable seminar setting. These shows comprise a concentrated schedule of workshops and educational symposia covering mutual funds, investing online, emerging markets, and investing overseas. Conferences/expositions occur in many convention centers around the country. Check your newspaper or look on the Internet to find out when these events may be scheduled in your area.

Action Step:

Call the event producer, InterShow, at 800–226–0323 and add your name to the mailing list and find out where and when it will be producing the next money show.

Day 76

STUDYING MONEY

The topic of personal finance is so popular that there's no doubt someone will be teaching a workshop or seminar that will answer some of your basic questions and get you started on the path to financial enlightenment. Your local YMCA or YWCA, junior college, or high school probably offers at least one class on money management in adult education classes on evenings or weekends. Many brokerage firms give free seminars to attract customers; you don't have to sign up for anything but you can get a lot of knowledge at no cost and probably meet some new neighbors who have similar interests.

Action Step:

Check with a college or university near you that offers adult education courses. The U.S. Department of Agriculture, Cooperative Extension Division, in your county gives regular courses at no charge. Find it in your phone book.

Day 77

RESISTANCE

Ultimately we know deeply that the other side of every fear is freedom.

—Marilyn Ferguson

Have you ever found yourself moaning and groaning for days about doing some task that you hate, like straightening out a closet, relining the kitchen shelves, weeding the garden, or grouting the tile in the bathroom? For most of us the biggest job to dodge is sorting out those bills, checks, and receipts to get ready for filing our taxes. Sometimes it's more attractive to clean the litter box or move furniture and shampoo the living room carpet. It can be the same with money issues in our lives. We often would rather replant all the trees in Yosemite National Park than open our bank statements and balance our checkbooks, because we don't want to know how badly we've let ourselves get behind in paying our bills. Sometimes the whole purpose of procrastinating is to let ourselves think it's better than it really is. Money issues don't go away because we want to blot them out of our minds; they just get worse. Financial problems grow like dust bunnies under the bed; if we don't get them out into the sunlight and look at them, they get bigger, darker, and more annoying to handle. How much time, energy, and mental anguish do we waste resisting the inevitable responsibilities of our lives, only to find that once we get started, they are so much easier to deal with than we thought they would be? As always, the resistance is in our heads.

Affirmation:

I can rid myself of all my delusions about money.

Action Step:

Make an appointment at your bank to get help with balancing your checkbook. The customer service representative will assist you in clearing up the confusion of why your balance doesn't agree with theirs. There may be some hidden fees and service charges that zapped your account. Be aware that the bank may charge a fee for this service.

Day 78

GIVE YOURSELF PERMISSION

There are two things to aim for in life: first, to get what you want, and after that to enjoy it. Only the wisest of mankind achieve the second.

—Logan Pearsall Smith

Most of us are afraid to admit our dreams to ourselves, let alone share them with someone else. But if your dreams remain dreams and you don't look for a way to fulfill them, sooner or later, they wither into dust. Give yourself permission to learn, to grow, to change, to be. Your outlook and attitudes about money are stepping stones to fulfilling those dreams because whatever your dream—a house in the country, a cruise on the Aegean Sea, a healthy child, or enough time to sit down and write the great American novel—it usually comes with a price tag attached. Just deciding that you want things to be different in your relationship with money is a start, but the thought has to be backed up by action steps that make them real. When an architect builds a house, he or she draws up plans, gets estimates of the cost of labor and materials, looks for the right setting, and develops the house step by step, brick by brick, day by day. Whatever your dream—losing weight, writing a book, learning to drive a car, or building a house—you get there by making it happen one day at time. Building a secure financial future happens the same way. Step by step, day by day, dollar by dollar.

Affirmation:

Affirmation:

I take my first step toward making my dreams become real starting today!

Action Step:

Make a calendar of the goals you can comfortably accomplish in the next six months. Calculate the weekly savings needed to meet the goal. Paste it on the bathroom mirror.

Day 79

PRAYING FOR ABUNDANCE

You can have anything as long as it's not against God's will.

—Yiddish Proverb

Have you ever seen a bird with a broken wing? The poor creature fumbles around sadly, grounded on the concrete streets, unable to lift itself above its predicament. In time, with proper treatment, the wing will be healed and the bird will be able to take off and rise above the trees, glide over the city, and disappear into the wind. Most of us are trying to fly with one wing as we constantly beg God for abundance, yet stick to the same self-defeating money habits and behavior that brought us down to where we are now. God's grace is like a bird in flight. Both wings must work together for the bird to climb into the sky. One wing is the blessing of abundance that is waiting for us. The second wing is our own effort. God cannot intervene and help you until you have exhausted all your own resources. Ask yourself first, "Have I done everything possible on my own to change my situation before asking God's help?" You can pray all you want and beg God to deliver you from the mountain of bills or help you find a better job or make more money, but if you turn over and go back to sleep without making a budget, sending out your résumé, or changing your habits and behavior with money, you're not making the best effort to help yourself. Next year you will be in the same place that you were last year; nothing will be different and you will wonder if God has forgotten you—again. It does no good to keep praying and asking for God's blessing unless you also create a budget plan and follow it. You'll also get in the way of the grace that is flowing your way if you decide that after two weeks of trying to save and budget, you've had enough and you go off to the mall as a reward. If you don't make the effort, you'll be like a bird that is trying to fly with one wing.

Affirmation:

I will follow my prayers with appropriate actions so I can soar!

Action Step:

Review your spending diary from the past few days. Did you observe at least one new good habit that you have included in your daily routine? Make a list of other habit changes you would like to make.

Day 80

A PRIVATE PACT

The world turns aside to let any man pass who knows whither he is going.

—David S. Jordan

What would happen if you told a few friends, relatives, or coworkers about a very personal goal you have that is slightly unusual. Let's say you want to go to Italy to La Scala to see a performance of *Aida* in which real elephants appear, or climb Mount Everest, go rafting down the Colorado River, take six months off to hike the Appalachian

Trail, or rent an RV to spend a year driving across country. What reaction do you think you'd get? If you expect laughter, derision, or some criticism or putdown, then it's best not to discuss it with them. The same goes for your money goals. Wait and surprise your friends—then see how much better you feel about yourself as you begin to get out of debt, pay cash for all your purchases, build a comfortable savings account, and start an investment portfolio. It's your money and you're doing this for yourself, so you don't need to tell anyone who will rain on your parade. Shock them with your fabulous results instead. Start today.

Affirmation:

Improving my financial prospects is something I can do for myself, and it's okay to keep it to myself.

Action Step:

Make a financial wish list that you share with no one else. Begin exploring what the price tag is for each of those wishes. It may be cheaper than you think.

Day 81

THE DEADLY SPIRAL

Nothing is a waste of time if you use the experience wisely.

—Rodin

It happened so easily and so subtly that Sarah P. didn't realize how she amassed that $4,800 worth of credit card debt. When she got her first job in September 1996 as a sales assistant in a brokerage firm making $20,000 a year, she intended to stay for a year and save some money so she could go to graduate school full-time. The credit card came in the mail two months later. Since it was Christmas, she decided it was okay to use it for holiday shopping. It had a $5,000 credit limit, and all she had to pay was a minimum of $30 a month. She could handle that. She spent $809. She also treated herself to three new business suits with matching silk blouses she found during the after-Christmas discount sales, for $517. In March, she sublet an apartment with another coworker. They needed a few things for the apartment. An afternoon at Home Depot came to $426. Whenever she worked late, Sarah would order dinner from the gourmet deli two blocks away from her apartment and pay with her Visa card. When her sister got married in April, Sarah was maid of honor. Her dress and the trip back home with presents ran up another $943. Sarah also treated herself and her roommate to theater tickets and dinner out for her birthday—$172 for the evening. By May, Sarah began to look at graduate school catalogs and realized she had no savings and could not remember what she had done with the money she had earned over the past year. Her dream of going back to school withered away.

Action Step:

Ask yourself these six questions before you use a credit card for anything:

Do I need this now or can I save for it?

Do I have enough in cash or savings that I can use instead?

How much will the interest add to the cost?

Do the extra payments fit into my budget?

How much will this purchase add to my total debt?

Is this a tax-deductible item?

Day 82

COUNT YOUR BLESSINGS AND YOUR TAX BILL

Those who have earned a fortune are more careful than those who have inherited one.

—Charles C. Colton

One of the best gifts you can give yourself and your family is a well-organized filing cabinet or a notebook of your financial records in an easy-to-find place. This is also what you will need to make a will, which should be considered a realistic financial planning techniques to avoid financial chaos if something should happen to you. Here's a recommended list of how your records should be arranged.

Make a list of all your assets. Include:

Stocks, bonds, money market accounts.

Retirement plans, pensions accounts.

Real estate, automobiles, and boats.

Insurance policies and annuities.

Outstanding debts, including credit cards, mortgages, and personal loans

Congratulate yourself on having done so well for yourself. Next to each item write a value for it and add it up. Now make a separate list of your outstanding debts, including credit cards, mortgages, and personal loans. If the result is more than $650,000 you have think about the taxes that may be owed on the total amount. Is there an insurance policy or savings account with enough cash in it to pay the taxes?

Determine what you want family members and charitable organizations to get and see if you can reduce your tax bill by giving away some of those items before your demise. $10,000 a year can be passed on to each child and relative to reduce your estate without creating a gift tax.

Action Step:

Review your net worth statement and think about how you would like to pass your assets on to your loved ones before you meet with an attorney.

Day 83

REVIEW AND REASSESS

Go back and review the spending diary that you kept in the first week. How many habits and expenses have you changed in the last few weeks? Have you been putting aside your extra change in your "dream jar"? Are your reading at least one financial publication each week? By now you should have attended at least one investment workshop or seminar. You should also be clearer about what goals are important to you, the price tag on them, and how your habits, attitudes, and daily behavior can direct you toward achieving them. Congratulate yourself if you have changed at least one excessive spending habit. Now we move on to dealing with debt, saving, and looking at the "B" word—budgeting and how to use it for your own well-being. If you haven't taken these steps yet, take your time and go back through the previous pages.

TWO

WEALTH
FOUNDATION

INTRODUCTION

Save money and money will save you.

—Jamaican saying

Now that you're clear about why money is important, how you feel about it, how it can help you accomplish things that really matter— how it can empower you to make a difference not only for yourself but in your community—let's move forward on the actual tools and skills for making wealth happen. You can't build a house without laying a strong foundation. The same is true for building wealth. The foundation for wealth has three simple components. None requires any special technical knowledge, and they are all within your control.

First you must have a budget—call it a spending plan if the "B" word makes your hair curl—so that you know where your money is going. Use all those diary entries you've kept for the last few weeks. You'll revise your budget as you find ways to cut your expenses, leaving more for savings. That's why the second element in the wealth foundation is spending less, every day. Take a look at your spending and become more conscious about how you spend. Plan it. Don't let it just happen. Use the savings tips in the following sections and start collecting your own. This section is full of savings tips on everything from clothes shopping to car buying, but once you develop the penny-pincher mentality, you'll find plenty of ways to save. Then you have to put those savings into Savings.

The final component of the foundation is—for some—the most critical: learning to manage credit and getting out of debt. Everyone needs credit, and we'll talk about how to obtain it if you've never had any. But for most Americans, the problem is too much credit—in the form of credit cards—and too, too, too much debt. Whether or not you feel that you are in over your head, you need to get out of debt to build wealth. Paying off your credit cards is job one; the whys and the hows are up ahead.

Make a spending plan, spend less, pay off your debts: That's the foundation you need to lay before you can start creating real wealth. Create a financial calendar. Set a timetable and follow it.

Day 84

BUDGET LAYOUT

It is very iniquitous to make me pay my debts; you have no idea of the pain it gives me.

—Lord Byron

Take all of those spending diaries that you have done for the last few weeks and now put them to use. Arrange all the information and notes you've taken along with your bills into the categories listed below. Wait until you have some quiet time on a Sunday afternoon or night, or whenever is convenient, and open your bills and diaries. Write out a list of what is actually paid out each month to each creditor in each of the categories listed below.

....

Income After Deductions

Salary
Alimony/Child Support
Social Security
Pension
Other (interest, tips, dividends, etc.)

Monthly Fixed Expenses

Rent/Mortgage
Installment Payments (car note, student loan, insurance, credit cards, etc.)

Other (saving and investing)

Monthly Flexible Expenses

Food

Utilities

Clothing

Recreation/Entertainment

Contributions

Other

Periodic Expenses

School Tuition

Medical/Dental

Vacation

Subscriptions

Home Maintenance

Auto Maintenance

Other

What's Left?

....

.

Action Step:

Click on http://www.household.com/trkcrech.html and print out copies of this worksheet as a starting point. You can also write for free copies of the "Money Management" series of booklets on saving, spending, and credit issues. Write to: Household International, Corporate Communications, 2700 Sanders Road, Prospect Heights, IL 60070–2799.

Day 85

YOUR DAILY "BREAD"

Nothing is so often irretrievably missed as a daily opportunity.

—Marie von Ebner-Eschenback

Each morning when we wake up, our minds automatically click on our mental "to do" list even before we hit the shower, all in the pursuit of earning a living. The average American spends 70 percent of his or her waking hours each day in the daily ritual of pursuing or managing money. Pause in the middle of brushing your teeth and ask yourself, "Why am I doing this if I don't have a goal?" Is your career going according to plan, or have you gotten distracted? Whatever the goal, getting there requires more than just thinking about it. Every payday that goes without a payroll savings deduction or a 401(k) contribution puts the prosperity and financial freedom you desire one more day out of reach.

Action Step:

Make that call today and fill out the form to have at least $25 taken out of your next paycheck and put into a savings bond.

Day 86

MILLIONAIRES' HABITS

The rich are different from you and me.

—F. Scott Fitzgerald

Want to become a millionaire before you retire? Then learn to think like one. In their best-selling book, *The Millionaire Next Door,* Thomas J. Stanley and William D. Danko listed some interesting habits of self-made millionaires who started from nothing and became successful without inheriting a dime from a rich relative or winning the lottery. They're primarily entrepreneurs, have only one credit card, pay cash for most purchases, drive three-year old used cars, preferably Fords, buy stocks and hold them for 20 to 30 years (not mutual funds that have annual year-end dividends that create taxes!), shop with coupons, and always look for sales when they do buy clothes at the end of a season. Their major focus is on saving, not spending! All of them have these three basic characteristics in common:

Live below your means.

Invest at least 10 percent of all you earn and hold on to it for retirement.

Pay top dollar for good professional advice about taxes and investing.

How many of these habits are a part of your financial life?

Affirmation:

I practice thinking like a millionaire when I review my spending plan.

Action Step:

Pick up a copy of *The Millionaire Next Door* at the library and make that your bedtime reading for the next three weeks.

Day 87

WHERE AMERICANS SPEND

Some couples go over their budgets very carefully every month,
others just go over them.

—Sally Poplin

In a 1997 study, the Department of Labor produced a study of consumer spending based on the categories below. Look at the percentages and categories and see where you fit in. Don't be surprised if your percentages are totally out of line here. Think of this as giving you a guideline to strive for!

	Average Household Budget	Your Average Monthly Budget
Housing	32 percent	_____
Transportation	17 percent	_____
Food	15 percent	_____
Insurance/Pensions	9 percent	_____
Education	8 percent	_____
Clothing	6 percent	_____
Health Care	5 percent	_____
Entertainment	5 percent	_____
Other	3 percent	_____

Action Step:

Review your spending diary and your monthly budget with your calculator and see how your spending compares with the national averages. Brace yourself! If too much is going into eating out, clothing, and entertainment, this is the time to find out.

Day 88

MYSTERY MONEY

Beware of little expenses. A small leak will sink a great ship.

—Ben Franklin

Old Ben was right. It's the little expenses that we don't pay attention to that seep out of our pockets each day which get in the way of building wealth: 50 cents for a newspaper that you throw away after reading it; $2.50 for a corn muffin and coffee when you could have eaten toast and jam at home. This is the one common problem of spending without a plan. You remember what the rent and the car note are but you never remember from day to day how the little expenses dribble away almost unseen, leaving you confused about where the money went.

Affirmation:

I will be more conscious and careful in my daily spending.

Action Step:

Review your daily spending log and carry only the cash you need each day.

Day 89

SKINFLINT, CHEAPSKATE, TIGHTWAD?

Being frugal is the cornerstone of wealth-building.

—Thomas J. Stanley, Ph.D.,
coauthor of *The Millionaire Next Door*

Never mind what people will say about you. If you need some guidance and direction in how to be frugal, there's more than enough help out there in the form of newsletters, books, and Web sites. You won't find many of the recent newsletters in the library, but you can locate them on the Internet. The most popular ones are:

The Tightwad Gazette, at http://www.tightwadmama.com.

The Cheapskate Monthly, at http://www.cheapskatemonthly. com.

The Living Cheap News, no Web site, but you can request out-of-date copies of books and newsletters by writing to: Living Cheap Press, 7232 Belleview Avenue, Kansas City, MO 64114.

Action Step:

For a free sample copy of *The Frugal Gazette*, send a self-addressed, stamped, business-size envelope to The Frugal Gazette, P.O. Box 3395, Newtown, CT 06470–3395. No, they don't have an 800 number because they are being frugal, but you can visit their Web site at http://www.frugalgazette.com.

Day 90

$$$—Savings Tip:

Balance that checkbook and watch those fees! The biggest expense in managing a bank account is the bounced check charges, which can be as high as $30 per check. The second highest fee is for the deposit-item-returned fees, which range from $5 to $15. Although the actual cost to the bank is only 50 cents to $1.50 to process these items, they are helping their bottom line, not yours, according to the Consumer Federation of America.

Action Step:

Review the expenses imposed by your bank for each service it provides. Find out if you can protect yourself by having a cash reserve line to avoid overdraft charges, and carefully follow your budget when you write those checks each month. And, what's more, too many bounced checks can also injure your credit rating.

Day 91

OUTLOOK ALIGNMENT

Make the most of yourself, for that is all there is of you.

—Ralph Waldo Emerson

Harry T. realized, at 30, that he would never achieve his goal of becoming a writer unless he changed his financial behavior. Working as a copywriter at a small ad agency in Boston, Harry planned to save enough to quit and write full-time. Experience taught him he couldn't put in ten hours at the agency and then come home and write a book. He had saved only $1,400 in five years—not enough for a year of writing at home. Budgeting had always seemed a bit shameful to him, like something a woman of his mom's generation would do, but if his book was ever going to become a reality he needed to change his outlook. He needed to *sacrifice*. Such an unpleasant word! But if you think of budgeting as a commitment to a goal instead of a painful reduction in life's pleasures, the sacrifice loses its sting and becomes a discipline that lead to self-sufficiency. Harry sold his gas-guzzling car and took the subway. He stopped buying books and used the library, cut out the restaurants and cooked at home, bartered his skills as a writer in return for free computer servicing from a teenager who needed help with his term papers. When he inherited a modest sum from a great aunt, he went to an investment adviser and bought stocks instead of taking a vacation in Barbados. By changing his daily habits and his outlook, he saw his savings grow every month, and his deprivations weren't painful because they were for a purpose. "If I'd done this from the beginning, I could have realized my goal at 30," he says. He's now 33, and six months into writing his book. If it doesn't sell to a publisher, Harry will still have the good financial habits he's acquired. He can keep them for a lifetime, whether he goes back to an agency or enjoys success as an author.

Affirmation:

I can change my financial behavior even if my mind isn't ready for it.

Action Step:

Review your goals and see if you have made any adjustments to them.

Day 92

CONSISTENCY PAYS OFF

People do not lack strength, they lack will.

—Victor Hugo

If you understand the ancient Chinese saying, "The journey of a thousand miles begins with one step," then you will also understand that the journey toward wealth begins with the first dollar. In this case you can start with $50. We have already established that you can find an extra $50 a month by simply taking the extra change out of your pocket each night and setting it aside. The next step is putting that money away in a blue chip equity mutual fund that will give you the growth you want to reach that million-dollar goal. (Blue chip stocks are those household names you recognize when you open the refrigerator or the medicine

cabinet, or when you look around your office or your living room—
names like Procter & Gamble, General Electric, Coca-Cola, IBM,
Disney, and Exxon.) Don't worry about the question of where to put
the money just yet. You just make the commitment to have $50 a
month deducted from your paycheck or your bank account. Do it on a
consistent basis. Approach it with the same discipline and personal
attention that you give to getting a haircut each month, taking your
vitamins each day, or paying your mortgage. Since you probably want
to play it safe right now, you may want to check out one of the oldest
mutual funds around, the Founders Blue Chip Fund, which was
established in 1938. The fund has been around for more than 60 years
and despite the ups, downs, dips, and dodges of the market, it has produced an average return of 19.1 percent per year over the last ten years.
Looking at the longer term, it has produced an average return of 15.5
percent since it started, which is an excellent achievement in such a
volatile business. Founders was also one of the first companies to allow
automatic monthly investments. Get out your budget sheet, put those
pennies away, clip those coupons, and set up that automatic monthly
savings plan. Now you know where to put that extra $50 a month.

Action Step:

Call Founders at 800–525–2440 and order a copy of the prospectus and application for the Blue Chip Fund and get started today!
You can also download a copy of it from the Founders Web site at
http://www.founders.com.

Day 93

PAY YOURSELF FIRST!

*Even the wisest among men welcome people who bring money
more than those who take it away.*

—G. C. Lichtenberg

You've heard this from every financial book, talk show, magazine, and adviser but you still don't put yourself number one because you think it's selfish and insensitive to think of yourself first. But who else is going to do it for you but you? First jobbers out of college think they can wait until they're 40 or later to worry about retirement. Parents think they must sacrifice retirement savings for college savings in an obligation to their children. Young married couples believe that the house, the mortgage, the car, the new sofa, drapes, appliances, and material goods of setting up a life together are more important than saving for retirement. Look at it this way. Were you born into the world, nurtured and educated by your parents, for the purpose of supporting Visa, MasterCard, AMEX, and the banks that have made the various loans to you? The reason for your existence is not to incur constant debt to support the lifestyle you think you should have. Above all else, you are working to create a comfortable life and creating a prosperous future for yourself and the next generation. You can only do that when you get on your own payroll. Start today.

Action Step:

Call one of the many money market funds or equity mutual funds listed in this book and put your saving and investing on automatic pilot. Build your budget around including this item at the top of the list.

Day 94

YOU, INC.

You must run a household like a business.

—Jim Jorgenson

Do this exercise. Think of yourself as an independent contractor, and look at your paycheck as the sales revenue for your business. You need to cover your expenses for the maintenance of the business and create enough of a profit so your business can grow. In your case, that profit is your savings and investments. The only way businesspeople know if they are making a profit is if they keep track of the money coming in and the money going out, and the income is greater than the outgo.

Action Step:

Take out all your receipts, ATM slips, and pay stubs from the past two months. Compare them with your spending diary to see if you have accurately recorded all your expenses. Keep track of your paycheck and your spending—even for a newspaper and coffee each day—for one month to see if you would be judged as a profitable business.

Day 95

$$$—Savings Tip:

The best software package you can purchase to help you demystify nearly every aspect of the financial planning process from budgeting and debt management to investment tracking and retirement planning as well as tax preparation and bill paying is Quicken by Intuit ($39.95). Remember that spending journal you've been keeping? Type in all those expenses in the various categories Quicken has laid them out for you: groceries, entertainment, prescriptions, dry cleaning, cat food, eating out, and so on. It will show you where most of your money is going, compare your money habits with some national averages, and make recommendations about how to improve your spending patterns. This program will also help you write checks, remind you when a bill is due, and keep track of your bank account on the Internet if you use computerized banking. All this saves tremendous time when you get ready to fill out your 1040 next April. Quicken also has an excellent Web site that offers great advice on all aspects of money management, investing, and taxes in a weekly newsletter.

Action Step:

Take a look at http://www.quicken.com or call 800–624–8742 to find a dealer near you if you don't find the Quicken software package in your nearest computer store. If you bought an IBM-compatible computer in the last year or two, with Windows 95 or Windows 98, the software may already be installed for you. Call for an upgrade for $19.95 if you already own an earlier version of the program.

Day 96

REVIEW AND REASSESS

Are you making an effort to balance your checkbook regularly? Have you set up a payroll savings plan yet? Review the budget you made two weeks ago and the spending plan. What changes can you make in these expenses to free up more money for savings? As you consider this question, keep your goals in mind.

Day 97

NET.BANK.COM

It was just a matter of time before it happened in the world of the information superhighway and electronic commerce, so if you're ready to start functioning in a checkless, cashless society, here's the bank of the future if you don't mind the lack of a human touch in doing your banking. No lines at lunchtime, no teller windows, because there are no branches to visit. Checkbooks are almost unnecessary because of the automated bill-paying service, but you do get 200 checks free when you open your account. If you get your paycheck by direct deposit and pay bills by automatic transfers and do investing by automatic deductions, this is the account for you. The bank offers self-addressed stamped envelopes for mail deposits and an ATM card to get cash when you need it. You'll have to be aware of ATM charges from the banks that you'll be using. The rarest benefit is the interest earned on your checking account without a $4,000 or $6,000 balance. It also offers telephone service until midnight and no fees for phone calls to check your balance.

Action Step:

Call 888–BKONWEB to get more information, but account opening can be done on the Internet at http://www.net.bank.com.

Day 98

THE "B" WORD

Don't cringe when you hear the word "budget"! Embrace it as a tool that you use for your financial well-being. There are three basic reasons for looking at your budget:

See what you think you're doing with your money.

See what you're actually doing with your money.

Make you think about how can cut your cost of living without diminishing your standard of living.

If you need help with getting the paperwork done on what you're spending, get *The Budget Kit* by Judy Lawrence, $15.95, Dearborn Publishing, 1997. Many software programs like Quicken and Microsoft Money will help you start getting control of your spending and planning ahead.

Action Step:

Browse through a software store and look at the various program available and ask for assistance on finding one that can help you.

Day 99

THE TRUTH ABOUT TAXES

Makes me wanna holler, the way they do my money.

—Marvin Gaye

The media is constantly reporting on Congress's plans to attack the budget deficit, and reduce taxes, but the average American still doesn't understand what it all means. Holler, scream, cry, but there's very little you can do as an individual about the Senate Appropriations Committee and the money mavens in the General Accounting Office—except write a letter to your senator or congressional representative and wait for tax reform. Meanwhile, don't pay one nickel more than you have to! Overpaying your federal taxes is no way to create a forced savings plan. Actually, the *last* thing you want is a large tax refund. According to the IRS, the average 1998 tax refund was $1,549—over $100 per month. That extra $100 could (1) clean up some debt; (2) add to your 401(k) plan; (3) shorten a 30-year mortgage by seven years; (4) invest in a growth mutual fund to save for your child's college education; (5) take a cash-paid vacation next year; or (6) build up that cash emergency account that you don't have yet. You weren't expecting to have that cash anyway, so why not put it to work for you? Look at it this way, would Uncle Sam give you an interest-free loan for a year? Then why are you giving it to him? Consider this: $100 a month paid into a blue-chip equity mutual fund with a 12 percent return adds up to $24,921 after ten years. Would you rather let your $100 pay for a bureaucrat's limousine, an inactive missile silo in Nebraska, or a study of grasshoppers in Alaska?

Affirmation:

I will pay my fair share of taxes but not one penny more!

Action Step:

If your last tax refund was more than $500, speak to a benefits counselor at work about adjusting your W-4 exemptions. Each extra exemption is worth approximately $50 per paycheck.

Day 100

TAX HELP

If you're comfortable with doing your taxes yourself, call the IRS at 800–829–1040 to order forms or click on http://www. irs.ustreas.gov to download them.

For useful prerecorded tax tips from the IRS covering at least 150 different topics, dial 800–829–4477.

If your taxes are simple but you want professional help, the National Association of Enrolled Agents at 800–424–4339 will refer you to a tax preparer in your area who will charge much less than the average $150 an hour of a CPA or a tax attorney.

Day 101

DO A CHARITY CHECKUP

The holidays are the time of so many solicitations. If you'd like to learn more about any of them, or to verify their legitimacy, call the Philanthropic Advisory Service of the Council of Better Business Bureaus at 703–276–0100.

Day 102

FIVE GUARANTEED WAYS
TO SAVE MONEY

Savings earn money; credit costs money.

—Anonymous

Don't play the lottery!

Don't buy anything unless you really need it!

Don't pay full price for anything!

Don't use credit cards for anything unless you have the cash to pay the full amount at the end of the month!

Don't buy lavish gifts—especially for people you don't like!

Affirmation:

I pay careful attention to how and when I use credit so I will not abuse the privilege.

Day 103

$$$—Savings Tip:

If you go to a small shop where an owner is behind the counter, you can negotiate a lower price on an item. A dress, jacket, or blouse that is missing a button can often be bought for 10 percent off the ticket price. A small dent or scratch on an appliance can save as much as $50 or $100 off a floor model, but you have to ask for that price reduction if it isn't already marked down.

Day 104

$$$—Savings Tip:

Shop on the "special midweek discount days" offered by many large chain department stores. Macy's, Dayton's, Hudson's, and most major department stores frequently have one-hour sales during the low-traffic morning hours on a Wednesday or Thursday when slow-selling items like sheets, towels, and small appliances may be offered at an extra 10 percent off if you purchase them between 9 and 10 A.M.

Day 105

THE HOLIDAY AMBUSH

Holidays are the biggest time of the year for irrational shopping and excess spending. Whether you celebrate Christmas, Kwanzaa, or Chanukah, chances are you end up spending far more than you should. Plan ahead by joining a "Holiday Club"—the bank automatically deducts $10 or $20 from your account each week, giving you a nice sum when the holidays arrive.

Adopt some commonsense rules when it comes to gifts for the family. Take a leaf from office parties, where all the names go into a bag and everyone picks one name. Uncle Walter or Cousin Amelia will be as pleased with one nice gift as with eight hastily bought knickknacks they probably don't want anyway. At Thanksgiving dinner everyone brings something, so why not make Christmas a communal effort and avoid that feeling that you've wiped out your bank balance on another stressful holiday.

Find some quiet time and get involved in some special craft. It's a way to relax, enjoy a silent moment with yourself, and make a special gift for someone that will be much more meaningful, and cheaper, than something purchased from a catalog or department store.

If you subscribe to magazines, check out their offers around the holidays; you may find you can renew your subscription and get another subscription for a fraction of the usual cost. A magazine subscription brings pleasure to the recipient all year long.

Action Step:

Curb the television watching that children do around the holidays. The toy ads are at their loudest and most hysterical then and make kids think they can't live without lots of expensive toys. Explain to them that they will receive two items under the tree. Put a limit on those overblown expectations. After the tantrum is over, they'll forget about it.

Day 106

NEEDS VS. WANTS

Rather to go to bed supperless than to rise in debt.

—Ben Franklin

Yes, you need a car to get to work, but does it have to be a brand-new $39,000 Lexus with all the toys and gadgets, or can you make it there each Monday morning with a three-year-old Honda purchased at an off-lease auction for $8,000? You need decent food to stay in good health, but you don't need to buy takeout meals every night or go to a four-star restaurant each weekend. You need shoes, but you don't need to be the next Imelda Marcos with a collection from the most expensive boutiques in town. A $30 pair of Keds on sale at the mall will serve as well as a $90 pair of Nikes as a walking shoe. Look for sales. Go to factory outlets. Check out garage sales for household appliances, dishes, lamps, games and toys for kids. You might find a lovely Mikasa dinnerware set for about 10 percent of what it would have cost you last year at a department store. Remember the Cabbage Patch craze of fifteen years ago and how you paid $60 for one doll? Now you can find one for about $5 at your typical garage sale! Learn to separate out the "must have" items from the "wait and negotiate" items. Try asking for an item from this latter category as a gift for your birthday, Christmas, and anniversary.

Affirmation:

I will be more conscious of spending my money only on things I truly need.

Action Step:

Pick up a local neighborhood newspaper or check out your community bulletin board and find a garage sale. Buy only what you need, and only if it's a real bargain.

Day 107

RULES FOR VISITING THE MALL

He who does not economize will have to agonize.

—Confucius

Leave the credit cards, checkbook, and debit card at home.

Take only $20 with you, and don't use it for putting something on layaway.

If you see something you "absolutely have to have," wait three days and come back. If you're supposed to have it, it will still be there.

Think of your visit as research for someone else's Christmas gift shopping.

Day 108

INTERNATIONAL BUY NOTHING DAY

The day after Thanksgiving is the beginning of the Christmas shopping season and is looked upon by retailers as a forecast of sales volume for the season. It has also been designated by the Voluntary Simplicity movement as International Buy Nothing Day to discourage unnecessary overconsumption. Since 28 percent of the world consumes 82 percent of all the material goods purchased, there's definitely a global imbalance in the patterns of spending. Anticonsumerism campaigns have been launched in shopping malls from Canada to New Zealand, aimed at making shoppers rethink what they are spending and why. They encourage people to spend the day reading books, playing chess or volleyball, engaging in any social activity that does not require money.

Affirmation:

I find creative ways to give gifts without spending money.

Action Step:

Find out more about how to enjoy a day without spending by calling the U.S. headquarters of Voluntary Simplicity at 212–966–5244 or visiting their Web site at http://www.netg.se/Oppem/Org/y/yee/mag-noshopping.htm.

Day 109

CATALOG TEMPTATION

$$$—Savings Tip:

Cancel all your mail order catalogs. They tempt you to spend when you don't need to, and make it easy to do so on a rainy afternoon when you're bored, depressed, or just "need a lift." Write to the Telephone/Mail Preference Service of the Direct Marketing Association, P.O. Box 9008, Farmingdale, NY 117335–9008 and ask to have your name removed from all those national solicitation mailing lists. Think of how many trees you'll save when you cut out all that unnecessary paper.

Day 110

TEN SMART WAYS TO HAVE A FUN DAY WITHOUT SPENDING MONEY

Attend a free concert.

Go to an author reading in a bookstore.

Take a nature walk or go for a bike ride in some nearby woods, or in a park.

Write a letter to a friend you haven't seen in a long time. Or send an audio tape if you feel like you're all fumbles with pen and paper. Make it a family event.

Go to an art museum on the free night.

Have a potluck supper with some neighbors, or invite the neighbors over to have popcorn and watch old videos.

Go to the library and pick up a couple of videos, an audio book, CDs, or even a book!

Make sandwiches and take the kids to the park for an impromptu picnic.

Volunteer for a special event (fund raiser, recital, holiday event, bake sale, etc.) at your church, mosque, or synagogue, or in your community.

Put those pictures from your last vacation in an empty photo album you have lying around.

Day 111

FIVE STEPS TO BUYING A USED CAR

Before you fall in love with a fender or get seduced by the metallic finish on a headlight, remember two things: (1) cars go down in value each year but your monthly payments don't, and (2) their basic purpose is transportation, nothing more, nothing less. If you see cars as a sex symbol, a status symbol, or any other form of psychological satisfaction, read that last sentence again. If you live in the city, take into account insurance, parking fees, tickets, and the higher cost of gas. Where you live determines what you pay.

Action Steps:

Follow these steps before you buy a car:

Consumer Reports Annual Buying Guide lists cars in price ranges from $2,000 to $25,000 rated as good buys over the last seven years, as well as the ones to avoid.

Go to http://www.edmunds.com on the Internet for a "reliability rating" on over 200 different used car models as far back as 1976.

Look in the yellow pages under "Automobile Auctions" and call to ask if the auctions handle "off lease" cars (vehicles that have been returned after a short-term lease of one to two years) and former rental cars.

Find an auto diagnostician—a mechanic/auto inspector who will go with you and for a fee of about $60 examine everything from the chassis to the carburetor to let you know whether you're getting a lemon or a good deal.

Get the crash safety rating of the car you want to purchase from the National Highway Safety Board at 800–934–8517 or 202–366–4198, or http://www.nhtsa.dot.gov/cars/testing.

Insurance companies use these ratings to set the cost of collision and comprehensive coverage on new vehicles.

Day 112

REVIEW AND REASSESS

Saving means planning for the future, but it also means changing your behavior now. Have you skipped one purchase in the last two weeks because you didn't have the cash and decided not to charge it? Great! Now take the cost of that unpurchased item and put it in your savings. You should also be much more conscious of how you used credit and why. .

Day 113

WRITING LETTERS

$$$—Savings Tip:

This old-fashioned art is so neglected in the age of cell phones and the Internet that writing letters will make you stand out as a very special person who will always be remembered fondly by the person you send them to. Your handwritten note will be treasured and reread many times over; long after the e-mail has been erased and the phone bill has been paid. And the cost of a stamp is much less than a 30-minute coast-to-coast phone call—even on nights and weekends.

Day 114

CARD BLOCKING

$$$—Savings Tip:

When you phone a hotel to make a room reservation, you are usually asked to guarantee it with a credit card. At that point, the hotel will contact your credit card company and put a block on your card for the cost of one night's stay. If you change your mind and go elsewhere, call the hotel, not the travel agency, and cancel that reservation before the 6 P.M. deadline. Be sure to get a cancellation number and the name of the person you spoke to. Otherwise, you'll find an item on your bill next month for a bed you never slept in.

Day 115

AVOIDING A CREDIT CRISIS

I owe, I owe, so off to work I go!

—California bumper sticker

"Congratulations, you've been approved!" Isn't it amazing how you can open your mail every few months and get one of those pre-approved credit card offers that sounds like it's a special honor? While it may feel great to know that another bank or department store thinks of you as a good credit risk, unfortunately, they aren't doing you a special favor. They're offering a temptation and selling you debt, which benefits them, not you. If you collect credit cards like souvenirs or status symbols, you're on the wrong track. All that accumulated credit does not enhance your social status as a consumer! Let's assume you want to apply for a mortgage but you have

17 credit cards, each with a $2,500 credit limit. Even with zero balances on all of them and a perfectly clean credit history, the lending bank will ask you to close most of those accounts, to avoid the risk that you might charge up to the limit on all those cards. It might also be concerned that your income might not cover the monthly minimum balance on all those accounts. Banks know better than anyone that the main one who benefits from your spending is the bank issuing the card, not you.

Affirmation:

I will learn to think like a banker before I apply for a loan.

Action Step:

Look at your credit cards and see how close you are to the limit on each of them. If you have several extra cards with low balances, call the bank and close those accounts or ask them to lower your credit limit.

Day 116

TEN PHRASES TO AVOID

No money down.

No payments (or interest) for 12 months.

Toll-free operators are standing by.

Here's your pre-approved credit card.

Fly now, pay later.

Bad credit, no credit, bankruptcy, no problem!

Sign and return our monthly purchase contract today.

Send no money now.

Time payment plans available.

Congratulations, you have won a free gift!

Day 117

PEACE OF MIND

If you're losing sleep over how much you owe, who to pay first, and what to say when the bill collectors call, you can take small comfort in the fact that you're not the only one. More than 135 million people filed bankruptcy last year. Nine percent of them were under the age of 25. If you're too embarrassed to go to a credit counselor in person, or can't find one that you trust in your community, or want to talk to someone at 3 A.M. when you're in a funk about money, phone Money Management International, a nonprofit professional organization that provides confidential counseling on debt repayment assistance by phone. Someone is there 24 hours a day to answer your questions and help you start turning your life around and relieve the pressure of owing too much money. A counselor will provide advice and negoti-ate with your bill collectors by phone, fax, e-mail, or snail mail. The service is completely free—no enrollment fees, no interview fees, no monthly program fees.

Affirmation:

I use whatever means available to me to improve my financial well-being.

Action Step:

Contact Money Management International at 800–762–2271 (24 hours a day) or visit its Web site at http://www.moneymanagement bymail.org.

Day 118

GETTING CONTROL OF DEBT

Solvency is entirely a matter of temperament and not of income.

—Logan Pearsall Smith

How do you get out of debt? Start with these basic steps:

Make a chart listing what you owe and the monthly payments for each debt.

Pay off the small debts first. That will make you feel better sooner.

Decide the amount you can pay each creditor each month. Write it down. You may have to ask your lender to help you determine how the interest on your debt is going to affect your timetable. For example, if you owe $2,500 on a credit card with an 18.1 percent interest rate, and the largest amount you can pay is $125 a month, you can safely assume that about $37 a month will go to pay interest charges. That means that only $88 will be applied toward reducing that $2,500 debt balance. Your $2,500 debt divided into $88 payments will take approximately 28 months to pay off, or slightly less as the balance decreases each month. This is why you should work on paying off the credit cards with the highest interest rate first. If you can, transfer the balance on an 18 percent card to a 12 percent card. That cuts your interest rate by one-third, so more of your money goes to the debt.

Write out a monthly payment schedule to follow. Mark a monthly calendar for your future "D" Day, the day you become debt-free. Think how much lighter you'll feel when your mailbox is empty of bills! You can do it!

As each debt is paid off, apply that same amount of money to the next bill until it is wiped out.

Once all the bills are gone, keep writing those same checks each month, but send them to a money market fund to build up your savings cushion.

Action Step:

Use one of the debt calculator formulas at http://www.fools.com to help you determine how soon you will become debt-free. Or go to http://www.smartcode.com/debt and download the Debt Analyzer. You can try it out for 21 days before you have to decide if you want to purchase it. By that time you should have learned what you need to know and can tell if you really need it.

Day 119

GROSS VS. NET INCOME

Perhaps you need to adjust your thinking to realize how much money you really have to work with! If you're single and earn more than $25,350, or married with a combined income of $42,350, you are in a 28 percent federal tax bracket. At $61,400 for singles and $102,300 for married couples, 31 percent. Take out state and city taxes, which can be as much as 3–7 percent depending upon where you live. Deduct 7.65 percent Social Security, known as FICA on your pay stub, 1.35 percent Medicare tax, disability, and unemployment insurance, plus union dues and retirement savings, and you can see at least 40 percent of your $50,000 disappears before you get your hot little hands on it. Even with exemptions for yourself and two children, you'll see why the average $50,000 salary should read "$50,000 gross and about $33,000 net."

> ### Action Step:

Adjust your thinking about your income to see the net rather than the gross income in planning your spending. If you can't afford a CPA which can cost $150 an hour, spend the money for a consultation with an enrolled agent, an IRS trained tax preparer, who can advise you on how to plan your taxes before the deadline. To find one in your area, go to the Web site for the National Association of Enrolled Agents at http://www.naea.org/find/us.htm or call 301–212–9608. The address is: 200 Orchard Ridge Drive, Gaithersburg, MD 20878.

Day 120

DEBT REPAYMENT PLANS

You want 21 percent risk free? Pay off your credit cards.

—Andrew Tobias

If it takes more than 50 percent of your take-home pay to cover the minimum payments on your credit card debt, the most important step is to get help and make a plan for repaying the high-interest cards, negotiating with your creditors to reduce the monthly payments if necessary, meeting the payments and not taking on any more debt until you accomplish your goal. If you're too intimidated to do this on your own or just too anxious to call your creditors yourself, then get help from one of these nationally recognized credit counseling agencies.

Consolidated Credit Counseling 800-SAVE-ME2 (728–3632); www.debtfree.org

Debt Counselors of America, 800–680–3328; http://www.debtcounselors.org

Natl. Foundation for Consumer Credit, 800–388–2227; http://www.nfcc.org

Each of these agencies can refer you to a local office in your area to get assistance on coping with bills. They charge low to moderate fees, such as $50 for the first visit and perhaps $10 to $20 per visit after that. Check with your local Better Business Bureau if you're uncertain about how such an agency works.

Action Step:

Make those calls today.

Day 121

SHOPPING FOR DREAMS

The chains of habit are too strong to be felt until they are too strong to be broken.

—Samuel Johnson

Love, success, self-esteem, and respect don't come in a package at Saks, Bloomingdale's, or Macy's. Yet these are the unfulfilled desires that drive most compulsive shoppers—though they are not cured with the use of the plastic. Do you tell yourself that you know you need to start being more serious about how much you use your credit cards, but first you have to get just one more thing at Home Depot? Is your main motivation for earning money a "gotta have it now" urge to buy up everything in the Victoria's Secret catalog? Are you entertaining yourself with constant trips to the mall, the movies, and calls to the Home Shopping Network, but finding yourself lacking bus fare and lunch money after the weekend is over? Hundreds of men and women who can't control their spending habits seek professional help for a problem that will make life worse until it's brought under control. Whether it's a credit counselor, a therapist, or a self-help group like Debtors Anonymous, there is help to turn your life around.

Debtors Anonymous, a national support group, like Alcoholics Anonymous, is for people who have trouble with excessive debt and reckless spending. Check your local phone book or call the headquarters at 212–642–8222 for a referral to a chapter near you.

Day 122

TROUBLE AHEAD

A little wanton money, which burned out the bottom of his purse.

—Sir Thomas More

FIVE SIGNS OF PROBLEMS WITH CREDIT CARDS

You pay only the minimum payment each month without thinking about the total balance owed.

You don't know for certain how much you owe on all your credit cards.

You're getting collection letters in the mail and nasty phone calls for missed payments or past-due bills.

You're close to the upper limit on your credit card and have gone over your credit limit twice in the past year.

You're using the credit card to pay for things that you never charged before, like groceries and haircuts, and using cash advances to pay for your daily living expenses, such as bus fare and lunch.

Action Step:

Take all the credit cards out of your wallet and leave them at home until you have found time to make an appointment to get help with your spending habits.

Day 123

THE TRUE COST OF CREDIT

Banks make money in several ways when they bless you with a credit card. Interest is just the beginning. Keep in mind that banks have the right to change interest rates, fees, and restrictions whenever they wish. They include a small legal-looking notice in your monthly statement informing you what changes will be put in force within 60 days. If you agree to the new rules you can continue using the card. If you don't agree, then you must stop using the card and pay off the full balance immediately (or convert it to a personal loan.)

Let's look at the major terms of your credit agreement:

Interest. The fee for the use of plastic money is interest, but it varies with each card. Interest can be fixed at a constant rate such as 18.1 percent, the national average, or at a flexible rate that will vary monthly, quarterly, or weekly. Did you get a credit card with a "teaser" rate of 5.9 percent for six months, which then changed to 18.1 percent after you moved your balance from another card? Read that fine print because the bank has a right to change the interest whenever it wants to! Credit cards with permanently low interest rates are out there, but only for good borrowers with squeaky clean credit records. The Pulaski Savings Bank of Little Rock, Arkansas, offers the lowest fixed-rate credit card in the country, with a 7.9 percent rate and no annual fee. However, it is very stringent with its credit scoring, and only one out of three applicants is accepted for this card.

Annual Fee. It used to be $20, but the average now runs to $35 to $55. The best cards have no fees at all, but these are extremely difficult to get.

Grace Period. This is the interest-free period before you begin paying interest on charged items, and usually lasts 25 to 30 days. But be forewarned: Some banks have begun shortening this time to 20 days so interest accrues faster.

Late Payment Fees. This is not a new idea in money lending but credit card companies used to wait 10 to 15 days for payment before they charged you an extra $10–$15 penalty. Now they sock it to you if you're so much as one day late. Some institutions have even given themselves the right to increase your interest rate by 2–3 percent if you are late, so get that check in the mail ASAP. Allow seven business days for a mailed check to arrive and be processed.

Fees for Exceeding Your Credit Limit. There used to be leeway for a $25 overcharge, but not anymore. Now you get a 2 percent automatic increase in your interest rate plus a $15–$25 penalty.

Nonusage Fees. Do you pay off your balance each month? Really? Then banks don't want you as a customer because they aren't making any money on your account unless you go into debt, stay in debt, carry a balance each month, and pay the annual fee. Nonusage can increase your annual fee or even cause cancellation of your charging privileges.

Action Step:

Bankcard Holders of America offers a brochure called "Debt Zapper" on how to shop for a credit card and understand the rules of borrowing. Get a copy by sending $4 to: 524 Branch Drive, Salem, VA 24153, or call 540–389–5445.

Day 124

CREDIT AND DIVORCE

When poverty comes in the door, love goes out the window.

—Anonymous

When Barbara and Frank recently ended their marriage, Barbara was allowed to keep their low-rent apartment, and Frank accepted the responsibility for paying the balance on the three credit cards they had shared, since he earned more money. Six months after the divorce was final, Barbara began to receive calls from a collection agency. She had sent the credit card company a copy of the divorce decree and assumed that the issue was settled. No such luck. As far as the creditors were concerned, Barbara was expected to make payments on the debts she and her husband created, since Frank had neglected to do so.

If your marriage ends, you need to be aware of your financial situation when it comes to credit matters. There are two forms of credit accounts: individual and joint. As an individual you are fully responsible for the assets, payments, and credit history attached to that account, even if you authorize another person to use your account. If two partners both sign the same account application, both of you are responsible for the payments and the credit history, regardless of which one of you has used the card and incurred the debt. When you end a relationship you'll need to resolve any outstanding debt issues with both of your attorneys before the final judgment is issued. As long as there is a debt owed on a joint account, both of you are responsible for paying it. If you are considering a divorce, you should consider closing all joint accounts and applying for your own credit status as an individual. Otherwise you might have to live with a frustrating situation for a long, long time!

Action Step:

Write to the Bureau of Consumer Protection, Federal Trade Commission, Consumer Response Center, Washington, D.C. 20580, or call 202–326–3650 and request a copy of its list of brochures on credit and money management. The booklet on "Credit and Divorce" is on their "best-seller" list.

Day 125

HOW MANY CARDS DO YOU NEED?

In 1950, when Frank McNamara and Alfred Bloomingdale created Diner's Club, it became the first nationally accepted charge card and was issued mainly to traveling salesmen in New York, Los Angeles, and Boston. It was intended for treating customers to lunch in 25 exclusive restaurants, with one bill at the end of the month as a means of avoiding the constant need to carry cash and collect receipts for business travel. Hotels and airline fees were added three years later— but everyone still paid the full amount owed at the end of the month. The card was a symbol of creditworthiness and affluence and was accepted at all the deluxe hotels and restaurants in the three cities. BankAmericard (later known as Visa) and the American Express charge card did not come into existence until 1958. Visa added the extended credit line with interest charges in 1971. Membership in one select group was viewed as license to join another, but having more than one card was discouraged until late into the 1960s. If those wealthy businessmen were able to manage with just one card, then perhaps you can aim for that same goal. Credit cards aren't souvenirs or merit badges to be collected and worn with pride in the consumer wars. At most, limit yourself to three credit cards: one for travel or business, a bank card for general purchases, and a gasoline card.

Action Step:

Count the number of cards you have in your wallet. If you have more than one, ask yourself why you carry so many with you all the time. Are you looking for an opportunity to get into debt? List the cards you have and look at your actual usage. Close the accounts of any cards you don't use frequently. Review your credit card statements from the past year and ask yourself how many of those purchases you would have made if you had only cash available to you. Make it one of your goals this year to reduce the number of your credit cards to only one.

Day 126

REVIEW AND REASSESS

Some people have a serious problem with credit card debt and some don't, but most Americans overuse the credit that is extended to them or are at risk of overexposure. Review your cards and their annual fees. If you can close any accounts, do. Now review the balances. Total them. Reread Day 120 and set up a repayment plan. If this seems too difficult, there's a lot of help out there for you. Getting out of debt is the most important step you need to take toward wealth building. In fact, it's essential. Do not go on until you have taken the steps to get started.

Day 127

PRACTICING SAFE CREDIT

Having more credit than money, thus one goes through the world.

—Johann W. Goethe

Are you careless about sharing your credit card information with some telephone salesperson? Have you let a friend or relative "bor-

row" your credit card and "pay you back next month?" Do you casu-
ally leave receipts or carbons with your account number lying around
for anyone to use or copy? Do you stop to think when someone calls
you saying you've won a "door prize" or with a too-good-to-be-true
deal but they need your Visa account number for verification and to
cover shipping expenses? Do you use your credit card when you
could easily pay cash and not get a bill the next month? Do you flash
a wallet full of plastic in the grocery store without regard to who may
be watching you? Watch out! Americans have created over $1 trillion
worth of credit card debt as of September 1997 and the figure is still
growing. Some of that is credit fraud caused by careless credit card
use, but most of it is plain old reckless and unnecessary charging. If
you need some encouragement to practice credit card control, get a
set of "credit card condoms." The National Center for Financial
Education provides these thin plastic shields that fit neatly over any
credit or department store card you wish to protect. The "condoms"
come with three distinctive warning labels, front and back: "Overuse
Can Be Hazardous to Your Wealth!" or "Should You Charge It?" or
"Can You Really Afford It?" The two extra seconds that it takes to
read the warning label and remove the card from its little plastic
shield may be just enough to catch you in the act of creating financial
mayhem and halt an act of reckless shopping that you'll regret later.
Remember, unnecessary spending can be detrimental to your financial well-being.

Action Step:

Order a set of credit card condoms and protection stickers from
the National Center for Financial Education by calling 619–232–8811.
A package of 10 condoms is $3 and a package of 20 peel-and-stick
warning labels costs $1.

Day 128

"IT'S ONLY $5 . . ."

What difference will a couple of dollars make in the weekly budget if you don't feel like cooking and treat yourself to a takeout meal? Plenty! That $5 that you blew on a fast-food lunch or a romance novel could mean the difference between being in debt for 17 years versus seven years. Take a look at the numbers:

Assume that you have a credit card balance of $1,000 with a 17 percent interest rate. The minimum payment is only $15 a month on such a small balance. But suppose you raised the monthly minimum payment to $20. A small but painless amount. Look at the difference in the time, money, and interest that will be saved. Take a look at the numbers:

	$15 a Month	$20 a Month
Total Principal Paid:	$1,000	$1,000
Total Interest Paid:	$2,082	$750
Total Money Paid Back:	$3,082	$1,740
Total Number of Payments:	205	87
Total Savings:	$1,332	

Any more questions?

Action Step:

Take a look at your credit card balance and your budget and work out how you can increase your monthly payments and be debt-free as soon as possible. Go to the Web site http://www.consumeraction. com to figure out your own debt repayment schedule.

Day 129

SAVINGS VS. DEBT PAYMENT

Can you walk and chew gum at the same time? Then you can save money and pay off debt at the same time. The cost of money and time is the major comparison here. Thelma B. has a $5,000 savings account that she wants to keep as her emergency fund, but it is paying her only 3 percent interest. Thelma also has a department store card with a $1,200 balance for the sofa and chairs she bought last year. This card charges her a 22.5 percent interest rate. She also carries two other credit cards, one with a $780 debt and the other with a $2,200 debt, and both with an interest rate of 18.1 percent. The monthly payments on all this debt are nearly $400, and Thelma can no longer deduct the interest on her tax return. It would be smarter for her to pay off the $4,000 of credit card debt with the savings account. This step would improve her credit rating, and give her some peace of mind, making it easier for her to begin to explore new financial options in her life.

Affirmation:

I will reconsider how I save and use debt in my life.

Action Step:

Use most of your savings in a low interest passbook account to pay off that 19 percent credit card debt. Set up a payroll deduction account to rebuild your savings account as you continue to make the monthly payments to get out of debt.

Day 130

CONQUERING THE STUDENT LOAN PAYMENT PLAN

Your college degree is your best investment. B.A. degree holders earn an average of 21 percent more over a lifetime than those without a college degree. Depending upon your field of study, master's degree holders earn 34–50 percent more than those with B.A.'s, so the expense does pay off over a lifetime of income.

At 8 percent, the interest rate on student loans is lower than the rate on most other debts, but it isn't tax deductible anymore. Though the minimum payments are usually as little as $50 a month, double them if you can and cut a ten-year loan down to five years— you'll save a bundle in interest.

Look into loan consolidation. Sallie Mae, the Student Loan Marketing Association, combines several payments into one. Unfortunately, if you don't pay close attention, you'll be paying for your degree as long as you'll be paying for your house, which could stretch out to 30 years. Call Sallie Mae at 888–2SALLIE (272–5543) or visit their Web site at www.salliemae.com

Day 131

REWARD YOURSELF!!!

After you pay off the debt and close your first credit card account, congratulate yourself for taking a big step toward financial control! You've earned the right to reward yourself and take a moment to enjoy the result of the struggle and sacrifice you have made so far. Treat yourself to some reasonable entertainment, but don't overdo it and dig your way back in again. Rent a video, pop some popcorn, and put your feet up. Savor the moment! You've earned it. If you do it right, the whole evening can cost less than $20 and you'll feel even better about enjoying yourself without spending a wad. Reflect on the lessons you've learned by making this sacrifice. Tomorrow you can begin restructuring your debt repayment plan, and put those same dollars toward paying off your next credit card. Soon you'll be able to take a look at some mutual fund brochures to see which one you're going to be investing in as soon as you finish whittling this mountain down to an anthill.

Affirmation:

I can turn my financial life around and start over again!

Day 132

"CHRISTMAS IN JULY"

$$$–Savings Tip:

Think ahead to your next family vacation, Christmas holiday, or week in the sun in February, and get some good airlines bargains. Here are two travel savings tips:

800–PRICE–LINE. You name the price you want to pay for your ticket. If this service can match it you get a nonrefundable ticket, and considerable savings. Check out the Web site at http://www.priceline.com to get an idea of the fares.

Global Discount Travel Services. Now owned by Carl Icahn, who negotiated a sweet deal when he stepped down as chairman of TWA. He has the right to sell all tickets on TWA at a 20 percent discount and at 25 percent off on some international routes. Call 800–977–7110.

Day 133

ANNUAL BARGAIN CALENDAR

When to Buy What:

You don't have to give up shopping to be a financially savvy person, but you should be careful about when you part with your dollars. Most items can be bought at bargain prices but only at certain times of the year.

Dresses:	January, April, June, November
Sportswear:	January, February, May, July
Lingerie:	January, May, July
Shoes (men and women):	January, July, November, December
Shoes (boys and girls):	January, March, July
Handbags:	January, May, July
Costume and Fine Jewelry:	January
Cars:	September
Furniture:	January and July
Appliances:	Major Holidays—President's Day, Memorial Day, July 4, Labor Day, and Columbus Day
Linens:	January
Air-Conditioners:	September

Since many sales take place in January, it's all the more reason to not spend all your money before Christmas. Give gift certificates as gifts or ask for them.

Action Step:

Identify which of the items you need, and make a note on your personal calendar about when you can expect to see them on sale. Watch the newspaper for special sales at those times of year. Note: The key word here is "need."

Day 134

CLOTHING CONSIGNMENT SHOPS

$$$—Savings Tip:

Have you ever wondered what happens to all the designer clothing that isn't sold at the after-Christmas sales? Nordstrom's, Macy's, Niemann Marcus, and other major stores frequently donate unsalable items to neighborhood consignment shops or hospital or charity-related thrift shops—sometimes with the price tags or labels still on them. Look in your local phone book under a listing for consignment shops to see if there are some in your area. Call them and find out what their hours are and what kind of merchandise they carry. They just might have that perfect Donna Karan outfit that you passed up last year because it was too expensive. Now it's probably 75 percent off the original price.

Day 135

$$$—Savings Tip:

Clip coupons out of the Sunday paper and use them for any product that you really need. Put the savings into your "dream jar."

Day 136

$$$—Savings Tip:

Use fluorescent bulbs. The $15 price tag on a Phillips Earthlight universal bulb may sound expensive compared to the $2.99 you might pay on a four-pack of incandescent bulbs, but think about the long-term savings. Fluorescent bulbs burn only 12 to 20 watts, compared with 60 to 75 watts of the regular bulbs that have to be replaced every 100 hours, while fluorescent lights last an average of seven years or so. That's a savings of about $120 a year—after you recover the initial cost of the bulbs. If you can't find them in your housewares store, call for a copy of the "Real Goods" energy saver mail order catalog at 800–762–7325, or visit the Web site at http://www.realgoods.com.

Day 137

STINGY MISERS

Most of the great investors are misers.

—Warren Buffet

John Paul Getty would charge his friends for meals and phone calls when they came for long weekends at his country estate. He would also wait until the last hour of the day to attend a museum exhibit because it was free then. John D. Rockefeller used to reuse the same tea bag. Hetty Green, the first woman in America to make $100 million, took her son to a public hospital clinic when he broke his leg rather than go to a private doctor. All of us have strange habits when it comes to money, so don't feel like you're weird if you use half a paper towel, save grocery bags, refold aluminum foil, or change the oil in your car yourself. Those are the habits that allow you to save those dimes and dollars for investing for long-term growth. You can learn to be much more frugal and careful with your resources. Less spent on necessities means more available for investing and saving.

Action Step:

On your next visit to the library, get a copy of Amy Dacyczyn's book *The Best of the Tightwad Gazette*.

Day 138

THE COST OF BANKING

Remember, bankers are so worried about holding on to things
that they put little chains on all their pens.

—Miss Piggy

Check and ATM fees, service charges, the high balance required to avoid monthly charges: They all add up each month. Have you heard of any banks apologizing for increasing the cost of a checking account by more than 60 percent over the last five years? Credit unions pay higher interest on savings accounts and have lower fees for services, because they are nonprofit organizations. They are also much more flexible on making loans to members, with rates that are the same as, if not lower than, a commercial bank. Checking accounts (called "share draft accounts" at credit unions) have no minimum balance and can usually be opened for as little as $20. Many credit unions can also provide low-rate credit cards, and the same kind of ATM cards and debit cards you find at a regular bank. Go back through your monthly bank statement and see what you have spent in fees over the past year. If it is more than $100, look around and talk to friends about finding a credit union or a smaller bank.

Action Step:

The rules for membership in credit unions have been relaxed in the past year. Call 800–358–5710 to see if you're eligible to join a credit union (usually you must have an association membership or be a union or company employee) and if there is one in your area. You can also get the number for your state's Credit Union League.

Day 139

$$$—Savings Tip:

Banks usually offer you the first 200 checks free when you open your checking account, but after that the cost can be as high as $22, depending on the design you choose. Order replacement checks from one of these mail order check-printing services instead.

Current Checks, 800–204–2244; http://www.currentchecks.com.

Artistic Checks, 800–733–6313; http://www.artisticchecks.com.

Designer Checks, 800–239–9222; http://www.designerchecks.com.

Each company charges only $4.95 on your first 200 checks. They need ten business days to print and mail new checks.

Action Step:

Check your bank's fee for printing checks and consider changing your next order.

Day 140

REVIEW AND REASSESS

Putting your financial house in order means changing your daily habits in small ways as well as large ones. Don't feel that a "discount" mentality is beneath you. If you're having trouble making small changes like going to a half-price matinee at the movies or using coupons at the supermarket, ask yourself why. Do you feel resentful? Deprived? You're not! The money that you save now will still be yours to spend—but it will be worth much more down the road. This is called delayed gratification, and it's the only way to steadily build financial security.

Day 141

CARD SHOPPING

When you buy a car, a computer, a stereo, or even a pair of shoes, you've learned by now to shop around in several places before you decide to buy. Do the same with credit cards for the same reason—to avoid paying a single penny more than you have to for the privilege of temporary borrowing. But be economical about how you put your time and money into this exercise. Some cards have no annual fee but a high interest rate. Others start with a low teaser rate that may go as low as 2.9 percent for six months, then change to 16.9 percent. Others may have an interest rate that changes every six months as the bank's prime rate changes. Some cards have no grace period—that time between the day you charge an item and the day he bank starts charging interest for the balance on the card, while others give 25 days. *Kiplinger's Personal Finance Magazine* and the Wednesday edition of the *Wall Street Journal*, section three, "Money and Investing," give you a list of the best deals on credit cards.

Action Step:

Get a copy of the monthly "Best Credit Cards" listing from CardTrak of America by sending $5 to P.O. Box 1700, Frederick, MD 21702, or calling 800–874–8999. Its Web site at http://www.card trak.com has only a partial listing. For answers to individual questions, call 301–695–4660 during business hours.

Day 142

PRIME RATE

This is the index by which most banks set their basic interest rates for lending. Only the best customers get to borrow at this rate. For the average person, credit cards, cars, home equity loans, and adjustable rate mortgages are usually set at anywhere from six to eight points over whatever the prime rate is. Prime rates are usually set each Wednesday morning. Why? Because banks wait to see if the Federal Reserve Bank has adjusted its federal funds discount rate up or down every Tuesday. The federal funds discount rate is the interest charged to the banks by the Federal Reserve. The adjustment is passed on to bank customers by changing the rates on CDs and money market accounts.

Action Step:

Look in the "Money and Investing" section of *Wall Street Journal* and find the "Yields and Rates" column. Compare the rates on a Tuesday and a Wednesday to see the changes. This list also gives the top CD rates at five banks around the country and the 800 number to reach them to open an account.

Day 143

$$$—Savings Tip:

Forget the incentives and rebates that credit card companies use to entice you to spend more. Frequent flier miles, a discount on buying a Ford Explorer, a free trip to Hawaii or a 2 percent donation to your favorite charity—all these come-ons appeal to our "something for nothing" mentality, but forget it. The interest rate is often higher than the average and there's definitely an annual fee of at least $25. That "free trip" to Hawaii happens only after you've charged about

$30,000 of merchandise. It would take 42 years to buy that Explorer, since the Ford Motor Company allows you to accumulate only $700 a year in credits toward the purchase of a new vehicle. Settle for a cheap card and open a savings account if you're shopping for a car or planning a vacation.

Day 144

YOUR FINANCIAL BILL OF RIGHTS

The Bill of Rights in the U. S. Constitution describes the basic liberties of Americans. There is also a series of laws that protect your financial rights. Here's a quick summary of the four most important laws that affect the typical consumer.

Truth in Lending Bill. All terms and conditions for the loan or credit agreement must be spelled out in "nonlegal" language so that you are aware of interest rates, fees, cancellation terms, and penalties for late payment or nonpayment. Banks, finance companies, and all legally licensed financial institutions are subject to this federal law.

Consumer Protection Act. You have a right to cancel a loan agreement or return a purchase within three business days without penalty under this law. You also have a right to a refund of your money as long as you have not damaged the merchandise that was purchased.

Equal Credit Opportunity Act. Originally created to protect women from credit discrimination, it now prohibits discrimination against anyone who applies for credit because of sex, age, race, religion, national origin, income from public assistance, or marital status. As long as the applicant has sufficient income to support the repayment schedule for the debt, he or she cannot be turned down for a loan or a credit card.

Fair Credit Reporting Act. Your consent is required for your credit report to be obtained by employers, landlords, lenders, and insurance agencies. You can dispute any inaccurate information but all information, positive and negative, remains in the file for seven years, or for ten years in cases of bankruptcy. You must be told if any information in the file has been used against you, such as being denied credit, insurance, or employment. You are entitled to a free copy of your credit report within 60 days of being turned down for any reason.

Affirmation:

I will learn my financial rights and act on them when I need to.

Action Step:

Write to the Bureau of Consumer Protection, Federal Trade Commission, at the Public Reference Branch, Room 130, FTC, Washington, DC 20580, for a copy of the free brochure on "Your Consumer Credit Rights" or call 202–326–2222. You can also print out copies or order several of the consumer credit brochures through the Web site at http://www.ftc.org. or at the U.S. government information Web site at http://www.pueblo.gov/gsa. The full text of these laws is available and can be downloaded from the Web site at http://consumerlawpage.com/nographics/brochure/36.shtml.

Day 145

YOUR HOUSE, THE VISA CARD

Some people refer to this is as the loan from HEL(L). Home equity loans became popular in the 1980s after the tax law made mortgage interest the only deductible debt. This financing technique, which was supposed to be for home improvements and renovations, has become a glorified Visa card with a checkbook attached to it. Now this financial product is being sold to cover debt consolidation loans, college tuition, and the new family car. If you can cut up the rest of your plastic and be very disciplined you can use this, but be aware, you're turning your house into a glorified Visa card. The difference now is that you can have a balance as high as 65 percent of the value of your home instead of $5,000 to $10,000.

Affirmation:

I will remember the true reason for borrowing money. I will not put my home at risk for frivolous spending.

Action Step:

Investigate the costs of a second mortgage vs. a home equity loan through your local bank. Send a $3 money order to HSH Associates, Department HEQ, 1200 Route 23, Butler, NJ 07405, for a copy of *Home Equity: A Consumer's Guide to Loans and Lines.*

Day 146

FREE ALTERATIONS

$$$—Savings Tip:

Women should ask for free alterations whenever purchasing a new suit or dress that requires adjustments to hems, sleeves, or shoulders. When men purchase expensive business suits they get free alterations for cuffs, sleeves, and seams. It can worth $50–$75.

Day 147

EASY SAVINGS

Learn how to cook! That's the way to save money.

—Julia Child

Would it surprise you to know that the number one expense in the average working person's monthly budget is food? Eating out, ordering in, and fast-food dinners take a huge bite out of our paychecks and diminish our disposable income. Janet S., manager of a clothing store in a Chicago mall, thinks she is a frugal person. She gets employee discounts on her clothing, sees movies at matinees when tickets are cheap, and always shops for the bargains when buying necessities. Why, then, doesn't she have a fat savings account? Janet kept a spending diary for a month and discovered that her eating habits robbed her of about $200 a month. Donuts with her coffee on morning breaks, deli sandwiches at lunch, and takeout meals at the end of a busy day cost more than she would have guessed she spent on food. Chinese and Indian takeout wasn't so cheap when she ate it every night, and the markup on the deli sandwiches meant she was spending $3 more for a sandwich she could make and bring to work. Janet set up an automatic investment plan for her retirement and a money market deduction from each paycheck and started brown-bagging it three times a week. She allowed herself lunch in a restaurant one day a week. Otherwise, she brown-bagged it! She'd never thought of herself as a cook, but how much skill does it take to roast a chicken for dinner, or to use a crockpot that cooks your stew on a low temperature while you're at work? Home-cooked food is better for you anyway, and you don't have to tip a delivery man. Now Janet plans her meals, especially since the dollars she saves now go into her IRA account.

Action Step:

Check out the inexpensive recipes, food storage tips, and bulk buying plans on the Frugal Family Network at http://www.frugal-family.network.com.

Day 148

MAKE THE EFFORT!

Economy is in itself a great source of revenue.

—Seneca

Frugality is a state of mind that can be developed with a little help from the many books, newsletters, and Web sites that can give you guidance and direction on saving money. Like most movements in America, it needs a name to define its direction. The new phrase is "Voluntary Simplicity," which has become the "back to basics" movement of the nineties. Its advocates have produced many newsletters, books, and directories to help you rethink your current lifestyle and learn how to get the most out of every dollar that comes through your hands. It's up to you to reach out and contact these resources that can help you find the extra money to invest and really teach you about stretching your dollars. *Your Money or Your Life: Transforming Your Relationship With Money and Achieving Financial Independence* by Joe Dominguez and Robin Evers, 1995 ($13, Putnam) is one of the best books written to trigger a new style of thinking about money and your life's goal. Pick it up on your next visit to the library. Put the $13 in your "dream jar" for your next goal.

Action Step:

Call the Simple Living Network at 800–318–5725 for a copy of its newsletter and visit its Web site at http://www.slnet.com for an extensive list of publications, consumer groups, and links to other organizations that teach and encourage frugality.

Day 149

THE TELEPHONE

Sorting out the various rates, plans, and special service packages of the different long-distance services is like trying to unravel a plate of spaghetti. Choosing the right one can save as much as 30 percent a month—if you can get an honest answer. For a simple comparison of the rates charged by the eight largest long distance carriers, send $5 and a stamped, self-addressed envelope to: Telecommunications Research and Action Center, Box 2729, Washington, DC, 20005, or call 800–344–TRAC.

Day 150

YOUR FINANCIAL REPORT CARD

They're talking about you out there. All those people who loaned you money, that is. Your credit report is like a character reference in the world of money. It documents in black and white how you're managing your borrowing relationships, and it is updated on a monthly basis. Unfortunately, because of human error, 42 percent of all credit reports contain errors. The only way to find out if there are any in yours is to read what's in the file. If there are, you can challenge them. Several states require that you be able to get one free report each year. If you have been denied credit from anyone, you're entitled to a free credit report from the agency that reported the data on you. Just send in your rejection letter within 30 days and the agency will send it to you at no cost. If you can't get your report for free you can expect to pay about $8 for it. Contact one of the big three credit reporting agencies:

Experian, National Consumer Assistance Center (formerly TRW)
P.O. Box 949
Allen, TX 75013
800–392–1122
http://www.experian.com

TransUnion—Consumer Relations Department
P.O. Box 7000
North Olmstead, OH 44070
800–851–2574
http://www.trans-union.com

Equifax—Consumer Affairs Department
P.O. Box 740256
Atlanta, GA 30374–0256
800–685–1111
http://www.equifax.com

Each of these Web sites gives you an idea of what a credit report looks like and the kind of information that is kept in your file. If you don't want to write each agency separately, you can order a combined file for $25.95 from: Confidential Credit File (Credico) 9444 Balboa Avenue, Suite 500, San Diego, CA 92123; 800–443–9342.

Day 151

DEBT DENIAL

When you come home and find a stack of bills in the mailbox, you'd probably like to stuff the bills in the trash and grab a ticket out of your life rather than open those envelopes and read one more past

due notice or collection letter. Escapist thoughts give us some temporary relief from the pressure and stress of not being able to make the
payments, but you can't treat your debts like the monster under the
bed at night, hoping it will go away if you pretend it's not there.
Hardly. Avoiding the bills by ignoring the mail when it comes will
not make the problem go away. Face it: You're not in control if you're
avoiding the problem.

Action Step:

Open the envelope! Then call someone who can be a "life saver"
in the form or a credit counselor at Metropolitan Financial
Management at 888–56–BILLS, ext. 987, or go to the Web site at
http://www.debt-help.com.

Day 152

DEBT IS A FOUR LETTER WORD!

The optimist sees the opportunity in every crisis.

—Anonymous

Nearly ten years ago, Mary Hunt and her husband, Harold, found
themselves in the worst of all possible financial nightmares—they
had over $100,000 of credit card debt! That's not a typo: $100,000.
Although they both had good incomes, Mary had built up a compulsive spending habit over a ten-year period. Even when they fought
over money, Mary continued to deny the seriousness of her problem.
When her husband lost his job and Mary's real estate business hit a
slump, they had to face themselves. Most people would have chosen
bankruptcy, but with the help of a very supportive minister, Mary
prayed for guidance to turn her life around. She started with a notebook, a pencil, and a calculator at her kitchen table one night in
1986. She wrote letters to all her creditors, offering as little as $10 a

month. For Mary, it was her dignity that she wanted to maintain. Twelve years later, Mary has repaid the $100,000 and has created a successful career as a financial columnist and writer of books on thrift and savings. Her personal story is a living example of being able to turn a life around, survive the ordeal of excessive debt. Now she promotes thrift and commonsense approaches to debt management in workshops around the country.

Action Step:

Take advantage of the excellent information Mary Hunt has to offer about paying off debt and saving money by reading one of her "Cheapskate" books, or order a year's subscription to her newsletter, *The Cheapskate Monthly*, by sending a check or money order for $18 to P.O. Box 2135, Paramount, CA 90723–8135. You can also take a look at her Web site at http://www.cheapskatemonthly.com, which offers an excellent "Tiptionary" list of ways to save money.

Day 153

WRITING YOUR CREDITORS

After you get a copy of your credit report, don't be surprised if some items on there are totally foreign to you. Some 42 percent of all credit files have mistakes due to human error, or confusion between similar names, addresses, or Social Security numbers. It's your responsibility to contact the lender, not the credit bureau, that filed the incorrect information and correct the error in writing. Phone calls don't count. If you do call and speak to someone, always, always, write down the person's name and the date that you spoke to him or her and keep it in your records. But you must follow up on each conversation with a letter. Here's a sample:

DATE:

Dear Name of Creditor
Address of Creditor
RE: Your Name and Account Number
Your Address
Your Social Security Number

TO WHOM IT MAY CONCERN:

I have just received a copy of my credit report from NAME OF CREDIT AGENCY and would like to bring some errors to your attention. According to this report, you state that my payments were missed or late (or were charged off). However, I have canceled checks that indicate that this did not happen (photocopies are enclosed). I also closed that particular account more than six months ago, but your company seems to have misplaced the letter of satisfaction that was not issued until a year later. I would appreciate it if you would investigate this matter and correct it with the above-named credit agency immediately, since it is producing negative and injurious impact on my credit rating. Your immediate attention to this matter is requested and I would like to be informed in writing of how this mistake has been corrected. Thank you.

Yours truly,
Your Name

Action Step:

Order the "Debt Busters" kit from the BankCard Holders of America at 524 Branch Drive, Salem, VA 24153, or phone 540–389–5445. It's worth the $15 to get it.

Day 154

REVIEW AND REASSESS

If you haven't obtained a copy of your credit report, do it today. If your credit is poor, you need to face up to it before you can move forward. If the report contains errors, you need to have them corrected. Then again, you may have an excellent credit history, or at least much better than you expect, and it's important to know that, too. Finding out that you have good credit is like getting a clean bill of health from your doctor: It may not tell you anything you don't already know, but it sure feels good to hear it from a professional!

Day 155

SOLVING MONEY PROBLEMS

We cannot solve life's problems except by solving them.

—M. Scott Peck

If you think your financial life is complex and messy now while you're in debt, ignoring the phone calls, reminder letters, and past-due notices that come each week won't make it any better. If you're secretly hoping to win the lottery to get you off the hook with your bill collectors, you're dreaming. There's no secret potion or fairy godmother who will wave her magic wand and wipe out your credit card debt at the bank or "make it all right" at the mortgage company. The first step toward finding a solution is to acknowledge your responsibility for the problem. What warning signals of mismanagement have you ignored? Buying things and hiding them from your spouse? Lying about the check being in the mail? Missing one month's payment and believing you can double up on payments next month? Ignoring past-due notices? Not being able to cover the minimum payments on your credit card? Using one card to pay off another? Your debts didn't happen overnight, so don't expect them to disappear overnight. You don't have to go through the process of turning your behavior around by yourself. There are credit counselors who will offer a sensitive listening ear, sane advice, and a commonsense plan to get control of your cash and credit problems. If you make the commitment to try, they will be there to help you with free or low-cost budgeting assistance and they will contact your creditors and arrange a plan to turn your life around. But remember, *you have to make the phone call and show up for the appointment* before they can help you see the light at the end of the tunnel.

Affirmation:

With discipline and professional help, I can turn my financial life around!

Day 156

STARTING OVER

Acceptance of what has happened is the first step in overcoming the consequences of any misfortune.

—William James

Eddie and Maria got married early and had two children, and both had decent incomes. Eddie was a construction worker in the warm months, did freelance carpentry, and moved furniture in the winter. Maria was the secretary/office manager for a small garment manufacturer. One spring Eddie injured his back and was laid up for three months. His unemployment check was $250 a week—quite a drop from the $700 a week he usually brought home. Later that year, Maria had a difficult pregnancy that put her in bed for five months. Rather than her usual $550 a week, workers' compensation only paid her $175 a week. The baby was born with a cleft palate and required additional surgery that was not fully covered by their health insurance. In less than a year, they had more than $25,000 worth of bills that they could not pay, so they applied for public assistance and eventually had to file bankruptcy. More than 2 million people in America filed bankruptcy in the last two years, so if you're in that boat, you're not alone and you won't be the last, either, but you don't have to repeat the same situation again. Starting over means learning from your mistakes and making a plan to avoid making the same mistake again.

Create a spending plan and review it weekly.

Get a secured card so you can have some credit, but only for emergencies.

Start a systematic savings plan. Put aside a bit of each paycheck—even if it's only $10! It does make a difference!

Action Step:

For counseling, support, and other questions about declaring bankruptcy, call Personal Bankruptcy Associates at 630–910–0306 for their self-help kit and questionnaire or go to www.nashbar.org/bankrupt.htm for an online brochure on the rules of bankruptcy filing.

Day 157

BANKRUPTCY

Failure isn't fatal.

—Reverend Howard Thurman

Changing your name, moving to Mongolia, hiding out in the Himalayas and becoming a monk won't solve the problem when you can't pay your bills, but don't race for the write-off option until you really understand what you're agreeing to. Bankruptcy comes in two flavors, Chapter 7—the total write-off of all your debts, but most assets are liquidated and distributed to your creditors (bitter); and Chapter 13—the "wage-earner" plan that helps you keep your house, your car (if it isn't a Benz or a BMW!), and your pride while you do a court-administered repayment/workout arrangement over three to five years (sour). You don't want to sample either one since the aftertaste lingers on your credit record for ten years. Since you must live with the results of this decision for such a long time, try to work out something with your creditors for the next ten years. Bankruptcy doesn't mean you're a bad person—you just made some bad decisions with your money. If you see no other hope for yourself, interview at least three different attorneys, find out what their fees are, and ask for references before you file. The fees can be as high as $500 to $1,000 which could probably pay off at least one of your debts.

Action Step:

Reread Mary Hunt's story on Day 152. That should be enough support and inspiration to encourage you to call a credit counselor and create a spending and repayment plan before you phone an attorney.

Day 158

DILIGENCE

Lord give me patience and I want it right now!

—Lucy in Peanuts

When you're buried under a mountain of debt, it can feel like you'll never get out from under it so why bother, right? It can feel very frustrating to see each paycheck eaten up by a three-year repayment plan with nothing to show for it but canceled checks. Patience means giving the process a chance to make a difference in your life. If all the changes took place overnight, you would forget the lessons that you need to learn from your situation. Like not using the plastic when you don't need to. Like spending thoughtlessly because you're bored. Like shopping as a hobby when you're feeling lonely. Being patient can be a learning time. Learn to develop new concepts and a new attitude about your own right to make your financial decisions. Learn about what goals really matter to you and what your financial priorities really are. When the debts are finally gone, where will you put that cash each month? A money market fund at Dreyfus or Vanguard to build up your savings cushion? A blue chip equity mutual fund at Fidelity or Neuberger-Berman to start a long-term investment plan? Make a promise to yourself that you will continue to write that same check each month that used to go to the bank for the car note, but this time it will go to a money market account to build up some savings. Or you can divide that amount between a savings account and a long-term mutual fund. You'll get your reward as long as you hang in there.

Affirmation:

I will begin investigating the possibilities for new wealth to come into my life by looking back at how far I have come and studying new ways to use my money each month when the debts are gone.

Day 159

SLOW AND STEADY WINS THE RACE

When he picked up his first tennis racket at age six on a run-down public playground in Richmond, Virginia, Arthur Ashe had no idea he would become a world-class tennis player—he was just excited by the chance to learn how to play. The discipline of daily practice had to strengthen his arm, his eye, and his swing before he could dream of Wimbledon and the U.S. Open. Saving money is the same way. It has to be done every day with discipline, the right attitude, and a commitment to make something happen. Effort and discipline come from you, not anyone else. Even if you can only put away $1 a day, do it. You won't miss that extra bag of potato chips. In fact, each time you think about buying a snack, put the dollar you might have spent into your "dream jar" instead of adding it to the poundage you already have on your hips. Think of how much healthier and wealthier you'll be after a year! At the end of the year it will be $365 more than you had before you started, and with 4 percent interest it will already have grown to $379.60. If one dollar is comfortable, why not make it $2? Then $5? You can work your way up to a comfortable commitment of $100 a month. Soon you'll surprise yourself and become quite excited as you see those savings pile up in an account with your name on it.

Action Step:

Look at the "Yields and Rates" section in *Kiplinger's Personal Finance* magazine, which lists the top five money market mutual funds—it gives Web addresses and 800 number as well as the current rates.

Day 160

YOU DO NEED CREDIT

Money and goods are certainly the best of references.

—Charles Dickens

Paul C. was offered his first job out of college as a junior marketing representative for a pharmaceutical company, starting at a decent salary and with the promise of good commissions. Paul had been raised by his mother, since his father died when Paul was ten. He remembered her anguish and humiliation over the phone calls, past-due notices, and collection letters. Paul refused all credit card applications offered to him in college. Now his prospective employer has requested a credit report as a character reference. He has also been asked for a credit reference by various real estate agencies while searching for an apartment. Paul must also provide a credit reference or pay a higher interest rate for the car loan and higher premiums for his auto insurance. Like it or not, you do need a credit card. Secured cards are an excellent starting point for first-time borrowers, students away at college, newly hired employees with no credit record, or those who have screwed up their credit history. As a new borrower, you will open a savings account or a one-year CD with a bank for $1,000. The bank will issue a Visa or MasterCard with that savings account as collateral against loss or nonpayment. Here are five major national banks that provide secured cards for new borrowers or recovering borrowers.

Bank	800 Number	Interest Rate	Annual Fee	Minimum Amount
Bank of America http://www.bankofamerica.com	242–5722	19.24%	$18	$300
Chase Manhattan http://www.chase.com	482–4273	17.9%	$20	$300
Citibank http://www.citibank.com	743–1332	17.9%	$20	$300
Citizens Bank http://www.citizens.com	438–9222	15.65%	$25	$300
Key Bank http://www.keybank.com	539–5398	19.4%	$35	$350

Action Step:

Contact CardTrak at 800–874–8999, or send $5 to Box 1700, Frederick, MD 21702 for a copy of *Secured Card Report.* You may also visit the CardTrak Web site at http://www.cardtrak.com for a current list of recommendations on finding the right credit card for your lifestyle.

Day 161

COLLATERAL

Collateral is any asset you own, free and clear, that can be pledged to a lender to guarantee repayment of a debt you owe in the event you are no longer able to make your payments. Remember your brother Fred, who borrowed $2,500 for a few weeks? If he had signed a letter of agreement giving you the rights to his furniture, his Rolex watch, or his television set if he defaulted on your loan, those items would be considered collateral. A mortgage is a form of collateralized loan, since the bank can repossess your house if you default on your loan payment. It's the same with a car note, or a loan to purchase furniture, a boat, a refrigerator, or tools or equipment for work. You agree to sign over ownership and possession of the asset in question to the lender.

Day 162

GETTING CREDIT

The mold of a man's fortune is in his own hands.

—Francis Bacon

Your brother Fred, calls one night and says he's in a tight spot and needs to borrow $1,500 for a few months. Fred has a good job as an assistant sales manager for a drugstore chain, so you know he has a solid income. What questions would you ask? Why does he need the money? How long will he need it? When will you get it back? Will he pay you interest? How much and when? Who will guarantee that you won't lose your money? Has your brother always been an honest person who was responsible with money, or is this an indication of mismanagement? These same issues come up when you apply for a credit card. The difference is that the credit card issuer doesn't know you, so it wants some proof from a third party that you're an honest, reliable person who will keep your promise to make good on the payment schedule that it establishes for you. Here are the three "C's" that the bank looks for in a borrower:

Capacity. Do you earn enough money to pay for your normal living expenses and the minimum monthly payments to this and any other lender listed in your file? Have you been responsible when borrowing money from other people?

Collateral. This is called "safe debt," since the bank or mortgage company can repossess the asset it is financing in case you begin to miss payments. A car, furniture, a house, and business equipment such as a computer can be financed with a collateral agreement. If you fall behind on more than two payments, the lender will call and start the legal paperwork to protect its investment, unless you phone, write, or show up to make some arrangement for payment.

Conditions. You will always have a good credit report if you follow these guidelines:

Never miss a payment.
Don't get too close to or exceed your credit limit.
Don't carry and use too many other credit cards.

Once you get it, how you handle the privilege of credit is up to you. Using it wisely is the difference between a life of comfort or chaos. How do you want it to be?

Action Step:

Read over one of your credit card agreements or the back of your monthly statement to learn what the terms are for the money you have borrowed.

Day 163

THE REAL ENEMY

What you don't know can hurt you.

—Anonymous

Ignorance is the real enemy when borrowing money. If you don't know what terms and interest rates you've agreed to for your credit cards, your mortgage, your school loans, or the car note, then you are probably paying too much. It's dangerous to ignore the fine print on these contracts as too small to take seriously or to dismiss it by saying, "Oh, well you can't do anything about it anyway." Reducing your interest rate by 4 percent from 19 percent to 15 percent can cut monthly payments by $100. Wouldn't you make the effort to find out where and how to do it? If the saying, "The devil is in the details," bears any truth, then you'll find him lurking in the small print of credit card contracts.

Action Step:

Take a magnifying glass if you have to and read the terms of any agreement in which you promise to pay back a loan. Phone the lenders and ask them to explain the terms and clauses that you don't understand. Do this before you sign! You could be locked into a rotten contract for a very long time. If you have a good payment record, ask to have your rate reduced or consider looking for another credit card.

Day 164

DEBIT CARDS

What looks like a credit card, moves money electronically like a credit card, but isn't a credit card? A debit card is worth a try if you don't trust yourself with a credit card and don't always want to carry cash, travelers' checks, or your checkbook. Most banks make them available to customers in place of ATM cards. When you present a debit card for payment it will immediately transfer cash from your bank account to the merchant's bank account. You get a receipt for the transaction and mark it in your checkbook. Note that you do have to have money in your bank account for this to happen smoothly. The only drawback to using a debit card for all your purchases is that you are not building a credit history. A debit card is basically a substitute for cash in the form of a plastic card. You also do not have the same protection as you would for any lost or stolen credit cards, since there is not necessarily a payment limit for unauthorized deductions from your account. Once a debit card is stolen, you could lose all the cash in your checking account before the card is blocked—the bank may take no responsibility for such a mishap.

Action Step:

Order a copy of "Debit Cards: Beyond Cash and Checks" from the National Consumers League at 202–835–3323 or write to: National Consumers League, 1701 K Street, N.W., Suite 1200, Washington, DC 20006.

Day 165

WHAT'S YOUR SCORE?

The human species, according to the best theory I can form of it, is composed of two distinct races, the men who borrow and the men who lend.

—Charles Lamb

You are not the sum of your credit history, but the bankers and department stores who do the lending don't know you personally, so they have worked out a system of evaluating whether you're a good credit risk. This system is based on criteria that might be quite enlightening to you. Take the test and see how you measure up.

....

Credit Points Scoring System

Employment	Points
1 year or less at present employment	0
1 to 2 years	1
2 to 4 years	2
5 to 10 years	3
More than 10 years	4

Monthly Income (gross)	Points
Less than $1,000	0
$1,000 to $1,500	1
$1,500 to $2,000	2
More than $2,000	3

Time At Present Address	Points
Less than 3 years	0
3 years or more	1

Savings Account	Points
No	0
Yes	1

Checking Account	Points
No	0
Account with this bank, but with five returned checks within past year	1
Account with this bank, but no returned checks within past year	2

Previous Loan with Bank	Points
No	0
Yes, but still open	0
Yes, but closed with two or fewer late payments	1

Credit References	Points
No	0
Yes	1

Obligations Past Due	Points
Yes	0
No	1

Monthly Obligations As Percent of Income	Points
50 percent	0
40 to 49 percent	1
30 to 39 percent	2
less than 30 percent	3

Own Real Estate	Points
No	0
Yes	1

Telephone Listed in Applicant's Name	Points
No	0
Yes	1

Automobile	Points
No car	0
Car more than one year old	1
Car less than one year old	2

Scoring System

The highest possible score is 22 points. Use the scale below to evaluate yourself and understand how a lender will evaluate your financial background.

19 to 22—Loan granted automatically.

15 to 18—Loan granted unless there is a good reason to deny.

12 to 14—Reasonable risk; review application toward approval.

9 to 11—Review application toward rejection.

10 or less—Reject application automatically.

....

Action Step:

Evaluate how you can improve your score by not making late payments, opening a savings account, and having a telephone in your name, then get a copy of your credit report and review how you would be rated by a lender.

Day 166

TAKING INVENTORY

Remember that sheet where you reviewed your income and your spending, the one that was intended to make you see where you were in your financial life? Take a look at it now. Did you change anything in your spending and saving habits? Unless you've managed to do an overnight miracle with your finances, take a new sheet of paper. Write down, on one side, all your assets, starting with your bank account, savings account, any credit union or money market accounts. Next list the value of your home, if you own it, and everything in it, remembering that furniture and clothing depreciates from the day you buy it. Add your car or computer, and call the dealer you bought it from or a bank to find out the current trade-in value. Don't forget any pensions or life insurance policies. On the other side of the paper, list any debts, whether credit card or personal. How're you doing? Are your assets keeping ahead of inflation? What is most of your money going to, and does it make sense financially? How much income are your assets earning for you each year? If you have debts on the scale of a Third World country, it's clearly time to find a way to cope. Keep this paper. It's your summery of assets, and whether it's a depressing summary or a cheerful one, you need to know where you stand in order to improve. This exercise is no good if you're not ruthlessly honest with yourself!

Action Step:

What you have created is a balance sheet, or a net worth statement, that shows you what you own and what you owe. If what you own exceeds what you owe, then congratulate yourself, you're heading in the right direction! The objective should be to keep increasing the assets and the net worth portion of this statement. Do this exercise every six months.

Day 167

GETTING IN TOO DEEP

We all live in a state of ambitious poverty.

—Juvenal

It's not a sin to be in over your head with credit cards and bills you can't pay. You're not the only one who is. We've all been there at one time or another. Job losses, overspending, and not reading the fine print in a contract until too late is an American phenomenon. Two million Americans filed bankruptcy in 1998—but you won't have to if you start making some good decisions early and getting some help with the debts you've got now. The real sin is in not working on changing the situation and believing that you have to be in it forever. Debt isn't fatal—just depressing, miserable, and embarrassing, like the new pair of shoes you bought on credit that look great but feel awful the next day walking home from work.

Action Step:

Debtors Anonymous, a national support group, like Alcoholics Anonymous, is for people who have trouble with excessive debt and reckless spending. Check your local phone book or call the headquarters at 781–453–2743 to find a chapter near you. You can also visit the Web site at http://www.debtorsanonymous.org or write for more information at: P.O. Box 888, Needham, MA 02492–0009.

Day 168

REVIEW AND REASSESS

If you are finding it difficult to set up a payment plan, contacting your creditors to begin paying off your debts, call a credit counselor. If despite the commitment you think you've made to yourself to budget more carefully and get out of the hole, you still find yourself borrowing money and spending compulsively, call Debtors Anonymous. No financial advice in the world will make you wealthy or even modestly secure if you keep hurting yourself. There is no shame in needing help, but it would be a shame not to get help when you need it. You owe it to yourself and the people you care about.

Day 169

GETTING DEBT-FREE

A creditor is worse than a slave-owner, for the master owns only your person, but a creditor owns your dignity, and can command it.

—Victor Hugo

"The hardest part was telling my father how badly I had messed up," said Raynard Jones, an accountant in Baltimore, as he talked about the process of cleaning up his $11,000 credit card debt. "I'm the educated one, an accountant no less, but when I lost my job, I didn't know what else to do with myself. For the three months that I was unemployed, I found myself at the mall every other day, buying shirts, shoes, CDs, anything to make myself feel better. I couldn't think about how to pay for it at the time. I just needed something to ease the pain and never really looked at the balance as long as I could make the minimum monthly payment. Unfortunately, the shopping opiate just made things worse. I didn't realize how deep I was in debt until it was too late." Three years later, after cutting up the cards, getting a second job, going to a local credit counselor to get some free advice from a financial planner, and supportive encouragement from his father, Raynard is debt-free, has $20,000 in his "house fund—a money market account," has another $5,000 in the bank for emergencies, and puts $200 a month into four different mutual funds. "My coworkers laugh at me now when I brown-bag it for lunch and tell them about the bargains I found at weekend garage sales, but I don't care. I've got money in the bank and I'm going to retire a millionaire. The best lesson I learned was how little I really needed for daily needs and how good it feels now to sleep at night knowing that I'm finally debt-free."

Affirmation:

I am not my debts but I must be responsible for them.

Action Step:

Go to the Web site for the Motley Fools at http://www.fool.com and use their debt calculator to discover how long it would take you to get out of debt: $11,000 of credit card debt with an 18.1 percent interest rate and a minimum monthly payment of only $200 can take 72 months to pay off, assuming that you never charged up another cent!

Day 170

THE OVERSPENDING DISEASE

Some people experience a basic social alienation from being left out of the ongoing national shopping spree.

—Juliet B. Schor, *The Overspent American*

Do you feel that you would lose your friends if you refused to go shopping with them every lunch hour or weekend? Are there members of your family who feel that the only activity worth sharing is a trip to the mall? The media tell us daily that we have never been so prosperous, or consumed so much, and some people seem to take that message to heart, feeling that they're social failures if they don't dine out at every new restaurant or conspicuously spend their money in shops and trendy hangouts. The truth is that you can't purchase social success. Overspending doesn't make you a hero or prove that you're prosperous—only that you might be a bit insecure. Don't let people who have different priorities for their money influence you, and don't be afraid to refuse those "shop till we drop" invitations. You're not a cheapskate if you choose to save your money, and if friends try to make you feel like one, they're friends you don't need.

Make a list of five activities that you can share with your friends
that don't involve spending money. Make it a game between you to
see how many ways you can enjoy your time together without shopping. Just to be sure you won't be tempted, leave the cards at home!

Day 171

I CAN'T AFFORD IT!

Jeannie P. wanted to treat herself to a Caribbean vacation for her
January birthday the year she turned 25, but the travel agent gave
her a staggering figure because of the season. Jeannie decided what
the heck, you only turn 25 once, so she used her credit card—for
everything! She could handle a $40 minimum monthly payment
with no sweat. Jeannie charged her plane ticket, hotel bills, meals,
duty-free shopping, and poolside piña coladas. She returned to
Chicago relaxed, tanned—and with a mountain of credit card bills.
Two weeks later she heard rumors of possible layoffs in her company
and decided to save every penny to be prepared in case she was suddenly unemployed. But she couldn't save money and pay off the
large credit card balance. Her minimum balance was now up to $125
a month with all the new charges! Soon the anxiety, guilt, and dun-
ning calls from the bank brought her a feeling of helplessness that
she had never experienced before. Was the one-week trip worth the
one-year of financial distress and pressure? Sometimes the healthiest
thing you can tell yourself is "I can't afford it." Being realistic about
what you can and cannot afford is honest, mature, and responsible to
the one person who matters most—you. You are not less of a person
by saying no to yourself, but rather, you are saying yes to something
else—a more sensible way of setting goals and getting there without
the anxiety, guilt, and worry of going into debt.

Affirmation:

I will use credit only for true emergencies!

Action Step:

Open a holiday savings account at your bank or credit union so you can spend only cash for your shopping.

Day 172

PLASTIC SURGERY

$$$—Savings Tip:

Perform plastic surgery—not on your anatomy, but on your pocketbook. Cut up your credit cards. Do a ritual burning. Or lock them in a safe deposit box and throw away the key. Do whatever you have to in order to stop yourself from adding to your debt. The problem won't get better until you decide you want help. Then pick up the phone and call a credit counselor or Debtors Anonymous. It provides a safe, comforting, nonjudgmental atmosphere for people who can't control themselves in the cycle of shopping, spending, guilt, depression, and charging again. For some people, cutting up the cards may be the only way to cope with the problem of endless spending until they gradually get a clearer idea of how to handle credit in their lives. Get to a credit counselor today and find out what's making you put yourself so deeply in the hole.

Day 173

THE "KOOL-AID" CURE

$$$—Savings Tip:

If you get heart palpitations and feel yourself growing faint at the thought of cutting up your Visa, AMEX, and MasterCards, here's a guaranteed way to freeze the bottom line on your credit statement— the next best solution to putting them out of reach. Make a jar of Kool-Aid (grape or cherry so you can't see through it!) in an old mayonnaise jar or an empty milk carton with the top cut off. Drop your credit cards inside and put the container in the freezer. Indefinitely. Or at least until you have paid down most of the outstanding balances. Don't even think of defrosting that Kool-Aid in the microwave oven—it will make the computerized magnetic strip on the back unreadable.

Day 174

GOING BROKE

Income one shilling, Expenditures, eleven pence, halfpenny. Result: Happiness. Income, one shilling, Expenditures, one shilling and a halfpenny, Result: Misery.

—Mr. McCawber in *The Pickwick Papers*

In 1822, Charles Dickens was forced to drop out of school and go to work in a shoe blackening factory for three years to earn money to feed his family because his father, a government clerk, had defaulted on several loans and was sent to debtors' prison at Marshalsea. Along with the shame, humiliation, and public scandal of being declared a defaulted debtor, those so accused were allowed only a drink of water each day under British law. While they were incarcerated, they had to depend on friends and family for food and clothing. Charles's job, in addition to working 12 hours a day in the factory, was to deliver his father's meals each evening. That daily experience of visiting the prison left such an impression on the young Dickens that in each of his books at least one character has some change of fortune that leads to a commentary on managing money, being in debt, and the miserable experience of poverty. Dickens would probably be appalled to see how being maxed out on credit cards has almost become chic now, in our present Golden Age of Debt. The shame of not being able to pay bills seems to have disappeared since they don't lock you in debtors' prison anymore for unpaid bills, or put you in stocks in the town square for late mortgage or credit card payments. Maybe they should.

Action Step:

Rent a copy of the old classic video of *Oliver Twist* and find out what happened to poor children in Victorian England, or borrow a copy of *The Pickwick Papers* from the library and read Mr. McCawber's story.

Day 175

EARN MORE, SPEND MORE

Joey and Marge B. both grew up poor. They knew all too well the humiliation of evictions, hand-me-down clothes, and going without Christmas presents, and when they married they vowed their children would never have to suffer the pain of poverty. Both of them started out with small salaries but advanced steadily. Each raise was a cause for celebration and spending. As their incomes increased they craved possessions and couldn't stop buying them, sure that another new dress, stereo, closet full of designer sheets, or costly trinkets would erase the memories of sadness of their youth. Marge has shoes she's never even worn; Joey feels he must get a new car every three years, even though the old one is working fine. Yet no matter how much they spend, they will never fill the emotional void left from their poverty-stricken childhoods. They don't have any savings and don't appear to consider the future at all.

Do you spend all your money in search of a toy or trinket that can't possibly cure your feelings of loss and lack? A new job with a better paycheck or a raise at your current job won't necessarily cure your overspending problem. You'll just find more things to buy! True wealth has nothing to do with owning all the toys or Tommy Hilfiger jackets you can buy. It's about assets in the bank and the brokerage firm. That's the only thing that will allow you to have the freedom to be in charge of your life, and can ease the painful of memories of poverty.

Affirmation:

My joy in life comes from inside, not from what I have!

Action Step:

Reassess why you spend so much time shopping and what goal is worth sacrificing for.

Day 176

PULITZER'S DREAM

Joseph Pulitzer arrived in New York from Budapest at age 19 after being rejected by the Hungarian army because of his bad eyesight. With no money and unable to speak English, he found his way to St. Louis and worked on a German-language newspaper. He studied English and law at night and saved a few pennies each week from his

meager salary. One day he hoped to become a lawyer and run for public office. Both goals would take money, and he wanted to be prepared.
Five years later, just after passing the bar exam, his chance appeared:
He was allowed to buy the *St. Louis Dispatch*, a failing paper, for only
$2,500. The deal wiped out his savings, but to Pulitzer this was his
chance to test his ideas on how to make newspapers more readable and
entertaining as well as informative. A year later, the paper's circulation
had doubled; within three years, it made a profit of $45,000. That
same year, Jay Gould offered Pulitzer the chance to test his journalistic
skills on the *New York World*. Gould structured a deal that allowed
Pulitzer to buy the paper for $346,000 in installments over a ten-year
period. Pulitzer sold the St. Louis paper at a handsome profit and
moved to New York. There he improved upon his newspaper theories
but he added another component to reporting that we take for granted
today: a standard for integrity and accuracy. He urged his reporters to
be original and dramatic without descending to poor taste or exagger-
ated stories. Within three years, the *New York World* was the most
popular newspaper in the country, with ad revenue of over $2 million a
year. Upon his death in 1911, Pulitzer's estate was valued at $30 mil-
lion. Two million was earmarked to establish the School of Journalism
at Columbia University and to create the Pulitzer Prize.

Action Step:

Imagine what would not have happened if Pulitzer had not saved
that $2,500.

Day 177

ROLE MODELS

*The secret of success in life is for a man to be ready for his
opportunity when it comes.*

—Benjamin Disraeli

Surround yourself with the stories, images, and examples of people who have become successful at building wealth in their lives. These prototypes can come from books, music, or a classic late-night movie. Think of the feeling you have walking out of a film that has inspired you to try something new and different. It's a springboard for breaking old patterns, reaffirming your commitment to fulfilling a dream that's gotten buried under the day-to-day of life's minutiae.

Action Step:

Go to a video store and rent some heroic movies, like the 1946 classic *Great Expectations*, or Richard Pryor's *Brewster's Millions*, that will inspire you to stay on the path. Better yet, go to the film classics section of the public library and save on the rental fee. That's an extra $2 or $3 you can add to your piggy bank now.

Day 178

INSPIRATIONAL MOMENTS

Great minds have purposes, others have wishes.

—Washington Irving

Pick up a copy of Barbara Taylor Bradford's novel *A Woman of Substance*, and read about Emma Harte, a woman who grew up on the wrong side of the tracks in the coal-mining slums and shanty towns of Northern Ireland at the turn of the century. She was denied an education, raped and abandoned by a wealthy landowner, then turned her life around and built a successful business empire despite her impoverished background. It's a good read and a reminder that you don't have to stay where you start in life.

Action Step:

Ask a librarian for similar books to read.

Day 179

DEALING WITH DEBT

When you get out cheap, you get back in quick.

—Reverend Charles Stanley

Repeat after me: *"There is no such thing as credit repair!"* Those ads you see in the classified sections of magazines and newspapers offering a clean credit report are promising something they can't deliver if you truly have not paid your bills on time. All they do is take a hefty sum of money from you and write lots of letters every month challenging the items in the credit bureau's files. You can write those letters yourself and save your money. Some credit repair con artists encourage you to apply for a new Social Security number with a "slight change in your name" so you can assume a new credit history. This is called fraud and will cost you a lot more than some late-payment charges if you resort to it. There are no quick fixes in the debt-repayment process, even though you may pray for an instant solution to an agonizing mess of past-due bills. Go to a credit counselor instead. Put yourself on a schedule and take the time to make things right. You'll remember and learn from the sacrifices you've had to make. It can be slow, painful, and aggravating at times, but it's the best way to learn from your mistakes.

Affirmation:

I am making every effort to conquer my irrational spending and improve the way I use my money.

Action Step:

Take a look at http://www.homefair.com/homefair/scams.html to see what services you should avoid in the credit repair racket. Then call 80–SAVE–ME2, for an appointment with Consumer Credit Counseling Service, a nationally recognized debt management agency.

Day 180

PENNY POWER

Have you ever walked past a penny on the sidewalk and decided that it wasn't worth the effort to bend over and get it? Pick up that penny! We pay little or no attention to the little red copper cents that turn into annoying bulges in the corner of our coat pockets, but think about it this way: Have you ever tried to buy a postage stamp with less than the full amount needed? No deal, huh? Take one penny and double it every day for 30 days and see how much that turns into. One cent, 2 cents, 4 cents, 8 cents, 16 cents, and so on. Doesn't sound like much, but if you try it you begin to get an idea of how money can grow quickly when you're not looking. After 30 days, your total should be $5,368,708! Now, still want to ignore that penny on the sidewalk?

Action Step:

Call 800–255–0899 for a sample of *The Pocket Change Investor* newsletter, which offers loads of tips on small ways to save that stretch small pennies into big bucks.

Day 181

$$$—Savings Tip:

Have you noticed that nearly all commercial laundromats have front-loading machines? There's a reason. According to the Department of Energy, front loaders save at least $100 year in operating costs. They use 38 percent less water, 58 percent less electricity, and spin your clothes dryer than top-loading machines, cutting down on the time your clothes spend tumbling in the dryer. The most efficient front-loading machine is a Maytag Neptune, which retails for a hefty $1,100, or about $950 at some discount outlets. It may take three years to recover the higher cost of the purchase, but the dryer is expected to last for an average of 15 years.

Day 182

REVIEW AND REASSESS

Now that you have taken an assessment of your life and decided to make some changes, you're in a hurry to start seeing the results of some of these new steps you've taken, such as the mutual fund you opened, the automatic payroll savings plan that you've started, and the cuts in your daily spending. Even if you've managed to pay down your debts, it still seems tough to save enough for the down payment on a home, or get near the goal of having a decent retirement plan. You're not the only one who has become discouraged about the slow process of seeing results from new habits. But don't worry—the results will happen! In the meantime, distract yourself. Start reading investment brochures about how to use that money wisely for retirement.

Day 183

$$$—Savings Tip:

Put a timer on your air-conditioner to avoid running it longer than you need to. Set the timer for one hour before you get home so you don't waste energy running your air-conditioner all day. If you adjust the temperature by even four degrees you can decrease your energy usage by 12 percent and still have a dry, cool environment. You can also reset the timer to turn the air-conditioner off one or two hours after you go to bed since nighttime temperatures are typically 25 to 30 degrees cooler, unless the outside temperatures are excessively high and humid. This can cut your summer energy bills by about $65 a month.

Day 184

$$$—Savings Tip:

Thinking about getting a pet? Call the ASPCA or the animal shelter in your neighborhood, especially at the end of the summer if you live in a resort area. The ASPCA costs less than a pet shop, and the animals already have their shots and have been spayed or neutered. Other fees are also about 40–60 percent less than at a vet's office. If there's an adjustment problem within 30 days, you can return the animal, no questions asked.

Day 185

$$$—Savings Tip:

Buy quality—not brand names. Do a taste test with two quarts of orange juice. Can you tell the difference between Tropicana at $2.50 a half gallon and the generic store brand at $1.50 a half gallon? I doubt it. Trade secret: Most store brands and lesser-known regional brands of juice all come out of the same processing plants in Ohio, Florida, or California. Save yourself at least $100 a year by buying the store brand.

Day 186

A MIND FOR THRIFT

To live is not merely to breathe; it is to act.

—Jean-Jacques Rousseau

Condition yourself to think in a frugal manner. Get a pad of Post-It notes and write a list of reminders and aphorisms about saving money. You can start with the quotes in this book, or with your grandmother's words of wisdom. Put them up all around your living space: on the bathroom mirror, the kitchen cabinet, the refrigerator door, and the steering wheel of your car so you will see them each day to remind yourself of your new approach to spending and saving. New habits can be learned and incorporated into your life with support, effort, and the right attitude.

Action Step:

Sign up for the weekly e-mail newsletter from *The Dollar Stretcher*, an excellent savings advice publication available at no cost at http://www.stretcher.com.

Day 187

FOUND MONEY!

Seven out of ten adults have unclaimed funds somewhere that are waiting for them to collect it. You may have forgotten the deposit you left with the utility company when you had your first apartment, the small savings account you started when you were a college student, or the joint savings account your grandmother set up and never told you about. Your name is on these inactive accounts somewhere, collecting interest and waiting for you to claim them. The average account for found money is $385 but some are as large as $65,000. Imagine what you could do with that unexpected find!

Action Step:

Contact Found Money International, Inc., at 302–996–5818 for a free search or visit the Web site at http://www.foundmoney.com and enter your name for a quick search. Found Money takes a 20 percent fee, which is a bit steep, but it's money you never expected to get. Go for it!

Day 188

REVIEW AND REASSESS

When you extend yourself through tithing, you get back so much more in so many ways that cannot be measured in dollars. Tithing, the act of making a contribution of a portion of your earnings to a spiritual cause, is a practice that is discussed and recommended in all forms of religion. It is a way of expressing gratitude, of saying, "Thank you" to the Universe for the blessing you have received. Reexamine your attitude about giving to others and how it can benefit you.

THREE

WEALTH
CREATION

INTRODUCTION

It takes courage to be rich!

—Suze Orman

You've analyzed your attitudes about money and you're working on adjusting them. You're educating yourself about financial issues. You have established financial goals for the near- and long-term future. You've created a budget (or a spending plan!) that includes paying yourself first. You're trying to spend more consciously and more carefully, you're setting aside a small sum from your paycheck, you've started to shrink your debts. You're developing wealth consciousness and building a wealth foundation.

You've come a long way in less than six months and we're just getting started!

Of course, wealth creation is the juicy part, the part you've been waiting for. Well, you're ready to hear about it, but there may be some surprises in store.

There are three basic ways to create wealth: building savings, investing in the stock market, and owning a home. Starting a business is another possibility but we won't cover that in this book.

Building savings can be fun. That's why you wrote out those goals. Building savings is also essential. Emergencies and investment opportunities don't send out early warning signals, so you have to be prepared. In this section, we take serious steps toward choosing the particular investment vehicle that matches your needs and goals.

Ahead is information on CDs and money market funds, bonds, mutual funds, and stocks. You'll put to use some of what you've already learned about finance, and you'll find out how to learn a lot more.

Understanding that your money has to grow is accepting a reality of life. Of course, true growth comes with an element of risk wrapped around it. Only you can decide how much risk is acceptable and appropriate: Money that's going to be needed soon belongs somewhere risk-free, whereas money saved for retirement can stand more risk in exchange for more growth (assuming retirement is a long way off)! Approach risk with a sense of adventure, not dread: Remember, your thoughts do manifest as a real living experience.

Investing in the stock market is full participation in the world economy for true growth. The market really is for everyone but first you need to understand the basic concepts of investing and why it is essential to your wealth-building plan. It doesn't matter if you have a lot of money to put in at once or just a little bit at a time.

Finally, if you already own a home, even a heavily mortgaged one, you know what an essential part of wealth creation it is. If you haven't thought of buying a home, or don't think you can, think again. There is a lot of help out there for first-time buyers. Read on.

Day 189

PREPARE FOR THE UNEXPECTED

A feast is made for laughter, and wine maketh merry: but money answereth all things.

—Ecclesiastes 10:19

The phone is going to ring one day to tell you that your elderly Aunt Martha has gone on to her Heavenly Reward. The trip home to the funeral, even with the discount bereavement rate offered by the airlines, will cost about $500. You'll also have to pitch in $300 to help pay for the funeral since she didn't have any life insurance.

Your son forgot to tell you about the slew of parking tickets he got when he used your car during his summer vacation. The parking violations department has towed your car away and wants $823 for tickets, towing charges, and interest penalties. In cash.

Someone dented your rear bumper in the parking lot at the grocery store and didn't leave a phone number. You have a $500 deductible and the repair will cost $450.

A thunderstorm left a tree on top of your terrace and the insurance company won't be able to reimburse you for the $1,100 removal cost for at least 30 days. The haulage company wants cash immediately.

Financial crises happen all the time and they all require cash. Earthquakes and tornadoes come with little or no warning. So do illnesses and accidents. If you've ever had to borrow from friends or relatives, or pass the hat to pay for a funeral, you understand why you must save money for emergencies. Cash cures problems faster than plastic. And not everybody takes plastic, especially tow trucks and out-of-town auto mechanics.

Action Step:

List two emergencies you have had in the past year that required cash. Think about it. This is why you need a savings account. Stop at your bank and see what the minimum amount is for opening a money market fund. Don't forget to ask about the interest rate, and compare that with the rate of the bank across the street or a money market mutual fund

Day 190

PURPOSE AND CLARITY

Great minds have purposes, others have wishes.

—Washington Irving

Remember the first section of the book where you asked yourself the simple question: "What do I want my money to do for me?"

Now is when you need a clear answer. If you're going to get serious about moving toward financial independence, you need a positively stated intention, an inner motivation that is much more exciting than seeing a zero balance on your credit card accounts. Saving money has to be built into your lifestyle, like brushing your teeth, taking your vitamins, and eating when you're hungry, but it must also start with a specific goal for how many dollars you are going to put away, and what you plan to use them for. And you must put it in writing—like creating a contract with yourself. Lay it out on the page so you can see what you really want. If you change your mind in a few minutes or a few days, that's okay. Keep writing and rewriting your goal until you have answered your own inner question: "What do I want to do with my life financially?" Write it out several times to become comfortable with the idea. Say it out loud several times until you really hear yourself speak out your belief that you can be financially independent. Look in the mirror and tell yourself what you want. Are the eyes of that person who looks back honest, clear, and strong? Do you believe what you hear yourself saying? Believing it is the first step toward making it happen. Take out your notebook and begin writing. No one but you has to know about your goal. Start writing!

Affirmation:

I carefully consider all my options on the road to financial independence.

Day 191

WHERE TO START SAVING?

Just about the time you think you can make both ends meet, somebody moves the ends.

—Pansy Penner, *Reader's Digest*

A logical place to start saving money is at work, with a payroll savings plan. This is the godsend that will take the money out of your paycheck before you get your hands on it. A fixed amount of money is deducted from every paycheck, and after a couple of weeks you won't even miss it. Unlike plans that put you on the honor system—swearing to put a certain amount in a coffee can every week, or promising yourself to bank a part of every paycheck—your company's payroll savings plan doesn't give you a chance to cheat. Join the company's savings plan, especially if it matches your contribution with a dollar for every $2 you kick in—that's a 50 percent return at no risk. Don't spend your next raise, but use the extra money to fatten your savings or investments. The same goes for your Christmas bonus or any other cash perks. Don't think of it as depriving yourself—you're building a bedrock of wealth for the future. *Hard fact*: By late middle age, you should be saving 10 to 20 percent of your income.

Affirmation:

Saving this way is painless and profitable.

Action Step:

Figure out how much you need to save annually, divide by 12, and make that sum your monthly contribution to your company's payroll savings or money market plan.

Day 192

CONSISTENCY PAYS OFF

Every time you get paid, take out your checkbook and write your name on the "payable to" line.

—Stephanie Gallagher

If you understand the ancient Chinese saying "The journey of a thousand miles begins with one step," then you will also understand that the journey toward wealth begins with the first dollar. In this case you can start with $50. We have already established that you can find an extra $50 a month by simply taking the extra change out of your pocket each night and setting it aside. The next step is putting that money away in a blue-chip equity mutual fund that will give you the growth you want to reach that million-dollar goal. (Blue chip stocks are those household names you recognize when you open the refrigerator or the medicine cabinet, or when you look around your office or your living room—names like Colgate, General Motors, Wal-Mart, Amoco, Scott Paper, and Citicorp.) Don't worry about the question of where to put the money just yet. You just make the commitment to have $50 a month deducted from your paycheck or your bank account. Do it on a consistent basis. Approach it with the same discipline and personal self-grooming attention that you give to getting a haircut each month, taking your vitamins each day, or paying your mortgage. Since you probably want to play it safe right now, you may want to check out one of the oldest mutual funds around, the American Century Select Fund, which was established in 1958. The fund has been around for more than 30 years and despite the ups, downs, dips, and dodges of the market, it has produced an average return of 19.8 percent per year over the last ten years. Looking at the longer term, it has produced an average return of 14.31 percent since it started, which is an excellent achievement in such a volatile business. American Century was also one of the first companies to allow automatic monthly investments. Get out your budget sheet, put those pennies away, clip those coupons, and set up that automatic monthly savings plan. Now you know where to put that extra $50 a month.

Action Step:

Call American Century at 800–345–2021 and order a copy of the prospectus and application for the Select Fund and get started today! You can also download a copy of it from the American Century Web site at http://www.americancentury.com.

Day 193

FREE LITERATURE

Banks, brokerage firms, mutual fund companies, and government agencies have tons of free literature explaining everything from FDIC insurance to investing in gold, commodities, and real estate that they can't wait to send to you. Just dial an 800 number, fill out a postpaid card and mail it, visit a Web site and fill in a form, or send a self-addressed stamped envelope. Here are a few key places to start:

"Take Charge of Your Money," published by AARP. Send a SASE to: 601 E St. N.W., Washington, D.C., 20049.

"Ask Questions," a list of questions you should ask any stockbroker, financial planner, or investment adviser. Call the Securities and Exchange Commission at 800–SEC–0330 or visit its Web site, http://www.sec.gov.

"How to Read an Annual Report," available from Merrill Lynch by calling 800–327–6748 or at its Web site, http://www.merrill lynch.com.

"What Every Investor Should Know . . . ," available from the Mutual Fund Education Alliance at 816–471–1454.

"Investor Expectations," one of several free publications available in English and Spanish from the Investment Company Institute. Call 202–326–5800, or write 1401 H Street, N.W., 12th floor, Washington, DC 20005–2148, or download it from the Web site at http://www.ici.org.

Action Step:

Order these brochures and read through them when they arrive. Share them with your friends for another discussion about money. See how your attitude has changed.

Day 194

AGE IS NO EXCUSE!

For age is opportunity, no less than youth itself.

—Henry Wadsworth Longfellow

A common excuse for many would-be investors is "I'm too old to start something that requires a long-term commitment!" Don't tell that to the Beardstown Ladies' Investment Club. This group is living proof that age should not get in the way of learning about money and investing. The average age of the 16 women in the small Illinois town was 68 when they established their investment club in 1983. These women started their own investment club because the average stockbroker ignored them because they were women, they were retired, and they had small amounts of money to invest. They went on to become recognized as successful investors and write the best-selling book *The Beardstown Ladies' Common-Sense Investment Guide.* The youngest member of the club was 41 when they got started; the oldest was 87. So you don't have to give up the idea of investing simply because you're over 40! According to the NAIC, the National Association of Investors' Corporation, the nonprofit organization that helps groups to start investment clubs, the average age of their membership is 52. The average investment club has 14 members, and each member contributes about $80 a month to the club's investment portfolio. The Beardstown Ladies have created a video discussing their philosophy of investing called *Cooking Up Profits on Wall Street,* which can be ordered from 800–359–EARN.

Action Step:

Contact NAIC at 711 West Thirteen-Mile Road, Madison Heights, MI 48071; 810–583–6242 for information on how to start an investment club. You can also download information from its Web site at http://www.better-investing.org.

Day 195

SAVINGS SCHEDULE

 W hat you're saving for determines where you do your saving and for how long!

Short-Term Savings	Time Period	Risk
Passbook savings	Six months to one or two years	Inflation impact
Money market funds	Six months to one or two years	Inflation impact
Treasury bills	Six months to one or two years	Inflation impact
Certificates of deposit	Six months to one or two years	Inflation impact
Short-term bond funds	Six months to one or two years	Inflation impact

Fixed Income	Time Period	Risk
High-quality intermediate bonds	Three years	Inflation rate risk
High-yield bonds	Three years	Inflation rate risk
GNMAs and mortgage bonds	Five years	Interest rate risk
Guaranteed interest contracts	Five years	Inflation risk

Action Step:

Review your list of goals and the timetable you created for reaching them. Choose at least one of the above investments to match each goal. Pick an appropriate mutual fund that supports that timetable and that goal.

Day 196

CDS

The magic of compounding interest is truly the eighth wonder of the world!

—Albert Einstein

Buying a certificate of deposit or CD is making a loan to the bank. In your contract you agree to let the bank lock your money away for a fixed period of time. The bank agrees to pay you as little as possible for it at the end of that deadline. Like any loan it has terms, conditions, a timetable, an interest rate, and penalties. But—there's always a but!—if you decide that you want to cancel the loan and take your money out of the bank before the deadline, the bank can charge you a penalty for breaking the contract—usually it won't pay you all the interest that was agreed to! CDs can be as short as one month and as long as five years. Usually, the longer you leave the money there, the better the interest rate that the bank pays you. There are exceptions. You can start with as little as $500. Shop around. Compare banks. Savings banks and credit unions offer better interest rates than large commercial banks. Rates change each week—usually on Wednesdays —because that is the day that the Federal Reserve Bank makes its adjustments on the rates that it charges all the banks it regulates.

Action Step:

Check out the Wednesday edition of the *Wall Street Journal* rates for the week. (It lists the five best bank rates around the country in eight categories of savings, from money markets to five-year CDs, and provides their phone numbers.) Or, if you're a member, you can check out the best rates in all 50 states each week at the BanxQuote Banking Center or the Bloomberg Web site at http://www.bloomberg.com. Call BanxQuote at 212–643–8000.

Day 197

REVIEW AND REASSESS

Have you picked up a copy of the *Wall Street Journal* and looked up the CD savings rates in the "Money and Investing" section? Each day that you delay doing this is a missed opportunity to earn better interest. For a weekly list of the top-rated money market funds, click on http://www.ibcdata.com or call 508–881–2800 for a faxed copy of the report.

Day 198

STASHING CASH

Gene P. was lucky enough to get a $30,000 fellowship to pay for his first year of graduate school to study psychology, but there was one catch—it came to him in one lump sum, and he's nervous about making it last from September to June. Lisa and Michael are a newly-wed couple who received a cash wedding gift that they are considering using for a down payment on a house or a condo within the next year. The stock market looks good right now. Gene, Lisa, and Michael are all wondering whether they could put this extra cash into a good mutual fund for about six months and get a better return than the puny 2 percent the savings bank is offering right now. Right? Wrong! If you plan to use any money that you have in savings for a major expense or big-ticket purchase within a year, you can't afford to invest it in the stock market. Stocks are good for the long term but can go south on you in a second—the recent Dow Jones decline went down 20 percent in less than six hours and took six months to recover. That would leave Gene wondering how to cover the tuition check due next month or Lisa and Michael wondering how to write the check for the closing on the mortgage that was set

WEALTH HAPPENS ONE DAY AT A TIME

for the next week. They should find a good money market fund
instead. Money market mutual funds (outside of banks) pay better
interest and maintain the stable value of your principle at $1 a share
at all times. They also give you a checkbook so you can write a check
to cover expenses over $500, which is the minimum amount most of
these accounts allow you to withdraw.

Action Step:

   Call the Berger Mutual Fund Group at 800–333–1001 and ask for
a money market application. It allows you to open a money market
account with only $250. Ask for the automatic savings option so it
can deduct $50 a month from your checking account.

Day 199

TOP MONEY FUNDS

All money market funds are not the same. The ones at most banks
are FDIC insured, which means that the government will protect
and guarantee your money up to $100,000 per account if the bank
should fold. The money market funds offered through mutual fund
companies are not insured. The difference boils down to this: (1) the
cost of the FDIC insurance that the bank provides and (2) the kind
of short-term debt notes that the mutual fund investment company
is willing to invest in. Banks will not invest in anything that isn't
insured or guaranteed, such as Treasury bills or other government
agency notes. Mutual fund companies will take a bit more risk and
invest in the short-term loans and discounted postdated checks of
major corporations, called "commercial paper," as well as Treasury
bills and government notes. The result is that independent money
market mutual funds companies are able to pay a slightly higher
interest rate on your short-term investment. A bit more risk, a
slightly higher return. You decide how much more you want to earn.

Action Step:

Look in the "By the Numbers" section of *Money* magazine for a list of the best current yields on bank money market accounts, money market mutual funds, tax-free money market mutual funds, and short-term bond funds. It also offers the same data on CD rates from six months to five years. Each month you can see which fund is offering the better rate for the week. The 800 numbers for each fund are included in the listing.

Day 200

PAINLESS SAVING

Start where you are, do what you can.

—Arthur Ashe

Your grandparents may have saved money under the mattress, but those days are over. Start small and make it painless. Can you find a dollar a week? How about a dollar a day? Don't laugh! A dollar a day is a pretty painless way to start saving. Just skip the extra coffee at noon or the dessert at lunch. Look at it this way. If your parents had started putting away a dollar a day when you were born, how much you would have now? A baby boomer now age 53 would have $19,345, and that's not including interest. What if that money had been invested each birthday in a mutual fund with an average annual return of 12 percent? Today that money would be worth $632,407.96! Even if you start today, you can still do rather well with a small amount of money if you consistently put it away and leave it there for the next 30 years. If you're 35 now, decide that no matter what happens you will put away $50 a month until you retire in 30 years. Choose a conservative equity mutual fund, like the Dreyfus Disciplined Stock Fund, which has never paid less than 10 percent in growth and dividends each year.

The total amount of money you will lay out over time will be $18,000. Even with the inevitable crashes and crescendos of the stock market, you will have accrued $113,024.40 when you are sixty-five. What are you waiting for? You don't have a day to lose!

Action Step:

Call for a prospectus and an application for the Dreyfus Disciplined Stock Fund at 800–874–8216, ext. 4504. This five-star fund averaged an annual return of 19.76 percent over the last ten years. A second choice would be the T. Rowe Price Dividend Growth Fund, which can be reached at 800–541–7853 or through the Web site at http://www.troweprice.com.

Day 201

THE INVISIBLE MONSTER

Twenty years ago it took two people to carry home ten dollars' worth of groceries. Today, a five year old can do it.

—Henny Youngman

Remember when you were a kid and you and your best friend could go to McDonald's and get Big Macs, fries, Cokes, and toys and still have change from the $5 bill your father gave you? Or afternoons at a Saturday matinee when $2 covered your admission and a large box of popcorn? Not anymore! Don't try to understand the bizarre economic formula behind inflation or even to predict it. One thing is unavoidable and guaranteed: Inflation is for certain. It's always going to push prices higher than you want them to be. Think about it, have you ever heard of the cost of a house, car, or bag of groceries going down? That means that unless your investment return is higher than the tax rate and the cost of living, your dollars are losing value, or your purchasing power is declining.

Compare the costs of a bus ride, a newspaper, a car, and a house in 1969, 1989, and 1999. Calculate the rate of increase. Now compare the rate of interest you get on a savings account with the increased cost-of-living expenses over the last few years. Which is growing faster?

Day 202

WHY INVEST?

Money begets money.

—John Ray

Investing is like farming. You don't know when it's going to rain or snow. You can't predict sun, floods, or locusts. But you trust in the seasons, so you plant your seeds, nurture the seedlings daily, and give them time to grow. Similarly, your money needs to have time to sprout, grow, and develop. In the stock market, the right soil would be good-quality stocks, primarily blue chip stocks that have stood the test of time and given good profits regardless of how unpredictable the economic weather may be at times. Would you plant a tree and pull it out by the roots at the first sign of a hurricane? Would you sell the farm after a first thunderstorm? If your tree is strong enough, you let it weather the storm and continue growing and blossom in spring after the bad weather is over. You must learn to do the same with money. Plant it, and leave it alone. Only $100 invested in the Dow Jones Industrial Average in 1950, the year the first baby boomers started kindergarten, would be worth $5,706 by the end of 1998, when many of those same kindergartners are thinking about retirement. If that same $100 had been invested in a 5 percent passbook savings account, it would be worth only $1,240.11.

Bad news about investing will always be there, like ants and flies at picnics. If you look for negative stories on the stock market and the frauds perpetrated against small investors, corrupt CEOs, and insider trading scandals that decreased a stock price, but you can also find some strong arguments and undeniable stories of successful investors.

Action Step:

Call the American Funds group at 800–421–4120 and request a copy of "Investment Company of America—An Investor's Guide." This 12-page brochure is an excellent example of how investing in an equity mutual fund over a 50-year period is still more successful than putting your money in CDs in the bank.

Day 203

THE RULE OF 72

This simple formula helps you figure out how long it will take for your money to double in value. If you put $1,000 into a CD earning 4.25 percent interest, and you want to know how long it will take for the $1,000 to become $2,000, divide 4.25 into the number 72. The answer you get is 16.94, which means it would take nearly 17 years for $1,000 to become $2,000 if it stayed invested at this same interest rate. By contrast, if you invested $1,000 in a stock mutual fund with an average annual total return of 11.6 percent, how long would it take for your $1,000 to become $2,000? Divide 72 by 11.6 to get your answer. The rule of 72 helps explain a long-term investment such as your 401(k) plan.

Rate of Return	Time Required to Double Investment
4 percent	18 years
5 percent	14.4 years
6 percent	12 years
7 percent	10.3 years
8 percent	9 years
9 percent	8 years
10 percent	7.2 years
11 percent	6.5 years
12 percent	6 years

Action Step:

Take out your savings account statement, your 401(k) plan statement, and your money market statement and look at the interest rate listed on each one. Use your calculator and apply the rule of 72 to each and see how long it will take to double your money in each account. Your 401(k) plan investments should double the fastest. If the investments in your 401(k) plan require more than ten years to double, you should reexamine your goals and your timetable for achieving some of them, and then decide if you want to change your investment options.

Day 204

THE LANGUAGE OF INVESTING

Money, which represents the prose of life and which is hardly spoken of in parlors without apology, is, in its effects and laws, as beautiful as roses.

—Ralph Waldo Emerson

If you have grown up in a family where money was never discussed, then any conversation about the stock market, banking, insurance, and real estate investments can feel like a foreign language to you. Financial talk shows probably make you lunge for the remote control, the tiny lines of the stock tables make you turn to the entertainment section, and the clauses in the mortgage agreement and the credit card application probably give you a headache, and make you walk out of the bank, dismissing the whole experience as if it is a conspiracy to keep you ignorant about how the whole game works.

Relax. You can find out what the folks on Louis Rukeyser's show and *Nation's Business* are talking about quite easily by checking out one of the Web sites that explains it all, or you can pick up one of the new books geared toward the financially impaired. Victoria Morris's *The Woman's Guide to Investing*, Neale Godfrey's *Money Doesn't Grow on Trees*, or Adriane Berg's *Your Financial Life for 18- to 35-Year-Olds* are good, simple books that don't make you feel like you've wandered into a corporate board room.

The New York Stock Exchange provides a collection of free brochures that explain the difference between stocks and bonds, index funds vs. blue-chip funds, and commodities vs. collateralized mortgages. It may feel like you're getting a crash course in Serbo-Croatian or translating some jaw-breaking Urdu dialect but, trust me, it's all in English and it's much easier that you think. If you can learn to drive a car, you can learn to speak investment-ese with ease but it takes time. Any financial book with a glossary will help you to master the language.

Affirmation:

Learning about money is as easy as getting to know a new friend.

Action Step:

Check out the list of investment terms explained on America Online's Personal Finance site, or visit another Internet investment information site called the Dictionary of Financial Risk Management at http://utah.el.com/amex/findic.

Day 205

"JUST THE FACTS, MA'AM"

Over the short term, anything can affect investor psychology. Over the long run, there's no doubt what drives the forces at work on a stock price—the earnings a company records.

—Robert Sheard, *The Unemotional Investor*

Turn off the daily market reports from CNN and CNBC about the hourly gyrations of a company's stock price. Forget all the rumors, half-truths, misinformation, and gossip. The unshakable historical facts are these: If you study the final returns of various investment choices over the 40-year period from 1956 to 1996, stocks have consistently done better than anything else available. These numbers should always be in the back of your head when you think about your investments, especially when your stocks and funds begin to gyrate in strange directions.

Investment	Total Return
S&P 500 Index stocks	11.18 percent
Corporate bonds	6.99 percent
Government bonds	6.51 percent
Inflation	4.47 percent

Action Step:

Visit the Web site for Ibbotson Associates at http://www.ibbotson. com to see an excellent chart on the long-term returns of stocks, bonds, taxes, and inflation on $1 invested over a 40-year period.

Day 206

FIVE MISTAKES TO AVOID IN THE INVESTMENT GAME

*Folly delights a man who lacks judgment, but a man [or woman]
of understanding keeps a straight course.*

—Proverbs 15:21

Expecting too much too soon. If you're paranoid and worried, with your luck the market will take a 500-point dip the day after you purchase your first stock. Don't panic! Remember the fundamentals of the stock market: Long-term investing always pays off better. If you're not willing to invest for at least ten years, don't open the account.

Not understanding where you're putting your money. Buying shares in cranberry bogs in Minnesota or in a catfish farm in Alaska wouldn't make sense to the most grizzled veteran of Wall Street, so why should you consider it? Blind trust can be lethal to your financial well-being. If you can't explain to a ten-year-old where you have invested your money and why, then perhaps you shouldn't do it until you can.

Following "hot tips." Stick with what you know. Quick hits can turn into long waits or ugly losses overnight. A University of Maryland study of investment styles concluded that investors who are fund switchers and quickly change from one stock to another earn 7 percent less than a patient investor with one asset allocation strategy who sticks with it.

Going for the greed. Chain letters, multilevel marketing, "insider information" schemes—none of them delivers what it promises.

Doing nothing. Leaving money in checking or low-interest savings and "waiting until next year" means losing a year of growth and investment returns. Playing it too safe can also be harmful.

Day 207

THE HIGH COST OF DOING NOTHING

You will never "find" time for anything. If you want time, you must make it.

—Charles Buxton

Every year that you postpone investing, you lose another 10 percent of growth on your retirement money. Think about it. Just $20 a week is $1,000 a year ($1,040 if you want to be exact!). If you had invested that money in a blue chip mutual fund or even one of the index funds, you would have earned at least 12 percent interest on your money over the last seven years, even with all the ups, downs, and swings of the stock market, instead of the 3.6 percent that is the average return for an FDIC-insured passbook savings account since 1991. Calculate the difference between 2 percent and 12 percent. Enough said. No, you can't buy last year's results with this year's dollars but you can get a head start on this year's results for $20 a week. You probably waste more than that on newspapers, coffee, and donuts each week. Which $20 is going to comfort you in your retirement?

Action Step:

The most popular index that the world pays attention to is the Dow, which until 1995 did not have a separate category on the mutual fund menu. If you want to invest in the top 30 stocks of the world's leading economic indicator, then consider $1,000 into one of the DOW–30 index funds. You'll be able to get a daily report on the performance of your investment on the evening news. Call Waterhouse Securities at 800–934–4410 and ask for a brochure and prospectus on its DOW–30 Fund. Its Web site also has an application and a prospectus at http://www.waterhouse.com that can be printed out and mailed in.

Day 208

GET RID OF THE "YEAH . . . BUT"

Some men have thousands of reasons why they cannot do what they want to, when all they need is one reason why they can.

—Dr. Willis R. Whitney

Investing skeptics specialize in excuses to procrastinate. "Yeah, the S&P ended the year up 24 percent, but what about next year?" Or, "Yeah, interest rates are down now, but how long will that last?" Or, "Yeah, Microsoft is hot now, but when will some other company beat them?" Or maybe, "Yeah, I understand historical trends, but what about market timing?" Recessions and market dips are like hurricanes, floods, and earthquakes. They are totally unpredictable and they happen all around the world, but somehow, no matter what corner of the globe they live in, human beings still get up each morning and start all over again, rebuilding their homes and businesses, restarting economies and market cycles. As for the perfect time to invest—there isn't any. Experts have proven that outsmarting the market is a myth. Suppose you started investing in 1963 in an S&P index fund (these funds invest in the 500 largest companies), and picked the worst day of the year (just before a 10 percent dip) to plunk down your $2,000 investment each year for ten years. If you'd let your $20,000 ride out the dips and turns of the market, you still would have accumulated $587,093 by 1997. Stocks go up two days out of three over a ten-year period. With these odds, you risk more losses being out of the market rather than in it.

Affirmation:

Timing and luck are nice, but I am a long-time market player today.

Action Step:

Call Dreyfus S&P Index Fund at 800–645–6561 or Vanguard S&P Index 500 Fund at 800–635–1511. Both funds earned 32.9 percent in 1997 and have low management expenses of less than .50 percent. Over a ten-year period each fund had an average annual return of 19.2 percent.

Day 209

YOUR INVESTMENT PLAN

Every successful investment manager I know has a sensible, logical investment approach and he sticks to it.

—H. Bradlee Perry

Investing starts with having a strategy, a plan, and a vision. The basic principles that you should follow begin with these simple rules:

1. Buy good-quality stocks that have favorable prospects for strong growth. Look at their prospects for earnings over the next five years. They should exceed the gross national product and be leaders in their industry.

2. Diversify your investments among several companies in different industries. If you own nothing but utility stocks your money is at a greater risk for being in one industry. Consider industries that show consistent growth, such as food and beverages, pharmaceuticals, entertainment, financial services, telecommunications, and medical supplies and health care.

3. Reinvest all dividends and capital gains to make your money grow faster. This is like compound interest on your savings, so that each dollar continues to work harder and grow faster.

4. Establish an automatic investment plan and contribute the same amount of money each month to each of the stocks or mutual funds that you choose. The is the "dollar-cost" averaging approach, which allows a lower overall cost on your investments.

Action Step:

For the Web site with the most interesting information on all aspects of investing, go to http://www.investorhome.com, which will link you to more than 60 other investment sites to help you research stocks and mutual funds. Get a copy of *A Guide to Financial Instruments* from Coopers and Lybrand, 1251 Avenue of the Americas, New York, NY 10020, which gives a simple explanation of the various types of financial investments that exist.

Day 210

DIVERSIFICATION

I am of the opinion that the boldest measures are the safest.

—Admiral Horatio Nelson

Basically, this means, don't put it all in one place. Like creating a balanced diet plan with the four food groups to get maximum results for good health, you can create a balanced collection of investments that allow you to get the most out of putting your money at risk, so that as one investment moves down the other moves up and the return on another category remains stable. Investment assets fall into three basic groups:

Stocks—as broad-based as science and technology stocks, international investments, established blue-chip companies, small startup companies.

Bonds—longer than one year. Five- to ten-year government bonds, corporate bonds with AA and AAA ratings.

Cash—usually a money market fund, short-term CDs of less than one year, U.S. Treasury bills and notes, short-term bonds from various government agencies.

If you purchase only one mutual fund, start with an asset allocation fund that give you the broadest diversification with one investment.

Asset Allocation Funds

Fund	Five-Year Return	Phone Number
Vanguard Wellington Fund	16.5 percent	800–635–1511
Mairs & Powers Income Fund	16.3 percent	800–304–7404
Vanguard Star Fund	14.9 percent	800–635–1511

Action Step:

Make those calls today and allocate $100 a month for this investment program.

Day 211

REVIEW AND REASSESS

Find a sympathetic friend and summarize for him or her what you've learned about investment options and mutual funds so far. How's your confidence when it comes to talking about money and asking important financial questions? Write down any questions your "student" asks that you can't answer: Those are questions whose answers you need to research for yourself!

BONDS

A bond is an agreement to invest in someone else's debt. When you buy a bond, you are essentially making a loan to a person, a bank, a government agency, or a financial institution. You agree to allow it to use your money for a limited period of time, and it agrees to pay you a fixed rate of interest for the use of your money. The largest and safest borrower is the federal government, which issues U.S. Savings Bonds, Treasury bills, notes, or 30-year Treasury bonds. The setup is the same for tax-free bonds from the city or state in which you live. The income from corporate bonds, mortgage bonds, international bonds, and any other form of bonds that are not issued by a government agency is *not* tax-deductible.

Action Step:

Order a copy of "An Investor's Guide to Bond Basics" from the Bond Market Association, Publication Division, 40 Broad Street, New York, NY 10017–2373 or download it from the Web site at http://www.investinginbonds.com/info/bondbasics/what.htm.

A SINKING FUND

When a large company or government agency sells long-term bonds that require annual interest payments, it doesn't wait until the week before the check should be in the mail to look for the money. It creates a "sinking fund," a separate account where the interest is collected each month to accumulate the needed cash for the payment. You can treat your savings the same way, especially for annual payments on items like car insurance or homeowner's insurance. Don't set yourself up for a nasty shock and a need to revert to the credit card again!

Action Step:

Check your calendar and calculate how much is needed for an annual payment and set aside that amount in your money market account each month in anticipation of that payment due date.

Day 214

THE NEW I BONDS

The biggest complaint among savers and financial planners is that U.S. Savings Bonds, while safe, insured, and guaranteed, do not keep up with inflation and taxes. Well, let me introduce you to the new bond for the new millennium: the I Bond. This new bond made its debut September 1998 to answer the problem of savings bonds being a money-losing proposition. The new bonds start at $50 and go as high as $1,000. They come with images of famous Americans on the face of each bond, from Helen Keller and Dr. Martin Luther King, Jr., to Marian Anderson, Chief Joseph, and Senator Spark M. Matsunaga, the first Japanese-American senator from Hawaii. I Bonds are an excellent investment if you want to lock up your money in a ten-year commitment. It is also great for grandparents who don't want to take risks in the stock market but want to give their grandchildren a gift that will pay dividends. It's also good for scared long-term savers who want to supplement their retirement accounts with extra cash for the future.

Action Step:

Ask at your bank branch or visit the U.S. government site at http://www.publicdebt.treas.gov/sav/htm for information on how the new bonds work. You can also download a copy of the application to purchase these bonds from the Web site of the U.S. Treasury. Call 800–USBONDS to find out the rate for these bonds compared with the Series EE bonds.

Day 215

ASSET ALLOCATION

To achieve satisfactory results is easier than most people realize; to achieve superior results is harder than it looks.

—Benjamin Graham, 1973

Asset allocation is a simple, but critical, concept of creating a comfortable formula that matches your feeling for risks with your need to grow your money, and choosing a balance between stocks, bonds, and cash to meet your long-term goals. Here's a simple example. If you had invested $100 in the Dow stocks the day before the 1929 stock market crash, even with reinvested dividends, it would have taken 16 years for you to recover your money. If you had invested $50 in stocks and $50 in long-term bonds and maintained this balance, you would have recovered your original investment in just six years. The return on investments and the protection of your original investment will vary according to which basket you choose and how much you put into each basket. Investment gurus recommended a balance of 60 percent in stocks—from blue-chip to aggressive growth; 30 percent in AAA-rated corporate bonds and long-term government bonds; and 10 percent cash—money market funds and short-term Treasury bills. These formulas are not hard and fast rules and the ultimate choice of investments and the percentage you put in each area depends on how you feel about taking risks with your money.

Asset Association	Allocation Percentages	Investment Time Horizon	Investment Risk Tolerance	Investment Objective
Capital Preservation	0–10 percent stocks, 45–55 percent bonds, 35–45 percent money market funds	very short (three years or less)	low	stability and preservation of principal
Moderately Conservative	35–45 percent stocks, 45–55 percent bonds, 10–20 percent money market funds	near term (three to five years)	low to medium	preservation of principal with some opportunity for growth
Balanced	50–60 percent stocks, 30–40 percent bonds	medium term (five to ten years)	moderate	growth of capital and desire for income with some stability of principal
Growth	60–70 percent stocks, 20–30 percent bonds	long term (ten years or more)	high	long-term growth of capital

The mixture is up to you, but you should remember that age is a factor in your choices, and life needs and income situations change over time. The younger you are—under 40—the more risk you can take, which would make you an aggressive investor.

Action Step:

Reassess your age and your risk tolerance. Review your retirement choices and see if you are too conservative for your age.

Day 216

WHAT IS A MUTUAL FUND?

A mutual fund is a collection of 20 to 80 stocks or 50 to 100 bonds with similar characteristics, that is, all international stocks, all science, and technology stocks, all small company stocks, mortgage bonds, government bonds, or corporate bonds. The investment company hires a fund manager and a staff of researchers to seek and follow these stocks. The company takes your money and the money of thousands of other investors and buys these stocks based on their potential for growth and income. The stocks make money in two ways: (1) the dividends earned by the stocks, or the interest paid on the bonds; and (2) the increased value of the stocks as the prices go up. As an investor you get a proportionate share of the income and dividends as they come into the fund. If the fund manager frequently buys and sells several stocks at a profit during the year, you will have a capital gain on your investment even though you requested that all your income and dividends be reinvested.

Action Step:

Write or call the U.S. Securities and Exchange Commission, Office of Investor Education and Assistance, 450 Fifth Street, N.W., Washington, DC 20549, 202–942–7040 for a copy of the brochure

"Invest Wisely: An Introduction to Mutual Funds." You can also order copies through the Web site at http://www.sec.gov. The Investment Company Institute at 1600 M Street, N.W., Washington, DC 20036, offers another useful free brochure, "What Is a Mutual Fund?" Call 800–876–5005 to get info about publications from Morningstar, the mutual fund rating service. Web site is http://www.morningstar.net.

Day 217

TEN MOST SUCCESSFUL NO-LOAD MUTUAL FUND FAMILIES

There are over 9,000 mutual funds out there, and unless you're a professional analyst with a full-time staff, you won't have time to look at more than four or five before you get totally confused and turned off. The ten mutual fund families I've listed below have been around for several decades and have excellent track records for management and profitability. Each of them is a "no-load" fund, which means no sales charge or commission is taken out of your investment and paid out to the broker or financial planner selling them to you. They also have good customer service representatives who will spend a lot of time on the phone helping you to understand their funds and which ones fit your needs. Take advantage of all the free literature and information they offer to learn how to start building wealth assets for yourself. Most of these funds allow you to open an account for $1,000 and then make automatic monthly payments for $50 or $100 from your bank account, the same way that you pay life insurance or make mortgage payments. This is how you put yourself on your own payroll and make yourself number one. Treat yourself like a creditor who has to be paid each month. Would you miss the mortgage or Visa payment and not feel upset or guilty? Then treat your retirement money the same way!

Stein-Roe	800–338–2550 or http://www.steinroe.com
Vanguard	800–635–1511 or http://www.vanguard.com
T. Rowe Price	800–401–4768 or http://www.troweprice.com
Strong	800–368–9044 or http://www.strong-funds.com
American Century	800–345–2021 or http://www.americancentury.com
Janus	800–223–4856 or http://www.janus.com
Evergreen	800–235–0064
Neuberger/Berman	800–877–9700, ext. 3600, or http://www.nbfunds.com
Berger	800–333–1001, Department A757
Founders	800–711–9558, ext. 875, or http://www.founders.com

Two well-known fund families that offer a mixed menu of no-load fund and low-commission funds are:

Fidelity	800–544–8888 or http://www.fidelity.com
Dreyfus	800–645–6561 or http://www.dreyfus.com

The best place to find objective advice about any mutual fund is the Morningstar directory that evaluates funds quarterly and annually. Most public libraries subscribe to it, or you can find the Web site at http://www.morningstar.net. Call the home office at 800–876–5005 for a free sample copy of the monthly report, though subscribing to it is rather pricey for a newcomer. Or purchase *Investor's Guide to Low Cost Mutual Funds* for $5 from the Mutual Fund Education Alliance, 100 Englewood, Suite 130, Kansas City, MO 64118, or at the Web site at http://www.mfea.com.

Day 218

READING THE PROSPECTUS

You can give yourself a headache trying to understand all the boiler-plate legalese in a mutual fund prospectus. There are only four things that you need to know when you read a prospectus.

1. What does the fund do? Does it invest in international stocks? Corporate bonds? Mortgages? Health stocks? Dividend-producing stocks for income and growth?

2. What will it cost you to participate in the fund? The list of fees, expenses, and commissions should be shown on a table indicating the average cost of fees on $1,000 invested over five years. Major question: Will there be a fee to get out of the fund?

3. What is the minimum amount required for opening an account? Is there a lower opening minimum for automatic investment from your checking/payroll account? What is the minimum for automatic investment?

4. Who is the manager and what is his or her track record of performance in managing the fund? In other words, what results have been produced in the past by this person?

Most of these questions can be answered by the customer service representative on the phone when you call to order a prospectus. Get all the answers you need before you write checks!

Action Step:

Contact the Investment Company Institute, 1600 M Street, N.W., Washington, DC 20036, and request a copy of the brochure "A Translation: Turning Investment-ese into Investment Ease." Vanguard mutual funds also offers several educational pages on its Web site at http://www.vanguard.com, including a glossary, chat groups, a multiple-choice test to judge your knowledge of investing, a complete list of all its funds (including prospectus and annual report), and an adviser who will respond to your questions by e-mail.

MUTUAL FUND TERMS

Net asset value. The daily dollar value of all the shares in the fund. Prices are set at the end of each business day at 4 P.M. when the market closes.

Load vs. no-load. A "load" is a commission or sales charge paid to the salesperson who sells the mutual fund to you. It's how the salesperson gets paid for the time and attention provided. The commission is from 3 to 8.5 percent of each deposit. "No-load" means no commission is taken out of your funds, but you must do the work of choosing, analyzing, and monitoring the investment yourself.

Front-end load. A 3 to 8 percent commission deducted from your funds when the account is opened.

Back-end load. A deferred commission that decreases one percent each year that you own the fund. If you purchase shares in a fund that has a five percent back-end load, you must hold the shares for five years to avoid paying the sales charge.

Rule 12b–1 fees. Another way of charging a commission that, like a back-end load, declines one percent a year over five to seven years.

Redemption charges. A withdrawal fee, usually one percent, charged to your account to close it.

Portfolio turnover. The frequency with which shares are bought and sold in a mutual fund portfolio. For example, a fund manager may buy and sell IBM stock fifteen times in one year to meet cash liquidity requirements of investors who redeem their investments. Each time those shares turn over, brokerage commissions are charged to your account as part of the expense/management fees. If a profit is made on the sale of those shares, the fund passes that profit along to you at the end of the year in the form of a capital gains payment which can give you a tax bill even if you choose to reinvest the earnings and do not take the taxable income—even if you are reinvesting all the dividends. Your favorite Uncle doesn't miss any opportunity to get his cut of your earnings.

Day 220

THE FUND MANAGER

When you invest in a mutual fund you hire people to manage your money; they make the day-to-day decision to buy and sell securities. Mutual funds—other than index funds—don't just happen to be successful by themselves, they are managed. The name Peter Lynch has become synonymous with successful mutual fund investing after his phenomenal success of making Fidelity Magellan fund the number one mutual fund in the country for all the years that he managed it. Witness the change in Magellan's size, portfolio, performance, and structure when Peter Lynch left it. Peter Lynch. Warren Buffett. John Templeton. These names have become almost legendary as Wall Street mutual fund managers. They are the stars of the investment world and manage millions of dollars and may purchase as few as 20 stocks for one portfolio or as many as 200. When you read the prospectus for a mutual fund, pay attention to the experience and background of the person or persons who will be managing the fund. They should have at least five to seven years or more of experience with buying, selling, and developing an investment portfolio. In a case like this, age is an excellent criteria for knowledge and experience. You want a fund manager like George Vanderheiden and John Templeton, veterans of several bear markets, who have been around long enough to have made money in both good markets and hard times.

Action Step:

Look at the Web site http://www.fundalarm.com to see the comings and goings of the investment professionals so you will know when a fund manager leaves the company and the effect that this may create on a fund. Pick up a copy of Peter Lynch's books, *One Up on Wall Street* (Fireside, 1997) and *Learn to Earn* (Fireside, 1996).

Day 221

THE $5000 PORTFOLIO

Here's a simple way to start a balanced portfolio without $10,000. This "menu" of choices offers a well-diversified selection that can be achieved using a variety of no-load mutual funds. Each fund listed here also allows you to start with a minimum of $1,000 to open the account and do automatic monthly investing for $100 month.

International—Janus Worldwide	20%	800–525–3713
Index—Vanguard S&P 500 Index Fund	20%	800–662–7447
Bonds—Strong Corporate Bond Fund	20%	800–368–1030
Aggressive—American Century Ultra	20%	800–345–2021
Sector—Vanguard Health	20%	800–662–7447
T. Rowe Price Science and Technology	20%	800–638–5660

Action Step:

Review your 401(k) investment menu and see if you have these kinds of funds available to you. If not, look at how you have invested your IRA money and decide if you want to adopt this menu of choices for long-term growth.

Day 222

GROWTH WITH CAUTION

For a more conservative portfolio, start with a group of mutual funds that specialize in stocks that only offer income. Funds that provide income through a combination of dividend-paying stocks and AAA-rated corporate bonds are known primarily as growth and income funds. Over the last ten years, five top-performing funds in this sector have been:

AARP	Growth and income fund	800–225–2470
American Century	Growth and income fund	800–345–2021
Invesco	Value trust/total return	800–525–8085
Scudder	Growth and income fund	800–225–2470
Vanguard	Equity Income Fund	800–835–1510

Action Step:

Call one of the above funds and ask the customer service representative to explain how the automatic investing option works and if you can have funds deducted from your paycheck.

Day 223

READY MONEY

When your dream appears as an opportunity you must have ready cash to take it home with you.

—Anonymous

For more than 16 years, Debra and Bob have dreamed of the day when they could sell their house in the city and open a bed-and-breakfast in Vermont. They had met there at an arts festival on an October weekend and revisited the same small town each fall to celebrate their anniversary. The idea of the B&B came to them quietly as they were having dinner in front of the fireplace at a favorite inn. Debra had been carefully saving $100 out of each paycheck in addition to her donation to her 401(k) plan. At the end of each year, she put her bonus checks in a growth and income fund and her nest egg slowly grew each year. She had no idea when she and Bob would find "that perfect spot" but she wanted to be ready when the opportunity appeared. One October weekend, on a leisurely drive along a country road, they found a small inn that was new to them. They stopped for tea and chatted with the owner, an elderly gentleman whose wife had recently died. He was anxious to sell but wanted a cash-only deal. That long-term investment account in the mutual fund had grown from $4,000 to $86,500 over 16 years of steady investing, and Debra and Bob's dream came true.

Affirmation:

I will clearly state my goal and apply it to my savings plan.

Action Step:

Ask yourself, if this opportunity presented itself to you tomorrow, would you be ready?

Day 224

COLLEGE GOALS

If you wait until your child is two you've already lost a possible $2,000 of growth if you had set up an investment fund for college before you changed your first diaper. College bills go up faster than inflation, and unless your child is scholarship material (which you don't know while he or she is still in the crib!), you need to start investing early for the long term. Each year you delay investing is like losing money. Use the gift money from the grandparents to open at least one of these mutual fund accounts and then put it on automatic pilot at $50 a month for the next 12 years. When you get within four years of needing the money, switch it over to some Treasury notes that mature about a month before you have to write those tuition checks.

Fund	Five-Year Return	Phone Number
Stein-Roe Young Investors Fund	34.1%	800–774–5567
American Century—Ultra Fund	23.1%	800–345–2021
Founders Blue Chip Growth and Income	21.4%	800–525–2440
Ivy International A	18.1%	800–777–6472
Benham Target Maturity 2015	14.5%	800–345–2021

Action Step:

If you call only one fund, choose the Stein-Roe Young Investors Fund. It invests in the products that children recognize (Reebok, the Gap, Nintendo, etc.) and sends quarterly educational materials to children to educate them about investing. Each of these investments can be used for a tax-deductible Education IRA, which allows you to put away $500 per year, per child as long as your adjusted gross income is less than $100,000.

Day 225

THE INVESTMENT CRUISE

Though it can be a very pricey way to learn about investing, you can work on your tan in the Caribbean or Mexico between seminars with investment gurus like Louis Rukeyser, Mark Skousen, and Paul Kangas. Travel agents that specialize in cruise line packages can tell you who will be on board and where you can sign up. Holland America offers quite a few such one-week trips several times a year. InterShow, Ltd. also specializes in them, departing from several ports of call including Acapulco, San Francisco, Jamaica, and Australia.

Action Step:

Call 888–684–SAIL to find out more about educational cruises. You can also log on to http://www.intershow.com/index for information on its packages, or call 800–970–4355.

Day 226

REVIEW AND REASSESS

Assuming that you have indeed requested (and received!) at least a few prospectuses and applications from the funds mentioned, go ahead and read them. If there is anything you don't understand, get someone to explain it to you. You can start with the representatives at the other end of most funds' 800 lines. Don't be embarrassed: You have a right to have your questions answered, and you are plenty smart enough to understand all this and more if you ask enough questions and give yourself enough time.

Day 227

START SMALL

Giant oaks from little acorns grow.

—Anonymous

Can you figure out which of these numbers is higher in value, two or ten? If you picked ten, then can you understand what the meaning of total return is all about? Don't let the numbers and the jargon make you crazy. Here's the basic premise. Total return is how much you can make on a long-term investment if you leave it in the bank vs. the stock market: 2 percent in the bank, 10 percent in the stock market. Simple. In the bank you earn interest. In stocks you earn two ways. The first is in dividends—often called yield—paid to you each quarter. The second is through price increases. The value of your share of stock goes up from $10 to $12. That's a 20 percent return on your money. Here are four well-managed equity mutual fund families that still allow small investors to open automatic investment accounts for $50 month.

Founders	800–525–2440
Fremont	800–548–4539
Janus	800–525–8983
Strong	800–368–1030

Action Step:

Open an account for yourself and set a monthly deduction amount to match one of your goals. This kind of account can also be used as a Uniform Gift to Minors Account (UGMA) or as an Education IRA, which allows you to contribute up to $500 a year for future college tuition bills. If your adjusted gross income is less than $100,000 a year, this is also a tax-deductible contribution beginning in 1998.

Day 228

INVEST WHERE YOU SPEND

The difference between rich people and poor people is where they sign their checks. Poor people sign on the front. Rich people sign on the back.

—Ric Edelman

You're just as smart as Warren Buffett and you don't need a Harvard MBA to pick stocks. Just watch where you spend your money. Look around your bathroom. Aleve pain reliever and Vicks VapoRub are in the medicine cabinet; Cover Girl and Max Factor are on a shelf above Crest toothpaste, and Scope mouthwash is beside the sink. Safeguard and Secret are your favorite soap and deodorant. You use Charmin toilet paper and Pampers for the baby. If you also find Folgers coffee, Jif peanut butter, Dawn dishwashing liquid, Cascade for the dishwasher, and Bounty paper towels in your kitchen, there's only one company you need to invest in: Procter & Gamble. P&G makes all the household and personal care products listed here. If you buy that many of its products, why not invest in its stock? P&G has been around since 1891 so it'll probably still be in business until the third millennium, especially if you keep buying its products. Procter & Gamble shareholders' services at 800–742–6253 will send an application for direct stock purchase. The minimum investment is $250 to open an account, and automatic monthly bank deductions of $100 are allowed for new investors. Next time you do laundry you'll also be earning dividends.

Affirmation:

I can start building wealth one share at a time, with discipline, vision, and $100 a month.

Action Step:

Call the shareholders' services line at Procter & Gamble at 800–742–6253 and request an application for the direct purchase of stock from the company. The minimum investment is $250 to open an account, and automatic monthly bank deductions of $100 are allowed for new investors.

Day 229

ONE COKE/SHARE AT A TIME

Wealth is when small efforts produce big results. Poverty is when big efforts produce small results.

—George David, M.D.

Suppose your grandmother had been in Atlanta in 1919 and bought one of the first shares of Coca-Cola when the stock was first issued at $40 a share. Imagine what would have happened if she had kept that stock and never sold it, never cashed the dividend checks, and let those payments from the company be reinvested in new shares of the company's stock. One share of stock and a small dividend of a few cents, paid out and reinvested four times a year, may sound like nothing, but hold on. Grandma held on to the stock as her "special little investment" through two world wars, the Great Depression, several recessions, 17 presidents, and numerous economic catastrophes. The price of the stock gyrated through numerous slides, slips, and bounces, from an all-time low of $19.50 a share in 1920 to a high of $183 a share in 1947. Imagine that Grandma held on for more than 75 years when, at the annual shareholders' meeting in 1996, the board of directors issued a historical brochure to show what one share of original stock would be worth. Grandma would now own 4,608 shares because of the many stock splits, and they would be valued at $5,150,146.12. Suppose Grandma had decided instead to cash all those dividend checks for a down payment on a house, to pay for a daughter's education and wedding, and to send a couple of grandchildren to college? She would still own 518 shares of Coca-Cola (KO), valued at $242,496. Not bad for hanging on through the gyrations and crashes of the stock market, is it? Think about it. Blue chip stocks are those companies and products that are household names. Buying them, even in small quantities, the same way you buy toothpaste or orange juice once a month, can make you rich. Starting small really does pay off.

Action Step:

You can buy one share of stock at a time of more than 350 blue-chip companies (including McDonald's, Procter & Gamble, Citicorp, General Motors, and Texaco) through some no-load company plans and no-load mutual funds, arranged by the Clearinghouse for Direct Stock Purchase Plans. Call 800–774–4117 for information on how to get started or visit the Web site at http://www.enrolldirect.com to request information.

Day 230

GET RICH THE SLOW WAY

He who hastens to be rich will not go unpunished.

—Proverbs 28:20

In 1944, Anne Scheiber retired from her job as an auditor at the IRS. Despite having a law degree, she had never made more than $3,150 a year on account of having been denied promotions and raises solely because she was a woman. Since this was long before the days of sex discrimination suits and affirmative action programs, the 51-year-old Scheiber had no choice but to tolerate the indignity. She took her lump-sum pension of $5,000 and decided to put it into three stocks—Coca-Cola, Exxon, and General Motors. From the time she left the IRS her mission was to invest her money and watch it grow. She continued to work part-time as an accountant, but she never touched her investments. In 1950, with some of the profits from her first investments, she bought 1,000 shares of Schering-Plough Corp., the pharmaceutical company that makes Oil of Olay, for $10,000. Today those original 1,000 shares are worth $7.5 million. Scheiber also bought other big-name brands like Pepsico, Chrysler, and Philip Morris, and continually reinvested her dividends. She never married and lived a quiet life in a small rent-controlled apartment on New York's Upper East Side. Despite her millionaire status, she continued to be frugal, often wearing the same black cloth coat year after year. Thumbing her nose at the IRS was one of her few enjoyments, particularly since she got the last laugh on it. Before her death at age 101, in 1995, Scheiber put all her money into a foundation and left it where it would help other women achieve professional careers. The complete estate—all $22 million of it—went to help other women who needed money for tuition to attend Yeshiva's Stern College for Women and Albert Einstein's College of Medicine.

Affirmation:

Building wealth allows me to help myself and others.

Action Step:

Order a copy of the *Directory of Companies Offering Reinvestment Plans* from Evergreen Enterprises, P.O. Box 763, Laurel, MD 20725–0763, or call 301–953–1861. The cost is $29.95 and it the directory is also available on computer disk.

Day 231

DRIPS

Man was born to be rich or inevitably to grow rich through the use of his faculties.

—Ralph Waldo Emerson

Beginning in 1994, the Securities and Exchange Commission—the granddaddy of watchdog agencies on Wall Street—insisted that it become easier for the "little guy" (or gal!) to begin investing. That opened the doors for the average working person with less than $10,000, $5,000, or even $2,000 to start buying stock in companies that he or she likes. The Society for Direct Investing (Web site: http://www.sdinews.org) lists the names of over 330 companies that allow you to purchase stocks directly from the company without a stockbroker. That's one way to save as much as $130 in fees for the purchase of 100 shares of, say, Procter & Gamble. The minimum investment for most companies is quite low.

Action Step:

Call 800–4–SDI–NEWS for more information on how to become a member and begin purchasing the stock of such companies as Home Depot, Bob Evans Farms, Johnson Controls, Duke Power, and Procter & Gamble. If you're too busy to write the check and mail it in each month, several of the companies have automatic purchase programs, which means that you can authorize them to deduct a pre-set amount out of your checking or savings account on the 15th of each month at regular intervals. Do this for a minimum of seven months and they will not charge you a setup fee.

Day 232

STOCK PICKING LITERATURE

If you want to start studying individual stocks and delving into financial newsletters don't spend a lot of time and money ordering sample issues from several publishers.

Select Information Exchange has a catalog of more than 50 investment advisory newsletters that offer trial subscriptions, which it will send to you at no charge. Contact it at: 244 West 54th Street, Room 614, New York, NY 10019, 212–247–7123.

The DRIP Investor will send you a free sample issue at no cost, and *The Dow Forecast Theory* will send eight issues for only $5. Both are written and published by Charles Carlson, author of *How to Buy Stocks Without a Broker*. Write to: *The DRIP Investor*, NorthStar Financial, 7412 Calumet Avenue, Hammond, IN 46324–2692 or call 219–931–6480.

Forecasts and Strategies, another excellent investment newsletter, written in a down-to-earth, coherent style, will provide a free issue if you call the publisher at 800–777–5005.

Action Step:

Go for it! What have you got to lose except the time for a phone call?

Day 233

DRIP PERKS

There's more to the investing game than just getting dividends. Many of the companies that offer dividend reinvestment plans also offer some exciting and fun fringe benefits for being one of their shareholders. Take a look at the following shareholders' offerings:

Hershey	A special "chocolate" catalog at Christmas
Sara Lee	A special 15 percent discount catalog of Coach leather products once a year and 50–70 percent discounts on certain Bali/Hanes underwear
Scott Paper	Special paper products for Christmas
Walt Disney	A 10 percent discount on admission to Disney World and Disneyland and a 10 percent discount on rooms at Magic Kingdom Hotels
Wrigley's	100 sticks of gum at Christmas
Goodyear	10 percent off on a set of four tires
Chalone	A 25 percent discount on the company's wines, access to special reserve bottles, and a special invitation to an annual gourmet feast at the Chalone Vineyard in Salinas Valley, California
Kodak	Free enrollment in the Kodak Friends First program, which provides discounts on selected Kodak cameras and perks at Six Flags, Universal Studios, and Paramount theme parks, as well as the Kennedy Space Center and Space Center Houston
Greyhound	A free round-trip ticket to the annual shareholders' meeting in Dallas
Carnival Corp.	$250 off a 14-day cruise, $100 off a seven- to 13-day cruise, and $50 off any shorter cruise.
Anheuser-Busch	15 percent off tickets to Busch Gardens and Sea World, and 25–50 percent off any merchandise you buy from the company's catalogs

Action Step:

Call the MoneyPaper at 800–388–9993 or 914–381–5400, or study the Web site at http://www.moneypaper.com, and request a copy of their directory of DRIPs. It will give you a free copy of one of its monthly newsletters. You can also purchase the DRIP directory for $25. It gives a listing of 1,300 U.S. companies that offer dividend reinvestment plans.

Day 234

"THE TEDDY BEAR LADY"

Each Christmas, the employees and administrators of Chicago's Children's Hospital could count on the "Teddy Bear Lady" to arrive on a Saturday afternoon bringing a large shipment of teddy bears and stuffed animals that she had ordered for the children in the pediatrics ward. She would supervise the distribution of the toys, making certain that each child received a present. It was her way, she said, of thanking the hospital for saving a favorite niece many years earlier. She also told the administrators that she appreciated their work so much that she planned to remember them in her will. They smiled appreciatively and nodded, thinking that the most they could expect from this modestly dressed secretary who drove a ten-year old car would probably be a few hundred dollars. A couple of thousand at best. When Gladys Holm finally passed on in 1996, she left an estate that included an $8 million gift to the hospital. Gladys Holm, the tall, red-haired daughter of Swedish immigrants to Chicago, had never earned more than $15,000 a year in her job as a secretary. To most people she was a soft-spoken spinster with a kind smile and a wicked sense of humor who lived in a small apartment in Evanston, Illinois, and drove an old car that she maintained well. She took one nice vacation each year, spent quality time with her family, and did volunteer work for her church and at the children's hospital. What no one knew was that for the forty-one years that she worked as a secretary to the president of American Hospital Supply Company, Gladys had invested her entire Christmas bonus check in the company stock. Her first check was for $500. When American Hospital Supply was bought up by Baxter International Pharmaceuticals, Gladys's company stock was transferred to the larger company and continued to grow in value. When Baxter created another company called Allegiance Corporation, Gladys also received shares. She followed the investing direction of her boss, buying small lots of utility stocks and blue chip stocks such as AT&T and General Motors.

When he bought 1,000 shares of IBM, Gladys bought 10 shares and held on to those stocks for more than 30 years, reinvesting the dividends and never selling a single share.

Action Step:

Call Pepsico at 800–226–0083 for an application to become a member of its direct stock purchase plan. It is one of the few blue chip companies that allows you to join directly without buying shares through a stockbroker. After you open your account you can make optional cash purchases whenever you wish for as little as $25 a month.

Day 235

PLAYING THE MARKET

Before you start writing checks and risking your hard-earned dollars in a game you're not sure you understand, get some practice with "play money." Look for one of the many board games that can teach you the principles of investing in stocks and bonds. One game by Milton Bradley, called Acquire, exposes you to all the typical ups and downs that can happen with any investment in the stock market. The object of the game is for each player to start with $100,000 and turn it into $1 million by buying stocks, bonds, and real estate, and withstanding mergers, buyouts, rising interest rates, government regulations, hostile takeovers, and market crashes. Sound like the way the real game is played? Another game, called The Game of Life, has similar rules and goals and is just as informative about the financial realities of Wall Street and building wealth. You don't have to be 12 or 14 to experience the fun, and it is also extremely educational. Another favorite is Stocks and Bonds from Avalon Hill, which teaches the same investment concepts.

Action Step:

Pay a visit to Toys "R" Us and see what board games are available for you to learn the investment game, or call Avalon Hill at 800–999–3222 to order Stocks and Bonds. You can also visit the Web site for The Stock Market game at http://www.smg2000.org and see how to enroll your children or a youth group in the program. Bloomberg.com is one of the many investors' Web sites that allow you to set up a mock portfolio, learn how to do stock research, and follow your picks to see how you measure up against the professional portfolio managers at choosing winners or losers.

Day 236

INDIVIDUAL STOCKS VS. FUNDS

You shouldn't own common stocks if a decrease in their value by 50 percent would cause you to feel stress.

—Warren Buffett

Investing in stocks is about taking a risk. No broker should ever make you think that it isn't. Mutual funds can diminish the risk by diversifying into several stocks with small amounts of money, but the drawback to funds is that you don't have control over what you own and when to buy and sell. Individual stocks are a good investment if you don't mind the concentrated focus of your investment dollars being less diversified, but they also let you exercise the buy-sell option when you prefer. Owning individual stocks on a long-term basis, particularly if you reinvest all those dividends, will avoid that nasty tax bill that comes at the end of the year when the mutual fund managers declare a capital gain—even when you reinvest. If you have the time to do the reading and research, the most important ingredients in the Wall Street wealth-building game are:

Simplicity. Pick three or four blue chips that you know and study them. Enroll in their DRIP plans and treat them like monthly bills to be paid along with the phone, lights, and gas.

Consistency. Ignore the news and noise of the market. Stick to your plan and keep writing those checks each month. If your stocks are solid companies in good industries with long-term earnings potential, they will recover from temporary setbacks and continue doing well for you.

Patience. Don't listen to the scaredy cats and the naysayers. Stocks have always done twice as well as bonds over a 10- to 40-year period. Commit that to memory and repeat it each day, even when the news sounds devastating. Those people who held on through the crash of 1987 have seen nearly a 400 percent increase in their investment since then.

Day 237

REVIEW AND REASSESS

Are you satisfied that the investment instruments you've identified match your investment goals? Did you start writing some kind of long-term plan? Did you look at some of the books, brochures, and Web sites? If so, fill out those applications and send them in. If not, you may need to do more research. If you cringe at the thought, it may be time to find a professional to consult. But don't delay any longer. Even if you've gotten in the habit of saving your money, if it's not invested, it's not earning, and you're cheating yourself.

Day 238

YOUR RISK PROFILE

Risk-takers fall into three categories: those who take poorly calculated risks, those who take half-thought-out risks, and those who take well-planned risks that usually succeed.

—Marsha Sinetar

"Risk" is the four-letter word that scares the heck out of most people, and never more than when money is at stake. If you play the lottery, it's a poorly calculated risk, but the price is cheap and won't bankrupt you. Investing in the stock market involves more money and more potential loss, but also a much greater chance of acquiring wealth. Investing isn't as risky as it sounds if you view it with the purpose of growing wealth and not as a gambling game. Risk is all around us and will never go away. You take a risk with food you eat if you don't grow and prepare it yourself. You assume your car is safe although some models have been recalled. You're at risk when you have surgery, have a baby, hike through the woods, or take a walk in an urban park. The chances of dying in an airplane crash are lower than the risk of dying in rush-hour traffic each day. It's there when you cross the street: Life is all about risk, like it or not. The most important thing is to evaluate carefully the risks you undertake. There is no such thing as a risk-free investment. The three issues in determining your feeling about risk are safety, growth, and income. The collapse of the savings and loan banks taught us that in the early 1990s, even though they were federally regulated and insured. "Risk" is the key word that stops most would-be investors. But careful investing is not a trip to Atlantic City. Take the time to apply some basic logic to how the stock market works and look at the historical patterns that appear over time.

Market risk. Sudden public scandal will impact company earnings and drive stock prices down—but not forever. The Tylenol tampering debacle hurt Johnson & Johnson's bottom line for about six months. If the balance sheet is strong and profits are good, the stock will recover.

Financial risk. Would a sudden change in company operations affect payments on bonds you bought? If a CEO died in a plane crash, could someone else operate the company profitably?

Economic risk. What external factors could affect company's profits, such as a shipping strike? These are events that the management has no control over.

Interest rate risk. If you invest in a company with a lot of debt, when interest rates go up, the stock price will go down because profits will go to the bankers rather than the shareholders.

Questions you must ask: Is the company large enough to withstand such a public assault? If you wanted to get out, are there enough shares on the market for you to be able to sell to a willing buyer without taking a major discount on the price of shares?

Action Step:

The Plain Talk Library, available from Vanguard, offers over 30 brochures that answer questions about different types of investments. Check it out at www.vanguard.com or call 800–523–8797.

Day 239

MARKET TIMING

Patience in a market is worth pounds in a year.

—Ben Franklin

When to get in? How long to stay in? Wait until Alan Greenspan makes his next prophetic announcement to see how it will effect the market? Wait until the year's end because you don't want any more taxable income? What's right for your brother-in-law, your neighbor, or your boss may not be right for you. Maybe you still don't understand what you're doing with the money. That's okay. At the other extreme, if you can explain it but still have a queasy feeling at the thought of signing the check, then you're not ready.

Action Step:

Next weekend when you're shopping, pick five items out of your grocery cart and read the labels. If there's an 800 number for customer service, call it and ask if the company has a dividend reinvestment plan for small shareholders.

Day 240

REVIEW AND REASSESS

Now that you have taken an assessment of your life and decided to make some changes, you're in a hurry to start seeing the payoff from some of these new steps you've taken, such as the mutual fund you opened, the automatic payroll savings plan that you've started, and the cuts in your daily spending. Even if you're managing to pay down your debts, the down payment on a home or four years' college tuition probably seem a very long way off. You're not the only one who has become discouraged about the slow process of seeing results. But don't worry—they will come! In the meantime, distract yourself. Start reading investment brochures about how to use that money wisely for retirement.

Day 241

MONEY WORKS

Money is a great friend, once you send it off to work.

—Peter Lynch

If your money isn't earning interest or dividends or building equity in some form of bricks and mortar it isn't working for you. You must think of yourself as the CEO of your own personal corporation, and your dollars must be thought of as employees that do your bidding and create profits for you in the wealth-building process. It must grow faster than inflation and outpace the taxes you will have to pay on the interest dividends it produces. A 12 percent average total rate of return on long-term investments will accomplish this goal. The surest way to get that 12 percent return is in real estate and the stock market. The biggest mistake most people who invest in the stock market make is to focus on what the market is doing today, rather than what it will do tomorrow. If the market is doing well, they'll jump in; if it's doing badly, they'll opt out. Yet they are overlooking the fact that the stock market itself is focused on tomorrow, not today. Any investments you make should be based not on where you *are*, but where you're going. The key to success is how long you invest. Over the long term, stocks rise more than they fall—though it's easy to ignore that fact because we react to the stock market emotionally, not rationally. The headlines in newspapers are designed to make us feel panicky and unsure but investing according to our emotions is a sure way to fail. You cannot escape the fact that for money to gain greater value in the future it will be impacted by *volatility*. A Treasury bill has no volatility. It's a mistake to think of volatility as merely risk, though, since volatility means your stock is just as likely to go up as down. If you are willing to invest on a long-term basis, chances are you will be a winner. If you let the idea of "risk" scare you off, you can only guess at the opportunities for financial gain you've passed up.

Action Step:

Make a list of your savings accounts, money market accounts, and insured investments. Compare the interest rates with the dividends from equity mutual funds and see the difference in total return.

Day 242

MARKET YARDSTICKS

You can't manage what you can't measure.

—William Hewlett

When you were a kid, you went to the doctor each year to get weighed, measured, and examined to see if you were growing normally. The stock market has its own measures of growth and performance, and you don't have to wait a full year to find out how your money is doing. You see and hear reports each evening on the news. Three of the most popular measurement guidelines are the Dow Jones Industrial Average, Standard and Poor's 500 Index report, and the NASDAQ, or the National Association of Securities Dealers' Automated Quote system. The success of a mutual fund is compared to the annual performance of the S&P 500, and fund managers are judged by whether they can "beat the market" or choose a combination of stocks that will be better than the S&P 500. Very few mutual fund managers are able to outpace this market index. If you invest money in an index fund, the index they are referring to is the S&P 500 index. An index fund is the first place you should start investing if you have no idea which fund to choose. That way, your first $1,000 will be widely dispersed among the stocks of the Fortune 500 companies, which are the broadest way to get diversification for a beginning investor.

Action Step:

Open an account with the T. Rowe Price Equity Index 500 Fund (800–541–7885), which tracks the S&P 500 stocks or the Vanguard 500 Index Portfolio Fund (800–992–0711) and you won't have to call to check on its status. Just watch CNN, CNBC, or your local newspaper each day for a week to see how the numbers change on your fund. Check out the Web site at http://www.indexfundsonline.com to choose specific investment funds that are designed to follow each of the above indices.

Day 243

SCAMS, SCHEMES, AND SWINDLES

A fool and his money are soon parted.

—English proverb

Of course, white-collar con men are out there, and they'll probably get your phone number from some mailing list if you send away for lots of investment literature. You'll be finishing dinner one evening and the phone will ring and someone will offer a charming deal that sounds so good you'll be itching to get the check in the mail. If a broker comes on to you with a high-pressure pitch or implies that this is a once-in-a-lifetime offer that won't last, do yourself a favor, just hang up. If he or she keeps bugging you, do the world a favor: Get the name and the address where you're supposed to send the check, and pass it along to the SEC, the Justice Department, or the state attorney general's office. It's rare but not unheard of for these kinds of brokers to call from a reputable, well-known firm. To be safe, only consider working with an investment adviser, stockbroker, or financial planner who has been referred by a friend or a professional person you know well. The most popular victims for these scam artists are retired senior citizens, usually women who don't have much of a social life and are often lonely and anxious to have someone to talk to at night. Competent, ethical professionals in the securities business will not push you into investments you don't understand, and will allow you to check references.

Action Step:

If you want to check out a broker before you deal with him or her call the National Association of Securities Dealers at 800–289–9999 or write to: 1818 N Street, N.W., Washington, DC 20036. Visit the Web site at http://www.nasd.com.

Day 244

$$$—Savings Tip:

There are telephone scam artists who prey on the elderly and naive and, according to an AARP study, those who are "open to anything" or "polite and vulnerable." These crooks take advantage of secluded senior citizens and pressure them with intimidating tactics to give up their credit card numbers or to send untraceable money orders to mailboxes. If you think you've been hustled or know of someone who may have been scammed in some shady-sounding investment deal, report it to the National Fraud Information Center, P.O. Box 65868, Washington, DC 20035. Call 800–876–7060 or check out the Web site at http://www. fraud.org.

Day 245

SAFETY AND SECURITY

There is no security on this earth; there is only opportunity.

—Douglas MacArthur

U.S. Treasury bills, bonds, notes, and government obligations are the benchmark against which all the others are measured and compared. No risks at all there. Financial protection for your savings and investments is available through these programs:

Federal Deposit Insurance Corporation (FDIC) insures your checking and savings account for up to $100,000 per account if your bank is a publicly chartered bank. Small state banks and some savings and loan associations are not protected under this federal program.

Municipal Bond Insurance Association (MBIA) is a private insurance association for the protection of municipal bonds. All bond issuers do not use it so read the fine print carefully.

Securities Investor Protection Corporation (SIPC) is a membership corporation of all securities brokerage firms that was created to protect customers' accounts if the firm has financial losses and difficulties resulting from mismanagement. Under this program, your investment account is insured for up to $500,000. This does not apply to bad investment choices in case your stocks go down in value.

Action Step:

Ask your bank for the brochure that explains your account protection and how the FDIC works.

Day 246

GIVING IT TIME

You've got to leave your investment alone long enough for it to increase.

—Oseola McCarty

Oseola McCarty, or Ola, as she was called by her family in Hattiesburg, Mississippi, hid the first money she ever saved underneath the mattress of a hand-me-down baby carriage. By the time she was in her late teens she decided to be the first in her family to put her money in a bank. Ola saved her money for many years in savings passbooks and Christmas clubs. Finally a teller at a bank suggested she get in touch with the bank's financial advisers. It didn't take Ola long to understand that with interest, compounded over time, she could have a tidy sum. No one suspected that sum could amount to over $300,000—that is, no one except Ola and her bankers. She made saving a lifetime habit and never took her money out once deposited. Her investments grew as her uncle, grandmother, aunt, and mother died and left her their estates. She continued to live a simple, reclusive life, paying for everything in cash, but she did not go lacking. If she wanted to paint her six-room house, she'd save enough to get the job done and buy a new china closet. Ola was not a believer in credit and prided herself on being a hardworking washerwoman and a thrifty spender. The key is that she didn't pursue extravagance. She was comfortable living in the same house she'd lived in almost all her life. She tended her flowers, went to church, and walked to and from the grocery store. She continued ironing for others until her arthritic hands and health failed her at age 87. Still wanting to do for herself, she decided it was time to do some estate planning. Ola's biggest regret had always been stopping school in the sixth grade to help her grandmother and aunt at home. Now she could help other children get their education. She instructed her bankers to set up a way for her to donate money to a college in her hometown. In July 1995, Ola established a trust fund, directing at least $150,000 to the University of Southern Mississippi. She made her first visit ever to a college campus on August 29, 1995. There, over 1,000 teachers and staff gave her a standing ovation. Since that time Ola has received national acclaim and many honors—from the President of the United States and from foreign governments—for her generosity. She also inspired one of the wealthiest men in America, Ted Turner, to donate a billion dollars to the United Nations. If you ask Ola what her secret to success is, she has a very simple answer: work hard and save your money for a rainy day. Sound advice.

Day 247

ABSOLUTE SAFETY

If sleeping at night is the most important criterion for you in developing an investment plan, then the debt instruments of the U.S. Treasury are the safest possible investment you can choose. They are backed by the full faith and credit of the federal government and carry no risk whatsoever. The ten regional Federal Reserve banks will sell you Uncle Sam's bills, notes, and bonds through the Treasury Direct program, starting at $1,000. They also have the added benefit of no state taxes on the interest that you earn.

Treasury bills. Short-term debt of 90 days, six months, and one year are bought at a discount, meaning that a $1,000 Treasury bill yielding five percent will cost you $950.

Treasury notes. These can be bought with maturity dates from two years to ten years. Notes are not sold discount but at face value and interest earned is additional income.

Treasury bonds (also called the "long bond"). These are purchased for 10 to 30 years.

Action Step:

Phone the Treasury Direct program at 202–874–4000 for forms or contact the Federal Reserve Bank in your region. You can also get forms at the Federal Web site at http://www.publicdebt/ustreas.gov.

Day 248

MODERATE SAFETY

The next level of investment safety can be found in uninsured money market funds, brokered CDs, and loan participation funds.

Corporate money market funds. Ford Motor company offers an uninsured money market fund through Ford Credit Corporation that pays .25 percent higher interest than the average money market mutual fund. Only $1,000 is needed to open an account, $50 minimum investments after the account is established. Checks can be written for $250 as needed. Enrollment forms can be downloaded from the Web site at http://www.fordcredit.com/moneymarket/intro.html. As one of the Fortune 500 companies Ford is highly unlikely to go out of business in a year or two. Do you drive a Ford?

Brokered CDs. Brokerage firms frequently sell FDIC-insured CDs in $1,000 increments for small out-of-town banks and savings and loan companies that offer slightly higher interest rates. If you have a lump sum of $100,000 or higher you can also negotiate a higher interest rate with the issuing bank or brokerage firm. No commissions are charged on these transactions.

Corporate short-term bonds. Corporate bonds from high-quality companies pay 2–3 percent higher interest than Treasury notes and are relatively safe since there is little indication that Exxon,

General Motors, or Xerox will be filing for bankruptcy in the near future.

Loan participation funds. These funds invest in collateralized bank notes from corporate customers with revolving credit lines that are based on the prime lending rate. The interest rate will float up or down depending on whatever current interest rates banks are charging their best customers. Average return is 1–2 percent higher than passbook accounts.

Day 249

TAX-BASED INVESTING

When you let taxes guide your investment strategy, you're making a big mistake.

—Bob Stovall

Tax-free investing helps some people sleep at night and believe that they are cheating Washington of a few pennies, but are you really doing the best thing for long-term growth and income? If you're young and want your money to grow, bite the bullet and go for the higher returns you get from stocks. On a 12 percent total return, even in a 36 percent tax bracket, after the IRS gets its cut and you adjust for a 3 percent inflation rate, you've still made a 4.68 percent return on your money. Apply that same concept to Treasury bills and money market accounts and see why brokers laugh at the idea of using Treasury bills, CDs, money market funds, and a bank savings account to build wealth.

If your tax bracket still looms larger in your investment planning than your need for growth, then consider building a portfolio of municipal bonds or buying tax-free mutual funds. Bonds can be bought for short-, medium- and long-term periods. You can build a "laddered" portfolio of bonds with various maturity dates and staggered interest rates to try to protect yourself against inflation but, on average, you will only break even so that you money keeps pace with inflation but will never grow in value. Here are some recent good choices in the municipal bond mutual fund area that can offer some decent returns:

Fund	Three-Year Average Annual Return	Phone Number
T. Rowe Price Tax-Free	4.9%	800–638–5660
Vanguard	6.8%	800–638–5660
USAA	5.9%	800–382–8722
Excelsior	5.6 %	800–446–1012

Action Step:

Review your investment strategy and decide if tax-free investing is more important than growth. You can also use tax-free money market funds to stash small amounts of cash for short periods of time when you don't care about earning higher interest.

Day 250

CONSERVATIVES GO FOR THE DULL

Dull companies with steady earnings growth may not make for stimulating cocktail party chatter, but over the long term they make the best investments.

—Fleming Meeks and David S. Fomdiller,
Forbes, November 6, 1995, p. 228

If you want to invest in the market without taking an outrageous risk, go for the dull. Boringly predictable stocks in industries that don't make the headlines are the ones you can usually rely on to maintain value and give dependable earnings. Industries like utilities, automobile parts, wallboard manufacturing, prefab housing, and building materials will never get the press coverage that Microsoft does, but you can usually count on them for fairly predictable 3.5 percent to 6.5 percent quarterly dividend. That's exactly what you want in a portion of your retirement portfolio. The closer you get to retirement, the better it is to shift your 401(k) investments into income-producing stocks that fit these categories. Utility funds are fairly predictable income funds although this may change as the deregulation of their companies goes into effect. Four successful utility funds with double-digit returns (yield plus growth) over the last five years are:

Fund	Five-Year Average Annual Return	Phone Number
Strong Utilities	14.5%	800–368–2945
Duff & Phelps Utility	16.5%	800–680–4367
Fidelity Select Utilities	23.5%	800–544–8888
Principal Utilities	18.1%	800–247–4123

Action Step:

Call each of the funds above for an application and a prospectus. Strong Funds offers *Why Utilities?*, a free guide to understanding utilities stocks. Find out about the procedure for rolling over your retirement money and taking your income from these funds after retirement.

Day 251

PEAKS AND VALLEYS

Here's a thought for the day to consider the benefits of long-term investing. If your grandfather had invested $1 in a mutual fund of stocks of the S&P 500 in 1925, and let it stay there through the 1929 stock market crash, the Great Depression of the 1930s, and all the other peaks, valleys, spikes, and dips of this well-known index, that $1 would now be worth $2,357.37. Imagine how much you would have inherited if Gramps had invested $10.

Action Step:

Reconsider your attitude about long-term investing and risk.

Day 252

USING A STOCK BROKER

Stockbrokers come in all sizes, shapes, colors, genders, and age groups, but if you look closely, you'll find that they have one thing in common: They want to make money with your money. If you're a small investor it isn't worth it to the broker or to you to pay full-service commissions and sales charges. If you feel nervous and uncertain as a novice, then be sure you choose someone who will have the patience to teach you what he or she is doing with your money and why. The services and commissions differ based on how much you expect the broker to do for you.

Full-service brokers such as Merrill Lynch, Morgan Stanley & Dean Witter, Salomon-Smith-Barney, Payne Webber, and Prudential Bache offer lots of hand-holding, many free brochures, extensive market research, and broad-based investment services from individual stocks, bonds, mutual funds, and Treasuries, as well as checkbooks and ATM cards for your money market account, along with loads of advice, but you're going to pay a pretty penny for it. They charge the highest commissions, averaging around $110 per trade for 100 shares.

Discount brokers like Quick and Reilly and Charles Schwab started out specializing in offering little or no advice but now provide more mutual fund research and portfolio management. They charge modest commissions, about $65 per trade for 100 shares and also have good fund management portfolio services, money market funds with checking and ATM cards, and some useful publications on retirement and education planning. Get Schwab's free "Investing Sourcebook" at 800–833–8633 or http://www.schwab.com or sign up for the weekly "Armchair Millionaire" newsletter available through the Web site.

Deep discount brokers are for sophisticated investors who do their own research and need very little advice. These firms, such as Brown & Co., Jack White, and York Securities are primarily order takers and specialize in the efficient execution of a trade. The commissions are low, around $19.95 to $35 per trade of 100 shares. Waterhouse Securities at 800–550–3535 was recently rated as the best of the bunch by *Smart Money* magazine.

With Internet brokers, if you're happy doing it all yourself and don't even need a human voice to confirm the transaction, you can save more than ever doing your investing on the Web. These are the lowest commissions, as low $5 per 100 shares. This is not for the novice. E-Trade, Ameritrade, Scottrade, and DLJ Direct are some of the leading firms competing for your business on the Web. Two words of caution: (1) You still have to put the check in snail mail to open the account or cover the trade, and (2) some transactions may give confirmations on the Net but can get fouled up if there's a glitch in the computer system.

Day 253

REVIEW AND REASSESS

By now you should be comfortable with reading financial magazines and watching some of the talk shows, and you should have discovered by now that this investment game isn't brain surgery. Once you're clear about what you want and where you want to go with your money, the opportunities and the information will show up—just when you need it! Make a list of the new things you have learned and the questions you have answered. Set a timetable for taking a personal finance course and starting a conversation with some friends to discuss how much you have learned about money in the last few months.

Day 254

INVESTING WITH PATIENCE AND FRIENDSHIP

There's no such thing as a self-made man. I've had much help and have found that if you are willing to work, many people are willing to help you.

—O. Wayne Rollins

Donald Othmer grew up in Nebraska in the early 1900s, living the proverbial frugal lifestyle, and earning money by delivering newspapers, tending cows for a farmer, cutting grass, and picking dandelions from his neighbor's lawns. After he got a Ph.D. in chemistry from the University of Michigan in 1927, he accepted a research position at Eastman Kodak. Within five years, Othmer had created more than 40 patents for the company, for which he received only a $10 bonus for each in his paycheck. He gave up the corporate arena for a college professorship in Brooklyn, New York, that allowed him to have his own lab and maintain ownership of his own patents in acid distillation. He was hardworking as a professor and careful with his money—a good catch for Mildred Topp, a high school teacher, whose mother, Mattie Topp, had arranged their introduction during a holiday vacation. Donald and Mildred married and bought a small townhouse in Brooklyn Heights, New York, which allowed Donald to walk to work and to save money by going home for lunch. When Mildred's mother mentioned that they should consider starting an investment program with a boyhood friend of Donald's from Omaha who was establishing a new investment management firm, Donald was able to open an account with him using $25,000 out of his savings account. That boyhood friend was Warren Buffett. It was 1958, Buffett was 27 years old, and had less than $1 million to manage. Donald's attitude was that he and Mildred were comfortable, and would not need the money for several years. As long as they saw growth they wouldn't worry about the investments. From time to time, they added more to the account but never withdrew a penny. Upon his death in 1995, Donald Othmer's estate was worth $210 million, which included 7,000 shares of Berkshire Hathaway stock valued at $30,000 a share. Three years later when Mildred passed on, the estate was worth more than $800 million, which has been donated to several charities.

Affirmation:

I will continue saving and be ready when the right opportunity appears.

Action Step:

Pick up a copy of *Julie and Debbie's Guide to Getting Rich on Just $10 a Week: How We're Making a Fortune-And You Can Too-Using Dividend ReInvestment Plans,* by Deborah Rosen Barker and Julie Behr Zimmerman, $9.95.

Day 255

COLLECTIVE PROSPERITY

The Prime Timers Investment Club of Akron, Ohio, is about as far from a typical Wall Street group of investors as you can get. The 17 men who work on an assembly line at the Firestone Tire Company started their group in 1972, with each person contributing $20 a month. The first stock they purchased was Polaroid. They liked the technology and the profit margins, and were comfortable with the *Value Line* rating for the company at that time. They could afford to purchase only ten shares, for about $800, but have held on to them for more than 25 years and reinvested all the quarterly dividends. After six stocks splits, those ten shares have now become 237 shares, with a value of $29,000. The club holds six meetings a year at the local library so that all of the members can read *Value Line* and share the responsibility for investment research before they discuss which stocks to buy and sell.

Action Step:

For more information on how to set up your own investment club, contact the National Association of Investors Corporation (NAIC) at 1515 E. Eleven Mile Road, Royal Oak, MI 48068 or call 248–583–6242. Its Web site also offers comprehensive information at http://www.better-investing.org

Day 256

GOING FOR VALUE

The "bible" for investors who want to purchase individual stocks is *Value Line*, a weekly financial newsletter that analyzes and ranks stocks according to their safety and volatility. It offers a detailed report of the performance of 1,700 of the most actively traded stocks available on the three major exchanges in the United States. *Value Line* ranks stocks for safety on a scale of 1 (least volatile) to 5 (most volatile). It also offers a rating of a company's financial strength on a scale from A++ (strongest) to C (weakest). Each issue provides buy/sell recommendations, ideas from various financial experts, and advice on other aspects of financial management, such as taxation and accounting. There are often special subscriber offers to new readers for as little as $55 for ten weeks. Call 800–833–0046 to take advantage of a special opportunity to begin learning to understand the stock-picking process. You can also see what *Value Line* has to offer by visiting its Web site at http://www.valueline.com. To find out about the CD-ROM software programs available to subscribers on a trial basis, call 800–535–9648, ext. 2373.

Day 257

"NO REGRETS" INVESTING

About 80 percent of what most stockbrokers are selling, you don't need. After you establish a core portfolio of four or five mutual funds and four or five blue chip stocks through dividend reinvestment programs, be content to sit back and monitor your investments and perhaps meet with a financial adviser once a year to review what you have and decide if you should keep those investments as your goals and financial needs change. Once you are on the mailing lists for certain investment publications, there are brokers who will call you with offers that may sound interesting, but unless you have a large fortune to play with, they can be dangerous to your long-term financial health. Certain investments can sound sexy and exciting, but once the hype has disappeared and the smoke clears you'll discover that they can easily turn a large fortune into a small savings, leaving you with a lot of pain, confusion, and absolute bewilderment about where your money went. To have a comfortable investment portfolio without outrageous risks, avoid any investments with names like:

Options and commodities.

Futures contracts.

Most real estate limited partnerships.

Film and entertainment partnerships/deals.

Over-the-counter/IPOs.

Horse-breeding syndications.

Currency exchange risks.

Joint venture partnerships.

Leveraged buy-out partnerships.

Gold, silver, and art objects unless you are collecting because you like them.

Action Step:

Keep it simple with a basic menu of four or five mutual funds, as shown in the $5,000 portfolio. If you study the portfolio of people like Anne Scheiber and Gladys Holm, you'll see that they owned only seven or eight individual blue-chip stocks. You can always go back to the safety and predictability of an index fund and sleep at night.

Day 258

Barron's weekly newspaper is not for the novice investor, since it is targeted primarily at the professional members of the investment community, but it is one of the most thorough financial publications available. It analyzes and summarizes the past week's events on Wall Street and comments on current trends in investing, and offers industry overviews and columns by the well-known financial columnist Alan Abelson. Each quarter, Barron's gives a thorough overview of the mutual fund industry, rating the quarterly performance of each fund.

Day 259

BECOME AN INDIVIDUAL INVESTOR

If you can't find a group of people interested in starting a club, don't wait around. Every year that goes by means a missed dividend check or opportunity to reinvest a dividend payment. If you have the discipline and don't mind going it alone, become one of the 700,000 individual members of the National Association of Investors Corporation (NAIC). The average age of NAIC members is 52, and each contributes about $82 month. In the past decade, NAIC has seen its membership increase by more than 300 percent to create over 37,000 clubs throughout the United States, and there seems to be no decline in their popularity.

Action Step:

To join NAIC, call 810–583–6242 or write to: 1515 E. Eleven Mile Road, Royal Oak, MI 48068. To find out more about other investment clubs and how to become an individual member, visit the Web sites at http://www.dripcentral.com and http://iclub central.com.

Day 260

DIRECT STOCK PURCHASE PLANS

Here's a list of the largest and most popular direct stock purchase plans. The minimum investment refers to the minimum amount you can use to open an account. Choose one company, call it, and get started—without a stockbroker!

Company	Minimum Investment	Minimum Monthly Payment	Phone Number
American Express	$1,000	$100	800–842–7629 or 800–851–9677
BellSouth	$500	$100	888–887–2965 or 800–631–6001
Bob Evans Farms	$50	$50	800–272–7675 or 614–492–4950
Walt Disney	$1,000	$50	800–948–2222
Eastman Kodak	$150	$50	800–253–6057 or 800–253–6057
Fannie Mae	$250	$25	800–289–3266 or 800–910–8277
Ford Motor Company	$1,000	$50	800–955–4791 or 800–279–1237
Gillette	$1,000	$100	800–643–6989
Home Depot	$250	$25	800–774–4117 or 800–442–2001
Mattel Toys	$500	$50	888–909–9922
Merck	$350	$50	800–774–4117 or 800–613–2104
Procter & Gamble	$250	$100	800–764–7483
Quaker Oats	$500	$50	800–774–4117
Wal-mart	$250	$50	800–438–6278
Walgreens	$50	$100	800–774–4117

Action Step:

Go look in your refrigerator and bathroom and see how many products you purchase from these companies on a regular basis. Why not get back some of the money you spend every month in dividends? Call 888–OWN–A–Stock to get a list of 900 direct stock purchase companies that offer DRIPS.

Day 261

INVESTING WITHOUT SIN

We have always known that heedless self-interest is bad morals; we know now that it is also bad economics.

—Franklin D. Roosevelt

Roosevelt tried to get Americans to become more conscious of the social impact of their investments before World War II, but the growth of individual investors evaluating companies for their political as well as economic sense did not gain momentum until the Vietnam War, when corporate issues such as nuclear weapons, apartheid, environmental pollution, and sexism and racism in the workplace became as important as profit margins. The problem with most mutual funds is that you don't always know what's in the portfolio. If you want your investments to match your ethics, you must choose your funds and advisers carefully. Doing social good while doing well financially has become primary criteria for many individuals, as well as churches, colleges, and universities. Many state and city pension fund managers now use various "social screens" to avoid investing in the stocks of tobacco, alcohol, and weapons manufacturers. Other use environmental and culturally sensitive standards for setting up a portfolio. The Morningstar Mutual Fund directory, which evaluates profitability, now has a separate category of socially responsible mutual funds. The largest group of socially responsible funds is managed by the Calvert Group, which has nine different funds. It also has a Web site called "Do You Know What You Own?" which helps you find out where your money is invested. The most profitably managed socially conscious funds based on three-year annualized returns are:

Fund	Three-Year Return	Phone Number
Domini Social Index Trust	30.03 percent	800–368–2748
Dreyfus Third Century Fund	29.53 percent	800–645–6561
Neuberger & Berman S/ Responsible Fund	27.69 percent	212–476–9100
Pax World Fund	19.99 percent	800–767–1729
Parnassus Fund	19.52 percent	800–999–3505

Who said you can't do well by doing good?

Action Step:

Visit the Web site for *The Good Money Journal* at http://www. goodmoney.com, which offers a complete list of all the mutual funds, banks, insurance companies, and credit unions that loan or invest money with a socially responsible philosophy. Call CO-OP America for its list of brochures on socially responsible investing at 800–713–8086 or order them through its Web site at http://www. coopamerica.org/ipfprrcv.htm.

Day 262

INVEST WHERE YOU EAT!

Eating out is a major expense in the typical family budget and probably will remain so as our lives get busier and busier. If you've ever taken a long road trip, you know that the major focus is on food. Since Americans like most of their meals to be fairly predictable, it's no wonder that fast-food drive-throughs and restaurant chains dominate the highway. If you eat out often, think about investing in your favorite restaurant chain. Here are some of the most well-known family-oriented national restaurant chains that are publicly traded and also have dividend reinvestment plans available for small investors.

Restautant	Number of Locations	Phone Number
Bob Evans Farms, Inc.	400 units in 18 states	614–492–4950
Cracker Barrel Old	380 units in 33 states	615–444–5533
		or
Country Stores, Inc.		800–568–3476
Darden Restaurants, Inc.	700 units in United States, Canada, and Japan (owns Red Lobster, Olive Garden, and Bahama Breeze chains)	407–245–7000
Luby's Cafeterias, Inc.	230 units in eight states	210–654–9000
Picadilly Cafeterias	130 units in 13 states	504–293–9440

Day 263

PENNY STOCKS AND IPOS

You pays your money and you takes your choice.

—Punch magazine

Penny stocks are defined as stocks traded for $5 or less. This is IPO territory, or initial public offering. Comparing most of these stocks with blue-chip stocks is like comparing a Rolls Royce with a Yugo. They both have wheels and qualify as a form of transportation but that's as far as it goes. This is a high-risk, totally unpredictable area that new investors should not enter unless they can afford to lose their money; truly the Wall Street version of Las Vegas. It's the area where you could have found Apple Computer and Microsoft when they first began to trade shares publicly ten years ago. A true penny stock will be offered by a small company that has less than $4 million in assets and whose stock is not traded on any of the large, recognized stock exchanges like NYSE or AMEX. You find them through small brokers who participate in a stock trading system called the

OTC (over-the-counter), which is linked to the NASDAQ (National Association of Securities Dealers Automated Quotation) system. These stocks are listed in the "pink sheets," and have such a small volume of shares available that they are not usually quoted in newspapers. If you don't mind risks and want to lay out an investment plan that allows you to play with a few pennies, then go ahead and enjoy yourself, but don't look for too much in return except statements in your mailbox. One last note—any losses you rack up can be written off your taxes as a capital loss against the profits you make in the blue-chip stocks and equity funds that you own.

Action Step:

The Bowser Report is a 20-year-old newsletter specializing in information on stocks offered at $3 or less. Call 757–877–5979 for a sample copy or visit the Web site at http://www.bowserreport.com to get more information.

Day 264

WHY $10,000?

When you look at investment ads, they show exciting graphics of what $10,000 would be worth today if you had invested ten years ago with the XYZ Super-Charged Hyper-Growth Fund managed by their company. If you're inclined to dismiss the ad because you believe that you need a minimum of $10,000 to invest in a mutual fund, think again. Most mutual funds will allow you to open an account for only $1,000. If you want to set up a monthly investment plan and have $100 a month deducted from your checking account, you can begin a plan for as little as $100. The real reason stockbrokers imply that you need $10,000 to open an account is that they don't really want small investors. They have to do the dialing-for-dollars routine each day to generate "new money" to keep earning a living. Brokers must generate at least $10,000 in gross commissions each month "to the house" in order to earn $3,000 of income for themselves. Your $1,000 in a mutual fund with a 5 percent deferred sales charge only generates about $17.50 for the poor broker—before taxes! What's left barely covers carfare and lunch money, so the broker prefers to go for the big fish with the big bucks to make it worth picking up the phone each day. Production contests and sales incentives encourage brokers to sell certain investment products like new mutual funds or partnerships that are not for your benefit, but for the trip to Hawaii, the red Jeep Cherokee, and the promotion to another executive level. *Caveat emptor!*

Action Step:

If you have established an investment portfolio that you're happy with, beware of any stockbroker or financial planner who tells you that it should be changed without a good explanation. Ask any and every broker, financial consultant, or investment adviser how they make money on each investment they recommend.

Day 265

CONSIDER THE SOURCE

Professional advice cannot be duplicated but you must always think about what investment recommendation you hear and why. Whom does your broker work for? Not you! The broker's primary goal is to produce dollars of commission income. The worst thing you can say to a broker is, "I'm not sure, let me think about it." Investments offered by advisers and brokers who work on a commission basis can have hidden charges and fees that they don't explain to you. Be suspicious if they can't give you a prospectus and offer, in writing, an explanation of what the investment will cost you. If you request no-load funds and Treasury bills, they don't want to know your name or they will urge you to consider a mutual fund that has Treasuries in it but carries a sales charge of 3–4 percent. You would have to get a year of earnings in a tax-free bond fund or a long-term Treasury bond fund to replace the cost of their commission.

Action Step:

Ask for a written explanation of what an investment adviser, stockbroker, or planner is earning on each investment recommendation that is offered to you.

Day 266

WHAT EXACTLY IS THE "DOW"?

When the evening news anchor intones: "The Dow was up 23 points today . . ." if you're like most people you probably wonder what the heck the "Dow" is. Although this index of the daily movement of the stock market has been followed since 1896, it is deceptive to believe that it is the most accurate measure of stocks. There are over 5,000 stocks traded each day on the two major exchanges, the New York Stock Exchange (NYSE) and the American Stock Exchange (AMEX), but the Dow measures only 30 stocks. It is supposed to represent a cross-section of major American industries from oil and entertainment to telecommunications and pharmaceuticals. The Dow average is the total price of one share of each of the 30 Dow stocks divided by a factor of slightly less than one, which is adjusted for the many stock splits, mergers, and divestitures that have occurred over the years. The stocks that are included in the Dow, which is named for Charles Dow and Edward Jones, who started the *Wall Street Journal*, are chosen by a group of editors at the *Wall Street Journal*.

The 30 Dow Jones Stocks

Allied Signal	Hewlett Packard
Alcoa	IBM
American Express	International Paper
AT&T	Johnson & Johnson
Boeing	McDonald's
Caterpillar	Merck
Chevron	Minnesota M&M
Citigroup	J. P. Morgan
Coca-Cola	Philip Morris
DuPont	Procter & Gamble
Eastman Kodak	Sears
Exxon	Union Carbide
General Electric	United Technologies
General Motors	Wal-Mart Stores
Goodyear	Walt Disney

Action Step:

Strong Funds now has a mutual fund that invests only in the "Dow 30." Get a copy of the prospectus at 800–368–2945 or its Web site at http://www.strong-funds.com.

Day 267

A CORE PORTFOLIO OF STOCKS

If you decide to build a portfolio of individual stocks that you will buy and hold indefinitely, you are the best resource for this decision. Read the research and decide if a company whose products you like also has a sound balance sheet, good management, and is a even if you use a stockbroker, you must be prepared to assume total responsibility for the final decision.

Do some homework and study the investments you are planning to buy and make sure you fully understand what you're getting into.

Buy quality stocks in three companies that produce products and services that you know well.

Hold those stocks for the long-term, reinvest the dividends, and don't sell them. Ever. After you've retired and want to cash a few dividend checks, you can take income from the stocks, but consider the inheritance you will pass on to your children.

Action Step:

Spend an afternoon at the library perusing *Value Line* to find its evaluation of the three stocks you have chosen to study.

Day 268

INVESTING FOR GROWTH AND INCOME

The creation of a thousand forests is in one acorn.

—Ralph Waldo Emerson

If you have decided that you want to invest in a comfortable combination of growing stocks and income-producing ones, then you should look at a select list that is touted as offering a relatively predictable combination of both. Each year Standard and Poor's, the financial research house that rates and reviews all publicly traded investments, prowls through its industry research and produces a list of the *100 Best Dividend-Paying Stocks*. In the most recent edition the following companies were given five-star or four-star ratings and listed as the best-performing stocks to purchase within the next year.

Company	Ticker Symbol	Transfer Agent	Minimum Purchase	First Purchase
Five-Star Stocks				
First Union Bank	FTU	704–374–6782	$25/month	One share/ from a broker
General Electric	GE	800–786–2543	$10/month	One share/broker
Merck	MRK	800–613–2104	$25/year	One share/broker
Nations Bank	NB	704–386–5000	$50/quarter	One share/ from a broker
Pfizer	PFE	212–573–3704	$25/month	One share/ from a broker
Four-Star Stocks				
Abbott Labs	ABT	800–730–4001	$10/quarter	One share/ from a broker
Anheuser-Busch	BUD	800–456–9852	$25/month	One share/ from a broker
Avery Dennison	AVY	800–649–2291	$25/month	$500/transfer from bank agent
Campbell Soup	CPB	800–446–2617	$25/year	One share/ from a broker
Clorox Corporation	CLX	800–466–2617	$10/year	One share/ from a broker
Eaton Vance	ETN	800–542–7792	$10/year	$100/transfer from bank agent
First Tennessee National Corp.	FTEN	800–486–9716	$25/quarter	One share/ from a broker
Hanna M.A. Co.	MAH	800–321–1954	$25/quarter	One share/ from a broker
Heinz H.J. Co.	HNZ	800–253–3399	$25/quarter	One share/ from a broker
Kimberly-Clark	KMB	800–442–2001	$25/quarter	One share/ from a broker

All these companies have dividend reinvestment plans that allow you to purchase their shares directly from the company after buying one share from a stockbroker.

Action Step:

Choose one of the companies above and call the transfer agent for a copy of the DRIP plan and enrollment information.

Day 269

REVIEW AND REASSESS

Congratulate yourself if you're still reading, learning, and looking forward to the new experience of being financially independent. You should be ready to buy stocks, start an investment club, open a mutual fund account, and explore new opportunities for investing. Go for it!

Day 270

$$$—Savings Tip:

Investor's Business Daily, an in-depth financial newspaper for the seasoned investor, frequently offers two-week subscriptions free of charge to new readers. Take advantage of one of these free offers to get a look at how investment information is presented and decide if this helps you learn about stocks, investing, and managing money. Like the *Wall Street Journal* it has detailed charts, technical graphs, and industry reports on investing; an excellent personal finance column appears each Friday. Every Tuesday and Thursday there is a chart called "How to Read a Mutual Fund Chart."

Action Step:

Call 800–306–9744 and request a free trial subscription or log onto the Web site at http://www.investors.com and register online.

Day 271

GETTING INVESTMENT PRACTICE

Before you spend real money on stocks, bonds, mutual funds, or real estate, get firsthand practice for how it's going to operate try it with a mock portfolio that you can create on the Internet. You don't have to use real money to enjoy playing the market, a "mock portfolio" teaches you about the real-life strategies and the ups and downs of stocks, bonds, real estate, hostile takeovers, mergers, and accusations. The stock market game can also be played each day by setting up a "mock portfolio" of securities that you buy and sell based on current information that you use from the research you collect from other Web sites.

Action Step:

You can visit the Web site for The MoneyCentral Investor at http://www.investor.msn.com, which will allow you to set up a mock portfolio, learn how to do stock research, and follow your picks to see how you measure up against the professional portfolio managers at choosing winners or losers.

Day 272

GOING INTERNATIONAL

Americans spend such a great deal of money on imported products that we almost forget they aren't made in the USA. Volvo cars, Sony audio equipment, Nestlé's chocolate, and BP (British Petroleum) gas are just a few. However, the idea of investing overseas often makes American investors nervous and uncertain because of the distance, language differences, potential for political instability, and hassle of currency exchanges. Despite these problems, international investing should be a part of everyone's investment portfolio because of the growth potential. If you look closely, many U.S. companies from Avon and Colgate to Ford Motor Company and Motorola are already major players in global markets because of the expanding economies that add to their bottom line. Mutual funds can serve you best in this area. Why not let portfolio managers and researchers take the angst and the paperwork out of making the fund choices, monitor the currency changes, and pass on the growth to you? According to *Morningstar*, five four-star-rated international stock funds with 10–12 percent growth over the last five years are:

Fund	Five-Year Return	Phone Number
Harbor International	14.81%	800–422–1050
Janus Overseas	17.04%	800–223–4856
Vanguard International	16.67%	800–662–7447
T. Rowe Price International	13.14%	800–401–4768
Scudder Global	12.88%	800–225–2470

Action Step:

Choose a fund and add it to your investment portfolio after you have created a asset allocation plan for yourself. Look at your 401(k) plan and see if any of these investment choices are included on the menu.

Day 273

ADRS—AMERICAN DEPOSITARY RECEIPTS

Most large U.S. companies are already international conglomerates that sell their products and services globally through foreign-owned subsidiaries. If you want to invest in the Mexican-based Coca-Cola or Amway Asia you have to purchase the stock as an American depositary receipt since it is traded on a foreign stock exchange. If you have a particular fondness for a non-U.S. based company like Sony, British Airways, British Petroleum, Reuters, or Nestlé, you may also purchase its shares as American depositary receipts. ADRs are a method of buying shares of international stocks outside a mutual fund. Keep in mind that your investment is impacted by currency exchange risks and political and economic events. Two U.S. banks act as trustee and collect investment dollars and pay out the dividends in U.S. dollars. You can buy direct from two sources: J. P. Morgan Bank, 800–749–1687, has a $250 minimum investment, and the Bank of New York, 800–345–1612, has a $1,000 minimum for opening an account. These investments have to be examined with the same caution and scrutiny that you would apply to any other security investment. Read carefully about the pros and cons before you start writing checks.

Action Step:

The DRIP Investor by Charles Carlson offers extensive research each month on over 100 international stocks sold as ADRs available to U.S. investors. Call 800–774–4117 for information or order prospectuses and applications at its Web site, http://www. enroll direct.com.

Day 274

THE WALL STREET "ZOO"

The "Bears." When stocks continuously fall more than 20 percent over several days from a peak point, as they did in July 1998, it is called a "down market" because stock prices are declining. When the closing index numbers for the Dow Jones

Industrial Average (DJIA) and the S&P 500 are lower at the end of the day than when they started, and if the trend continues for more than two weeks, the market is said to be in a "bear market" phase. People who are negative about the market and do not believe in the continued upward growth of stocks are called "Bears." The longest "bear" market on record lasted from October 1929 through June 1933. If you want to invest with the bears, Mutual Series Beacon "Z" Fund, 800–342–5236, and the Prudent Bear Fund, 800–711–1848, have been successful mutual funds in down markets, with an average 29.3 percent return when the Dow is in trouble.

The "Bulls." When stocks rise consistently for more than two quarters, and the three major indexes—the DJIA, the S&P 500, and the NASDAQ—continue to set new records at the close of each business day, it is considered to be a "bull market." The longest bull market on record started in October 1990 and did not have a major downturn until July 1998.

The "Chickens." This means anyone who is afraid to take even the slightest risk and will only invest in insured bonds, FDIC-insured certificates of deposits, bank money market instruments, or Treasury bills, notes, and bonds.

The "Pigs." The greediest of all investors take outrageous risks and are attracted to bogus opportunities as they search for the one "big hit" that will make them rich "overnight." They bounce around from one investment to another, trying to milk every investment opportunity for all they can get and usually end up earning less than the average small investor who has a consistent long-term strategy and a stays put in good investments that fit an asset allocation plan. Few of these people succeed at long-term investing.

Day 275

GOLD!

Gold speaks sense in a language all nations understand.

—Aphra Behn

In all the James Bond action-thriller type movies, the traitorous villain is usually some international terrorist who wants to be paid in gold. Why? Because gold is one universal form of portable wealth that is recognized as negotiable anywhere in the world. Although the Hollywood plot makes sense on the screen, in reality, gold as an investment is cumbersome and complicated to buy, own, and maintain. Although gold and other precious metals have a universal attraction, they don't really deliver on their glittering promise of constant wealth or even as an inflation hedge anymore. If you want to invest in gold, don't focus on this as your first investment or as more than 5 percent of your total investment portfolio. You can purchase shares in gold mutual funds that buy shares in gold mines or get your own gold bars by purchasing gold bullion coins and bars that must be appraised, certified, insured, and protected in a safe deposit box. Gold certificates can also be bought and held in your safe deposit box. As with most precious metals, the glitter of gold's reputation offers more than its actual return as an investment.

Action Step:

Order a copy of the brochure "Your Introduction to Investing in Gold" from The Gold Institute, Administration Office, Suite 101, 1026 Sixteenth Street, N.W., Washington, DC 20036. Call 202–835–0185 or visit their Web site at www.goldinstitute.com.

Day 276

HETTY GREEN

Contrary to social conditioning, men are not genetically superior in managing money. What matters are exposure, knowledge, and discipline. Take Hetty Green, the "Witch of Wall Street," for example. Henrietta Howland Robinson Green was born in 1834 to a family of Quaker shipowners in Massachusetts. When her grandfather began losing his eyesight, Hetty spent her mornings reading him the financial news. She listened to the morning business discussion between her father and grandfather before going to school. At 31, she inherited $6 million from her father after his death. Hetty refused help from the bankers and brokers who had served her father. She was quite capable of managing her money herself, which her male advisers considered "undignified" and "unhealthy" for a woman, and they treated her as a pariah because of her insistence on being independent. She tried to inherit her aunt's entire estate by producing what some thought was a forged will. She disappeared to England for eight years to avoid disgrace. When she came back, she plunged into the stock market with a new fervor, buying stocks and real estate and offering mortgages. She thrived on lending money to distressed traders so she could reap the interest from personal loans or take over their business on default. Hetty earned the nickname the "Witch of Wall Street," living in a boardinghouse and wearing musty old clothes, and she was accused of eating grimy sandwiches. When her son hurt his knee, it was rumored she dressed him in rags and tried to pass him off as a charity patient at a free clinic. She was a detested figure who paid her son $3 a day while she trained him to look after business. Pleading poverty and persecution to the end, Hetty died in 1916; she was worth $100 million!

Day 277

STOCK SPLITS

Stock splits create an increase in the number of shares outstanding without an increase in value. After a two-for-one split, a shareholder with 100 shares valued at $20 per share would have 200 shares valued at $10 each. When a stock has run up in price, a split is often declared by the board of directors at the annual shareholders' meeting to make the stock more affordable. Most stock splits occur in the second quarter after the annual shareholders' meeting held in the first quarter. There is an investing concept that stocks that split frequently rise 8 percent faster in value than stocks that do not split regularly.

Action Step:

Take a frequent look at such Web sites as http://www.stock-watch.com, which keeps a calendar of announced stock splits and all previous stock splits for the past 12 months.

Day 278

TAX PLANNING

Suppose you won the lottery for $10 million tomorrow. The choice you would be given is to take the money all at once or spread it out over a 20-year period. The greedy and the needy part of us would grab the bundle and take it all at once, but that's not a smart idea. Do you know how much would go to taxes on such a lump sum? Paying the IRS is the smartest move you can make to avoid aggravation and save thousands of dollars and the surprise of an unwanted tax bill. Whether you get an inheritance or a raise in pay, or get married and combine salaries, which puts you in a new tax bracket, professional advice and planning ahead is worth the expense. Don't wait until

April to ask questions when your financial status changes; do it before December 31; it's too late to take the tax-saving steps then. A good CPA will cost you $150–$200 an hour—if you are organized!

Action Step:

If you feel comfortable doing it yourself the best tax planning software is Kiplinger's Tax Cut, which will cost you about $49.95 and can be purchased and downloaded through your computer from http://www.beyond.com.

Day 279

MANAGING A WINDFALL

Once the money is gone, you can't get it back.

—Anonymous

Be very, very careful with once-in-a-lifetime gifts. Whether you win the lottery, get an inheritance, come into an insurance settlement or a trust fund, you don't want to blow it with a poor investment strategy.

SIX STEPS TO MAKING IT LAST

1. Don't tell anyone that you have money until you talk with an accountant and an attorney. Be prepared to spend $300–$400 on a consultation with a good CPA to learn the tax implications of this blessing that just fell into your life. The last place you want to screw up is with the IRS.

2. Ask the CPA for recommendations on "fee-only" financial advisers who will teach you about investing before asking you to write checks. Interview a few of them to get an idea of how they work and if you feel comfortable with them.

3. Pay off all unsecured debts like credit cards, car notes, and student loans (but not the mortgage yet), if you have them.

4. Treat yourself to one nice vacation, but don't get extravagant. Put a limit on the vacation so this won't be your last one.

5. Put the money in a money market fund or lock it away in a CD for six months or a year and give yourself time to think about what you really want to do. Don't worry! The money will wait for you. If your lump sum is greater than $250,000, ask that the bank give you a "jumbo rate," usually at least ½ percent higher than what is available to smaller depositors. Now you'll begin to learn some of the special banking privileges that come with having money!

6. Read, study, listen, learn, and ask every question you can think of before making big financial decisions. Take your time. Enroll in a money management class at a junior college or adult education program. Study the language and concepts of investing. Don't rush into any investment that you can't explain to a ten-year-old. If you don't understand it, don't do it just because a friend said it was a good idea.

Action Step:

Call NAPFA, the National Association of Personal Financial Advisers, at 800–366–2732 and get names of three "fee-only" advisers. Make appointments to see them, for the free 30 minutes "getting to know you" consultations they provide for new clients.

Day 280

ANALYSIS PARALYSIS

We know too much and are convinced of too little.

—T. S. Eliot

You've read every book and magazine out there, taken every course, gone to every seminar and workshop you could find, spoken to three different financial professionals, ordered dozens of brochures and prospectuses from all the mutual funds you see in the personal finance magazines, subscribed to three publications, and even bought a couple expensive newsletters, but you still can't write that first check. Then maybe you're not really an investor! These excuses can keep you floating along on a fine line between frustration and procrastination—what's right for your brother-in-law, your neighbor, or your boss may not be right for you. Maybe you still don't understand what you're doing with your money. Maybe you need a bit of humor to lighten up your attitude about money. Check out the cartoons at http://www.investorhome.com/humor.htm.

Action Step:

Review your long-term goals and determine if you would be comfortable putting at least 10 percent of your money into blue chip stocks. Take the risk tolerance quiz at http://www.moneycentral.com to see where you fit on the investment scale.

Day 281

REAL ESTATE INVESTING—WITHOUT BEING A LANDLORD

Real estate investment trusts (REITs)are corporations that buy, develop, and manage all forms of property, from multifamily apartment complexes to shopping malls and industrial park sites, until the trustees decide that it's time to sell the property. As an investor you get a share of the income from their management expertise since they are legally required to pay out 95 percent of their profits each year. Here are several worth looking at if you want to own property without being a landlord:

REIT	Ticker Symbol	Yield	Phone Number
Crown American Realty Trust	CWN	9.92%	814–536–4441
Duke Realty Investments	DRE	5.98%	317–846–4700
Redwood Trust, Inc.	RWT	7.3%	415–389–7373
Taubman Centers	TCO	6.65%	248–258–6800
Great Lakes REITs	GL	8.16%	630–368–2900

Action Step:

Do a little homework and decide if you want to take the risk and invest in some large commercial real estate projects. Call the National REIT Association at 800–3NA–REIT or get a copy of their brochure, "Investing in REITS" from their headquarters at 1875 I St. N.W., Suite 600, Washington, D.C., 20006. Visit their Web site at http://www.nareit.com

Day 282

PLANNING FOR THE FUTURE

John and Alice R. were happy renting their apartment in Baltimore, and when the landlord offered them the opportunity to buy it for $90,000 in 1976, they initially resisted the idea. "Why should we saddle ourselves with a mortgage and maintenance payments when we can rent for much less?" they asked. What they were overlooking was that they were paying for the privilege of living on someone else's property. Any money they invested in improvements would be lost if they moved, and their home would in no way be an asset if they ever had to borrow money. When they came to understand the advantages of owing their home, they borrowed to meet the low, insiders' buying price and tightened their belts to pay the monthly mortgage and maintenance. Fewer dinners out, a reduction in impulse buying (no extra shoes for Alice, no additions to John's huge collection of compact discs) and the couple found themselves enjoying the security of ownership more than they could have thought possible. Instead of paying rent for a place to live, they were contributing to an investment whose value steadily increased. In 1998, the market value of their apartment was $250,000. Not bad for a couple who had only counted their wealth in compact discs and beautiful shoes—commodities that will not help out in a financial crisis or send your kid to college.

Action Step:

Keep in mind what new career or lifestyle changes you want to create for yourself after retiring while you're still in your first career. It takes time to make it happen.

Day 283

REVIEW AND REASSESS

Give yourself a day off. Relax and see if you can pass a day without spending, charging, or thinking about money.

Day 284

GETTING SHELTER

Owning a home is still the number one American dream. It is a major asset that may support you in your retirement and can be a valuable legacy for your children. Other than your retirement plan, it is also the only legitimate tax shelter still available for the average working person. But buying a house is likely to be the most expensive and time-consuming financial transaction you'll ever make, beyond buying a car, paying for a college education, and planning for retirement. It's okay to be scared and uncertain as you consider this step, but be aware that there's lots of help out there for achieving this wonderful goal. Just keep your mind focused on one fact: After you get past signing the contract, making the down payment, finding a mortgage, and surviving the shock of paying the points, the closing costs, and the moving expenses, you get to move into a community where everyone else is likely to share your values. They are there to put down roots and contribute to the improvement of your neighborhood.

Day 285

HOME-BUYERS SCHOOL

There are times when the process of buying a house seems so complex that you might want to go to school and take a course to understand how to handle it. If you don't have time for a full-time course, how about a full-day workshop? The Federal National Mortgage Association (FNMA) is a government agency on a mission to help you and 20 million other Americans become first-time homeowners in the next five years. You have seen the infomercials on TV, the ads in your local paper, and full-color brochures in your bank. Since buying a home is so complex and time-consuming, the Fannie Mae Foundation has created a series of one-day Home-Buying Fairs around the country. Whether you live in Denver or the District of Columbia, Fannie Mae seminars bring together mortgage lenders, credit experts, real estate professionals, and members of local community housing groups to answer all your questions with multilingual presenters who will assist you with credit issues, understanding mortgages, and all the legal and financial aspects of buying a home. Best of all, the workshops are free of charge.

Action Step:

Visit Fannie Mae's Web site at http://www.openthedoor. org/events to find out when it will sponsor a Home-Buying Fair in your area. Call 800–833–7500 to get a list of FNMA-approved mortgage counselors in your area who may be conducting workshops on buying a home. Get their free brochure "Opening the Door to a Home of Your Own."

Day 286

ACORN'S SCHOOL

The challenge in buying a house is to get solid advice on the financial issues and to feel comfortable with what you're getting into, because you're going to live with the results for a very long time. If you want more than a one-day workshop on the issues involved, you might be lucky enough to live in one of the 16 urban areas where Fannie Mae is sponsoring an Acorn Pilot Program—a six-week course for first-time home buyers. This series of consumer education workshops helps you clean up your credit report, fill out mortgage applications, and understand the language and the process of home buying.

Action Step:

Contact Acorn national headquarters in Chicago at 312–939–1611 to find out where its special programs for first-time home buyers are located.

Day 287

YOUR HOME-BUYING TEAM

Buying a house is probably the most expensive investment you will make in your lifetime, so don't do it alone. You need a team of seasoned professionals to guide you through the process.

Real estate broker. The broker should show properties, make full disclosure about any faults or flaws in the property, answer all your questions about neighborhood facilities, and inform you of any legal restrictions on the property, but remember, the 6 percent commission is being paid by the seller, not you, and therefore the broker's loyalty is geared toward making a sale.

Inspector. He or she is worth the $200–$350 you will pay for a report that can uncover termites, weak beams, wet basements, and plumbing or wiring problems that may not be evident to you. Call the American Society of Home Inspectors at 800–743–2744 for a list of members in your area.

Lawyer. Choose an attorney who is familiar with the Fair Housing Law and has had considerable experience in negotiating on real estate contracts and closing procedures. Expect to pay about 1 percent of the purchase price for the service.

Banker/Mortgage Broker. This person is the key to helping you find the right loan program to suit your needs. Mortgage brokers have broader access to various lenders outside of banks, although they will charge 1 percent of your purchase price for their services. The Mortgage Brokers Association of America suggests that you check your local phone book for its members.

Action Step:

Review your goal list. If buying a home is a major item, set up a monthly date to talk to brokers and bankers, attend workshops, and begin collecting data. The average home purchase takes a minimum of one year to negotiate.

Day 288

DOING AN "FSBO"

"FSBO" stands for "For Sale By Owner." You must decide if you want to spend each weekend for the next six months showing your house or condo, answering the phone for prospects who may or may not show up for the appointment, writing up and handing out the information sheet on your property to "just lookers." If you're willing to do it yourself and have the time to invest in this exercise, you can save the 6–7 percent that you will pay a real estate broker. Before you forgo the services of a broker, read *Tips and Traps When Selling a Home* by Robert Irwin (McGraw-Hill, $12.95), the best guide available to help you decide if you want to do this yourself.

Action Step:

Register your home with http://owners.com on the Internet, which lists over 300,000 condos and homes around the country for people who are looking. This is also an excellent site to compare home prices to see if you're asking too much, which can slow down your sales process.

Day 289

THE MORTGAGE MAZE

More than a dozen different forms of mortgage exist in the financial marketplace, but here are the most popular mortgage types that you can usually find at most banks.

Fixed. Interest rates and monthly payments will stay the same for the life of the loan. You can choose a 15-year mortgage or a 30-year mortgage.

Adjustable/variable rate. The interest rate changes every year or every six months, based on some financial index such as the six-month U.S. Treasury bill rate, which changes your monthly payments. A ceiling on the payments can keep this from getting too unbearable.

Two-step or graduated mortgage. An excellent choice for new homeowners with low incomes and little money for a down payment. After five or seven years the payments will increase as the buyers' income increases.

Action Step:

"Choosing the Mortgage That's Right for You" is another excellent brochure that Fannie Mae offers to explain the different types of mortgages available and how to choose one that fits your income and expectations.

Day 290

"HOW MUCH HOUSE CAN I AFFORD?"

Don't try to buy a mansion your first time out. Look for a home that fits within your budget and your lifestyle. Bear in mind that the average American relocates from one home to another or from one city to another every seven to ten years as career opportunities develop, family size grows, and needs change. Perhaps a two-bedroom condo will be sufficient as you start out. Do you really need your own four walls and your own backyard and all the maintenance that involves? The size of the home you buy depends on your earnings, your debts, and your savings. Banks believe that you can only buy something that is 2.5 to 3 times your earnings, therefore a $50,000 income can support a $125,000 mortgage. They also review your monthly gross income and estimate that 28 to 33 percent of that income before taxes can be allocated for monthly mortgage payments. $3,000 a month gross income times 28 percent is $840. That's what you can afford to spend on monthly mortgage payments. About 36 percent of your monthly gross income is the maximum debt (including credit cards!) that you can comfortably carry.

Action Step:

Take out your pay stubs and apply these ratios on your annual income to see how much house you can afford.

Day 291

PREQUALIFYING

Planning and preparation are the best way to avoid getting your heart broken in the home-buying process. Don't fall in love with a three-bedroom, two-bath condo with terrace and view of the park and then try to manipulate the numbers to afford it. Before you start reading real estate ads and spending weekends talking to brokers, sit down with a home-buying counselor or a mortgage broker to learn how much house you can afford. Lenders look for four things:

Current income. How much do you earn from salary, investments, and interest? Bankers will ask for a copy of your 1040 and pay stubs as proof of income.

Current debt. Review your personal assets and liabilities statement to see your total debt.

Current savings. The down payment should be in your account for a least 90 days before you make your mortgage application.

Past credit history. Get a copy of your credit report to see what the bank will be looking at before you fill out a mortgage application. Bankers don't like surprises!

Don't overuse credit. Pay your bills on time. Late occasionally but not consistently. What's your ability to repay? Are you a good risk? What was the reason for it—divorce, lost a job, illness, death in the family. Show that you are now making more money now, and have cleaned up credit. Bring six months of canceled checks. Lenders want to see that the last two years of credit are good, clean, and consistent. Wait for a year or six months to clean up your credit, and get rid of some debt.

Action Step:

Call 800–688–HOME and order Fannie Mae's booklet "Buying Your First Home."

Day 292

DOWN PAYMENT

There are no set rules on how much money you should put into the down payment on your first home, most lenders expect you to have at least 10 percent of the purchase price of a house for the down payment; some will settle for as little as 5 percent down, depending on the current interest rates, the competition for mortgage money, and the location, although they will require private mortgage insurance (PMI), which will cost you a whole lot more in the long run. In some cases, as with the Federal Housing Administration (FHA) and a few other special government mortgage programs, 3 percent is acceptable. If you are a U.S. military veteran, you may not have to make a down payment at all. For a small fee the federal government will guarantee your mortgage up to $100,000.

Action Step:

Visit the Web site for the American Homeowners Association at http://www.ahahome.com for information on various ways that you can get the down payment.

Day 293

RELOCATING

With the new technology and the easy access to housing information, you can shop for a house without leaving home. If you want to get an idea of home prices and mortgage rates in another city where you plan to relocate, visit the Home Scout home listing service at its Web site at http://www.homescout.homeshark.com/scripts/listingssearch. It lists over 800,000 homes in more than 200 cities around the United States. It also has an excellent mortgage referral service to lead you to a bank in your area that may be offering mortgages at a reasonably lower rate.

Day 294

$$$–Savings Tip:

PMI—private mortgage insurance—is an arrangement with an insurance company to guarantee your payments to the bank on your mortgage if you don't have 20 percent of the total price for the down payment. The cost of PMI can add about $75 to $100 to your monthly payments on a $100,000 mortgage. Once you reach the point of having 20 percent equity in your home, usually after a year or two of payments, you can have this monthly insurance payment canceled.

Action Step:

If you have been paying PMI insurance for a year or more, ask your bank for a reevaluation of your loan and your property to determine if you qualify to cancel your coverage. You can use that extra money to reduce the principal on your mortgage or add it to a retirement plan.

Day 295

CLOSING COSTS

Be prepared to pay for a lot of expenses that include more than just the house, the appraisal fee, and the mortgage application. This list can seem long and expensive, but you will spend 4–6 percent of the purchase price of your house to cover your attorney's fees, the bank's attorney's fees, land surveys, title insurance costs, and mortgage recording taxes. In some urban areas a community development agency will help first-time homeowners to pay these closing costs. Ask the real estate broker, the banker, or the mortgage counselor that you meet with to give you a list of what these charges are and if you qualify for a subsidized program.

Action Step:

All mortgage lenders are required to give you a copy of the HUD booklet "Settlement Costs: A HUD Guide." Download a copy at http://www.usmall.com/hbc/closing/index.html or call 415–974–2163 to order it.

Day 296

BUYING FORECLOSURES

Whether you're looking for a condo in Chicago, a single-family home in Tucson, or a townhouse in Toledo, you can probably find it listed as a foreclosure. Income properties as well as residences can be bought at 35–50 percent less if you're willing to do some homework.

FHA, VA, Fannie Mae, and HUD are all government agencies that guarantee home mortgages must resell properties when they have defaults to recover their invested capital.

Your local bank branch manager can refer you to the division within the corporate structure that handles foreclosures.

Check the classifieds of your local newspaper. Property foreclosures for taxes must be listed in the public notices at least a month before the date.

HUD has regional offices that manage foreclosure sales. It will also provide a list of real estate brokers in your area that it has designated as its representatives for these sales.

Action Step:

The Internet is indispensable for foreclosure information. Three Web sites are an excellent resource.

Foreclosures, USA at http://www.foreclosuresusa.net lists properties around the country.

Foreclosures OnLine at http://www.4close.com offers a weekly e-mail newsletter giving listings in your area by county and zip code for $19.95 a month.

National Foreclosures at http://www.nationalforeclosures.com lists properties in 50 states from government agencies, bank trustee sales, and tax lien sales. One free listing of a sample report is available by calling its 24-hour hotline at 800–5BANK–REO (522–6573), ext. 30007.

Day 297

HOME IMPROVEMENTS

Spring is the season for home repairs, maintenance, additions, and renovations. The average homeowner spends about $3,250 per season, but the greatest concern should be what percentage of those repairs you will recover when you eventually sell your home. Here's how real estate brokers rank the improvements and additions:

Kitchens—cabinets, floors, appliances and tile work—102 percent recovery.

Bathrooms—new tubs, faucets, tiles, shower stalls—98 percent recovery.

Sundecks and patios—treated redwood or flagstone and slate—86 percent recovery.

Extra closets and hardwood floors—oak or cherry are most popular—91 percent recovery.

Family/recreation rooms—basements for children and guests—82 percent recovery.

Two items to avoid are hot tubs and poorly constructed extra rooms. Skylights and fireplaces draw mixed reviews. Doing some homework can save dollars, anxiety, and disappointment.

Action Step:

Call the National Association of the Remodeling Industry at 800–440–NARI for a free copy of *How to Select a Professional Remodeling Contractor*. At http://www.askbuild.com you can get a standardized checklist of questions to ask any contractor, along with a list indicating the costs related to more than 25 major jobs that can be done in a house, from heating and air-conditioning installation to a new roof. Another site, at http://www.home-help.com, will advise you on the cost of materials.

Day 298

$$$—Savings Tip:

Hire a buyer's broker if you feel totally intimidated and uncertain about what you're doing and need help. They have been professional real estate brokers so they know the jargon and the sales techniques and can find an honest inspector to protect you. Their fees can be negotiated on an hourly basis, which may cost less than the 1 percent of the purchase price that your attorney will charge.

Day 299

MOVING DAY!

Try to close on your house and move into it at some time other than the most popular months of May through August. These are the most expensive months, and professional movers are extremely overwhelmed then, especially on weekends. Get estimates from three companies and check their references with the Better Business Bureau. If the move is job-related, some of the expense may be tax-deductible, so keep records and receipts. Call 800–829–3676 for IRS publication #521 *Moving Expenses.*

Action Step:

Allied Van Lines, rated number one as a national and international moving company, offers *Guide to a Good Move,* a checklist to guide you through the planning process, which can be downloaded from its Web site at http://www.alliedvan.com. Or you can call a local office in your area and request a copy.

Day 300

PAYING OFF THE MORTGAGE

When you own your home you can count that as 100 percent equity on your asset statement and not worry about the bank anymore. Then it will really belong to you! Four ways to get rid of the mortgage as soon as possible:

Pay an extra $100 a month to shorten a 7 percent, 30-year mortgage to 21 years.

If you can't afford $100 a month, make one extra payment each year on the same mortgage and you can shorten the mortgage to 24 years and 7 months.

Make two extra mortgage payments per year and you will shorten the mortgage to 20 years.

Four extra mortgage payments will reduce your 30-year mortgage to 15 years.

Plan a mortgage-burning party but keep a copy of the mortgage satisfaction notice in your safe deposit box.

Day 301

REFINANCING—YES OR NO?

If you bought your house more than five years ago you probably have a mortgage rate that is closer to, if not above, 10 percent interest. Or you have an adjustable-rate mortgage and want to obtain another loan with different terms. Standard guidelines are that if mortgage rates fall more than 2 percent below your original interest rate, you should refinance. Refinancing means getting a brand-new mortgage, which could reduce monthly payments by $75–$100 a month on a $150,000 mortgage, or if your mortgage is more than ten years old and you have considerable equity, perhaps you should refinance for 15 years. Closing costs will still be at least 2 percent of the new loan amount. This is a numbers-crunching exercise to be done individually with a professional, but ask yourself these questions first:

Will I be staying in this house until retirement?

Is my income going to remain stable enough for higher payments if I get a 15-year mortgage at a lower interest rate?

Is it worth the additional fees and expense if I plan to sell within three years?

Action Step:

Use the refinancing calculator at http://www.kiplinger.com to get an idea of what can be saved by refinancing. Ask your lender if you can get a modification of the payment schedule and terms of your existing loan instead of refinancing.

FOUR

WEALTH
PROTECTION

INTRODUCTION

Unless you're very rich, the only way a responsible person can meet all your obligations is with insurance.

—Walter S. Kenton, Jr.

Investing is about taking risks. Insurance is about eliminating risk. Of course, you can't eliminate danger and accident from the world, but you can decide to protect yourself if it comes your way. You've committed so much time, energy, and thought to accumulating assets, don't gamble with them and with the people who depend on you by not protecting them at all or by not protecting them adequately. We will learn how to protect and insure your home, your paycheck, your car, your health, even your life. Insurance can't prevent small accidents or great tragedies from happening to you, the things you own, or the people you love, but it can sometimes prevent small accidents from turning into large tragedies, and it can certainly replace the value of what's lost.

Day 302

GETTING THE FACTS

Test your knowledge of insurance and your questions about how insurance works at the Web site for the insurance industry information center at http://www.life-line.org. The facts, figures, and useful data and the links from that site will be very enlightening and profitable for you—without talking to an insurance salesperson!

Day 303

FINANCIAL PEACE OF MIND

I finally know what distinguishes man from beasts; financial worries.

—Jules Renard

Life insurance has been around since the days of the early Roman Empire, when the legionnaires pledged a portion of their pay to a fund for the families of the soldiers who did not survive the various wars. As old as this concept is, buying insurance has become more complicated and confusing in the last two centuries since bankers and brokers decided to start investing the pool of premium payments while they waited to pay off policies. Let's keep it simple. The only reason to buy life insurance is to meet your obligations to your family in the event of your death. Before you talk to anyone about buying insurance, the critical question you should ask yourself is: "Who would starve or be homeless if I were to drop dead tomorrow?" If the answer is "no one," then you can skip the next few pages and go on to the next section of the book. You don't need life insurance. Regardless of what you may read, or what the agents may tell you, the only reason to purchase a policy is to replace your income in the household. If you have made a commitment to a life partner, business partner, elderly parent, spouse, or young children to provide the income necessary to sustain their lifestyle, then you need life insurance. Life insurance is not a savings plan. It is not an investment. It is not a hedge against inflation. It is not the place to put money for the children's education. There are far better investment choices than an insurance policy to meet your financial goals.

Action Step:

Review your savings and retirement plans to see how much income you would leave behind before you choose an amount for an insurance policy.

Day 304

THE GREAT DEBATE—WHOLE LIFE OR TERM?

Every insurance agent will tell you that your best choice is to buy whole life or universal life for the forced savings and the cash value. Don't believe them! Like stockbrokers, they have their agenda, too, which is to make money. The highest commissions are earned by salespersons selling whole life, but it is so expensive that the average breadwinner who needs at least $500,000 of life insurance cannot afford adequate coverage with a whole life policy. Forget the projections, the charts, the long columns of complex numbers and formulas! Ask for—no, demand—term insurance. Term life is like your homeowner's or auto insurance. You renew it each year, get the maximum amount you can afford with very few dollars—and the agent doesn't like that idea!

With adequate long-term planning you will need a large life insurance policy for only the early years of your life. While the mortgage is being paid off, the children are at home, and you're still building a retirement portfolio, you can't afford to put every dime into life insurance premiums. Get what you need while you need it but don't overpay for it, and let it lapse when you no longer need it.

If you're more comfortable having a "permanent" life insurance policy, search for a "low-load" policy such as the Veritas/Ameritas universal policies that are much more affordable for the average family but aren't available in all states. If you're fortunate enough to be in the military or related to someone in the military, you have access to one of the best insurance companies available. Call USAA Life in San Antonio, Texas, at 800–531–8000 and inquire about its life and disability policies.

Action Step:

As with investments, do some homework and get objective advice before you sign on the dotted line. Call Insurance Information, Inc., at 800–472–5800 for a review of your existing coverage for a fee of $50, and a recommendation of the best coverage available to you from up to three companies in your area.

Day 305

JUNK INSURANCE

Don't waste your money on these policies. Use the dollars instead for your retirement savings, college tuition savings, or your emergency savings plan.

1. Insurance on children. Unless your children provide income, use the $60–$75 for this special add-on to your policy for an Education IRA rather than for life insurance.
2. Dread disease insurance. Improve your overall medical coverage rather than waste money on special disease insurance. With all the exceptions and prohibitions, these policies don't pay off until you exhaust your other medical coverage. Unless you have a crystal ball that forecasts a cancer diagnosis, don't waste your money. Think positive and you'll die in your sleep after your 92nd birthday party.
3. Flight insurance. If you take 10 to 12 flights a year and buy this out of fear, a better use of your money would be an additional term insurance policy. Flight insurance is overpriced coverage.
4. Hospital indemnity insurance. The insurer promises to pay $100 a day while you're in the hospital, but with today's HMO coverage you probably won't be hospitalized more than three to five days.
5. Credit card insurance. This protects the bank's interest, not yours. The overall cost of this is very expensive. Carry enough life insurance and let your family decide when and how they want to manage your remaining debts.

Day 306

SHOPPING AROUND FOR LIFE INSURANCE

Before you begin calling agents and brokers to get coverage, spend some time doing a bit of homework and collecting some free information to learn how to get the most inexpensive coverage available. Several national insurance quote services are available and will charge you nothing for their services. All you have to do is phone the company and give it your vitals: name, address, age, gender, and how much life insurance coverage you think you'll need. Within three to four days you'll get a package in the mail that will give you the breakdown on at least five different insurance companies in your area that can provide reasonably priced term insurance for you. The best part of this deal is that no salesperson will call you!

Action Step:

Phone at least one of the following quote services to get a proposal for comparison with your current insurance costs. Don't be surprised if you have never heard of many of the companies that are presented to you. There are more than 3,000 national insurance companies, and many of them have good ratings but are not that well-known.

ConsumerQuote USA	800–552–SAVE (7283) or http://www.consumerquote.com
Direct Quote	800–845–3853
MasterQuote	800–337–5433 or http://www.Masterquote.com
Quotesmith	800–431–1147 or http://www.termquotes.com
Veritas/Ameritas*	800–552–3553

*Low-load universal life insurance.

Day 307

YOUR INSURANCE COMPANY'S HEALTH

Don't let low premiums be the basis for choosing an insurance company, especially in the health and life insurance area. With the payment problems of Oxford Health Coverage and the demise of companies like Mutual Benefit Life and Executive Life, your first concern should be whether they can deliver on what they promised. Check out your company's financial health by looking at the ratings reports from four sources.

1. A. M. Best, http://www.ambest.com, or use the *Best's Review* in the library.
2. Duff & Phelps, 312–368–3657.
3. Moody's Investor's Services, 212–553–0377.
4. Standard and Poor's, 212–208–1527.

Day 308

HONEST ANSWERS ABOUT BUYING INSURANCE

You can get quick simple answers to all your questions about every aspect of life, health, disability, and homeowners insurance at the National Insurance Helpline. This free service is maintained by the Insurance Information Institute at 800–942–4242 during normal business hours. Another source of straight answers is:

National Insurance Consumer Organization (NICO)
121 North Payne Street
Alexandria, VA 22314
703–549–8050

Action Step:

Two publications from NICO will guide you through the process without obligation. *A Buyer's Guide to Insurance* for $3.50 with a self-addressed stamped envelope and *Taking the Bite Out of Insurance*, for $12.95.

Day 309

HOW MUCH LIFE INSURANCE DO YOU NEED?

Industry pundits tell you to buy from five to eight times your current income, but that formula doesn't work for everyone. The average policy sale is $100,000, which isn't nearly enough for a young family with a mortgage, children, and credit card bills. Think about it. After burial expenses of about $5,000, $95,000 would barely replace your income in the family for three years. Is that enough to take care of mortgage payments, a car note, the normal cost of bringing up your children, their medical and dental bills, and future tuition payments? Definitely not. The average family breadwinner needs at least $500,000 in life insurance protection to replace his or her paycheck for at least ten years. In the event of a sudden demise, this money should be moved into some income-producing investments that would provide at least $40,000 to $50,000 a year. Take a look at your total savings, retirement plan, private insurance, and group life coverage available through your employer, to determine how many years' income could be replaced by those total assets. Each person's needs are as different as his or her fingerprints. The real answer depends on three items in your financial profile:

1. Your yearly income and how many years are left until the children are out of the house.
2. The standard of living the family will want to maintain if you
   were absent.
3. The amount of debts that need to be paid off.

Action Step:

Review your own assets, debts, retirement plans, and other obligations before you settle on an amount of coverage. Use
http://www.smartcalc.com to help you determine how much life
insurance you need before you call a broker. You can also get objective answers without a sales pitch from the customer service reps at
Insuremarket at 800–695–0011.

Day 310

THE "SINGLE" FOCUS

If you're young, single, and have no dependents, then your main
insurance concerns should be a health policy and a very strong disability policy. If you're under 35, there is a 65 percent chance that
you'll experience an accident or long-term illness that will keep you
out of work for at least six months and possibly for two years. And
the bills don't stop when you're incapacitated. Social Security won't
take care of you, because less than 30 percent of Social Security disability applications are approved. The rules are so restrictive that it is
nearly impossible to receive. There are a few more grim statistics: 48
percent of all mortgage foreclosures occur because the homeowner
did not have sufficient disability coverage; 36 percent of all small
businesses fail for the same reason. After you use up your sick leave,
most employers provide workers' compensation, but that may offer
only short-term disability coverage for up to 90 days at approxi-

mately half your current salary. Longer payments require lengthy applications, and compensation board hearings that may take six to nine months to approve a payment plan. Disability insurance replaces up to 70 percent of your income if you're ill or injured for a lengthy period of time.

Action Step:

Call the human resources department of your company and find out how the company's disability and workers' compensation coverage works. This will give you an idea of how much you will need to keep in a savings account for an emergency.

Day 311

GUARANTEED SAVINGS ON YOUR HEALTH EXPENSES

The five leading causes of death in the United States in 1997 were heart disease, diabetes, cancer, strokes from high blood pressure and hypertension, and AIDS. Each of these diseases is related to diet, exercise, and behavior, which means your health is in your hands. Change your behavior, improve your health.

Affirmation:

My health is also my wealth and I am worth the effort.

Action Step:

Check with your insurance company to see if it will give discounts on your premiums if you lose weight, stop smoking, and lower your cholesterol.

Day 312

PROPERTY INSURANCE

If you own a house, you need property insurance or you were required to buy it when you got your mortgage. If you haven't reviewed your policy in the last few years, you may be overinsured or underinsured. Real estate values have increased dramatically in the last five years in most states. Have your insurance company do a reappraisal and find out what it would cost to rebuild your house in today's dollars. Make sure that the policy itemizes the appraisal and separates out the cost of the land from the cost of the house. Property insurance should cover only the building–not the ground it sits on.

A homeowner's policy should be sufficient to replace up to 90 percent of the value of the property but not the land. Some policies provide guaranteed replacement cost coverage with an inflation protection option. You should review the amount of protection and adjust it every two to three years.

To cover the contents of your house or apartment, you must provide an inventory list of the contents to assure yourself of correct protection. You can get insurance to cover up to 80 percent of the value of all the items in the house. Write down serial numbers for the television, VCR, microwave, stereo, computer, and any other such items in case of theft. Make a copy for your insurance agent and keep the original inventory list in your safe deposit box. You don't want the list to get lost in the house in case of a fire or water damage.

Day 313

TEN WAYS TO SAVE ON
HOME OWNERS INSURANCE

1. Raise your deductible. A $500 deductible can reduce your premium as much as 10–12 percent. Raise it $1,000 for a 24 percent savings. Your savings should cover the difference.

2. Look for group coverage. Business associations and alumni organizations can get 10–15 percent discounts on rates. Ask your association's director if it offers such a benefit.

3. Improve your home security. Dead-lock bolts, smoke detectors, and burglar alarms can reduce premiums by 5–15 percent.

4. Insure the house, not the land under it. Land does not disappear in a flood or fire. Review your appraised value and deduct the portion allotted for land.

5. Ask for discounts. If you are retired, a senior citizen, or work at home, you can probably get a 10 percent discount.

6. Stay with one company. Longstanding policyholders get a 5 percent discount on annual premiums after two to three years.

7. Get all insurance—home, auto, life, liability—from one company. Purchasing several policies from one company can give you leverage to negotiate a 5–10 percent discount on each.

8. Stop smoking. Cigarettes cause 23,000 home fires each year. Being a nonsmoker can save another 5–10 percent discount.

9. Buy a new house. New structures have fewer problems with wiring and plumbing, which can save you 8–15 percent on your premiums.

10. Shop around and compare policies each year near your renewal date. Call three other companies for rate comparisons or visit http://www.insuremarket.com, which will give you comparable quotes for up to five companies in your geographic area.

Day 314

SHOPPING FOR CAR INSURANCE

Auto insurance varies from state to state, neighborhood to neighborhood, but don't let that dismay you. The Ohio-based Progressive
Auto Insurance Company has links to auto insurance agents in 47
states (except New Jersey, Massachusetts, and South Carolina) and
provides a free comparison quote by mail for up to three companies in
your zip code. It can be reached at 800–AUTO–PRO (288–6776) or
at its Web site: http://www.auto-insurance.com.

Day 315

CUT THE COST OF COLLISION AND
COMPREHENSIVE INSURANCE

"Nine Ways to Save on Auto Insurance" is the most popular
brochure that is offered, free of charge, by the Insurance Information
Institute. It will give you some useful insights into the fine points of
how insurance rates are set. It also gives the highlights of the crash
tests of the National Highway Safety Board, which determines how
the model of your car affects your insurance rate. You can print out a
copy of the booklet at http://www.iii.com. Read it before buying a car.

Day 316

$$$—Savings Tip:

If your car is more than five years old, consider joining the AAA
Plus program. For an additional $32 a year above the basic member-

ship fee, you can be guaranteed the protection of a friendly tow truck operator in every one of the 50 states—one who won't drain your wallet and ruin your vacation if something goes wrong with your car. The AAA Plus Program allows you up to 100 miles of towing free of charge instead of the usual three miles. Use it once and it will have paid for itself.

Day 317

"AM I COVERED?"

Hurricanes, earthquakes, and floods are natural disasters that no one can predict and we all pray we never have to experience, but they happen. The people in North Dakota didn't plan on getting washed out of their homes in the spring of 1998. Nor the families on the coast of North Carolina or in the fire-ravaged area around Orlando. What you may not realize is that your normal homeowners' insurance policy does not cover the cost of home replacement after natural disasters. You may be covered for fire, but not for floods and earthquakes, unless you specifically requested it in your policy application and paid extra for such protection.

Only your insurance agent can answer the question of whether you are covered. Don't wait until tragedy has struck to make the call to find out if you're covered. Since many private insurance companies charge exorbitant rates for this kind of protection, the federal government provides flood insurance at reasonable rates based on where you live and the historical record of previous natural disasters in your area.

Action Step:

Call 800–CALL–FLOOD, ext. 696, to find out the cost of such coverage in your area, or look at the Web site at http://www. fema. gov/nfip.

Day 318

CREATING EVIDENCE

$$$—Savings Tip:

Make a videotape of the interior of your home and the various possessions that you want to protect. The insurance agency can't argue with you about the contents of your home and their quality if it can see the dining room suite, the bedroom furniture, the microwave oven, and the Persian rug in the living room. This smart move can add 15–20 percent to your claim in case of fire, flood, or theft.

Day 319

REVIEW AND REASSESS

Have you reviewed your insurance needs and current coverage and determined how much more (or less) you need? If you need additional coverage, especially life or disability, start investigating where to get it right away. If you are already paying too much in premiums call your insurance companies and ask about lowering the premiums. Yes, you need the coverage but you don't need to overpay for it. What you save on insurance should go into savings, investments, and your retirement plan. This is how millionaires become wealthy! Pay as little as possible for the necessities.

Day 320

RENTER'S PROTECTION

Lydia and Carlos just moved into their first apartment as newlyweds. One evening, a candle that was left burning didn't just fizzle out as expected when they left the apartment after a party to go out for a late supper. They came home to smoke, charred furniture, water damage, and an uninhabitable apartment. Your landlord is only required to provide insurance coverage for accidents that occur on the property that result from building fixtures that are his or her responsibility, such as a pipe that bursts in the closet and ruins half your wardrobe or a cabinet that falls off the wall in the kitchen and destroys all your dishes. However, you'll need your own policy to cover theft, fire, or water damage that is your fault. It is your responsibility to have your own separate policy. You can estimate that the average cost for renter's insurance is $10 per $1,000 per year, or $100 a year for $10,000 protection.

Action Step:

Call three different property insurance companies for estimates of the cost of protecting your assets. Three nationally known companies that offer excellent rates are Allstate, http://www.allstate.com; Liberty Mutual, http://www.libertymutual.com; and Geico, http://www.geico.com. Try Geico first at 800–861–8380. It is the only company that gives quotes by phone or Internet.

Day 321

THE HOME OFFICE

If you have anything that comes close to a home office full of the latest electronic gadgets, equipment, and toys, such as a laptop or desktop, software programs, a fax machine, a flatbed scanner, a copying machine, an answering machine, and a cell phone, you may exceed the limit of what your company is willing to pay to insure these items in a home office environment. Check your homeowner's or renter's policy to see what the maximum payout is on such items. It may be only $1,500, which won't replace your whole system in case of fire, theft, or water damage. Since the value of computers and technical equipment depreciates so quickly, some companies may refuse to provide any supplemental coverage at all.

If you have office equipment for yourself it's worth asking your insurer for a special floater for your high-ticket items, otherwise the total replacement value on all such equipment in the home is limited to $2,000.

Action Step:

Call your insurance agent and ask for a special rider on your policy for your most expensive items. The added cost of about $150 a year will help you sleep at night.

Day 322

$$$—Savings Tip:

If you purchased a home in the last five years with a down payment of less than 10 percent of the purchase price, you were required to buy PMI—personal mortgage insurance—payable to the bank. This extra coverage is probably costing you as much as $400–$500 a year. If the equity in your home after several years of payments is now more than 20 percent of the appraised value of your home, and your credit rating with the bank is still good—meaning no missed or late payments in the last few years—then you can request that the PMI be discontinued. This can shave an extra $40 or $50 a month off your mortgage payment. It's another place to find the dollars you need to invest each month in a retirement plan.

Day 323

STATE INSURANCE POOLS

No national regulatory agency like the FDIC exists for insurance companies. Each state sets its own rules. Companies must join a pool of other insurance companies and contribute to a collective cash cushion that protects investors in the event that one of the companies gets into financial difficulty and goes bankrupt. This is not a government program and is under a "voluntary" regulation arrangement, so even though each state has an insurance commissioner and various state laws that dictate how they operate, no separate government body like FDIC will step in and reimburse you for the full payout on your policy if your insurance company goes under. Rule and regulations vary from state to state, so you need to find out how they operate in your state. Get the number for your state insurance department from the Web site for the Insurance Information Institute at http://www.iii.org or call the insurance hotline at 800–942–4242.

Day 324

SPECIAL RIDERS

If you keep special items at home that would be expensive or difficult to replace, such as furs, jewelry, paintings, antiques, and coin or stamp collections, you should inform your insurance company and request a special floater. Without this supplementary coverage the insurance company will limit your loss to a preset amount that is quite low—about $2,500 on silverware or gold, $1,000 on furs or jewelry, and only $200 on any cash in the house or a stamp and/or coin collection. Regardless of what precautions you take with alarm systems, iron gates, and other electronic security measures, you may still find it difficult to get sufficient coverage for your home, office, or business, depending on location. Check with your state insurance department and, where necessary, you may be able to get coverage through the Federal Crime Insurance Program, 800–638–8780.

Day 325

"NOTHING PERSONAL, BUT YOU'RE BEING SUED"

Your best friend Pam thinks she's found the man of her dreams, a young surgeon, but she want your opinion. You invite them over for dinner and after a great evening together, just before they leave your cat makes a mad dash across the living room, causing the young doctor to trip on the loose edge of a throw rug. He hits his head and fractures his wrist on the edge of your coffee table and ends up in the emergency room for three hours. You offer to pay his medical expenses, which he declines and assures you he'll be fine. Three weeks later, you are served with a summons from an attorney. Pam's "intended" is suing you for $2 million since he will be unable to work in his chosen profession for at least the next couple of years. With the litigious society that we now live in, don't be shocked or angry at Pam. If you have renter's or homeowner's insurance you also need umbrella liability protection since you are responsible for any such accidents that occur on your premises.

Action Step:

Check your homeowner's policy to see how much coverage you have for such accidents and if there is some additional liability coverage. For $1 million coverage for everything from dog bites to personal liability suits you will pay approximately $100 a year.

FIVE

WEALTH PRESERVATION

INTRODUCTION

RETIREMENT

*The irony is that investing for retirement is not rocket science.
It's vision and diligence.*

—Dave Ramsey

Preserving wealth is about your own retirement and the estate that you'll pass along after you go. It's natural to think that these topics are relevant only to those in the latter half of their lives (or third, or quarter, or tenth—depending on how much denial you're in), but it's simply not true. You can't wait until you're 50 or even 40 to think about this period of your life. Nobody ever starts out in life with the goal of ending up in poverty and penury, but that's exactly where you'll end up if you don't give serious attention to planning for this stage of life. This is one of the most important periods of your life, but if you don't take it seriously and include it in your long-term plans, reaching 70 could be financially painful and unpleasant. You can't afford to wait another day. At 70 it's too late to do any saving; you'll end up with a minimum-wage job at a fast-food drive-through window to supplement your Social Security check. Is that direct enough?

Likewise, though estate planning may become more complex if you're older, have more money, or have complicated family relations, wills are for *everyone*. An 18-year-old with a child needs a will. So does a single 25-year-old with a new condo. Writing a will is essential if you want any control over how your assets are dispensed. And the process of writing one is an excellent way to take stock of where you are, what you have, and what you might still like to do

WEALTH HAPPENS ONE DAY AT A TIME

about that. Writing a will also give you the opportunity to make a statement of how you would like your final passage out of this life to be arranged. Death does not discriminate. The desire for death with dignity transcends gender, race, culture, and financial status. Straightforward handling of the legal and financial issues surrounding your death and the transfer of your assets will make your funeral and the dispersal of your estate less agonizing for your survivors. And knowing that you've planned for it will give you peace of mind for however many, many, many years you still have ahead to enjoy what you have accumulated and the people you want to share it with.

Day 326

JAMES CHATMAN

James Chatman, born in Atkins, Arkansas, worked hard all his life, going from field work to the U.S. Air Force, all the way to the CEO of his own business. Hard work was Chatman's middle name. He worked his way through St. Louis University, earning a degree in economics, and then spent 24 years in the U.S. Air Force, never losing his drive for learning and work. In the interim he took time to get married and had four children. After leaving the armed services at age 58, not one to rest on his laurels, Chatham decided to set up a business. With his years of experience and contacts, he founded Technology Applications, Inc., a consulting firm for government agencies. He put all his energy into building this business, paying careful attention to his books. After ten years his firm was grossing revenues of $40 million a year. At 70, Chatman sold the company for a handsome profit and set up a $400,000 fund at the Northern Virginia Community Foundation to create a Grandfathers' Group to mentor young black boys. Now Chatman could help young boys develop the all-important work ethic he had always lived by.

Chatman is living proof that hard work, knowledge, and ambition don't end when you qualify for Social Security. His attitude and energy combined to make him a winner regardless of his age. His story is an example of using the know-how you have already acquired in a particular field to open your business. It is also important to save your money as you build your business. Use solid bookkeeping practices. And recognize, like many of the folks mentioned in this book, that if you invest your energy up front you can relax in the end.

Affirmation:

Retirement is not the end of my creative years!

Day 327

RETIREMENT MYTHS

1. Your taxes will be lower! Don't believe it. If you saved and planned carefully your income will still be in the 28 percent tax bracket if you have more than $15,000 a year.
2. Your living expenses will be lower! Although there are many discounts for seniors the budget may not change as much as you think if you haven't paid off your mortgage and other debts. What you don't spend on business lunches will be spent on other items like travel and medical care not covered by insurance.
3. You can work and collect Social Security without consequences! You will still have to pay income taxes as long as you are alive and earning money. If you start collecting Social Security and work part-time you will lose $1 of benefits for every $3 of earnings over $14,500.

The rules change after 65 so review your income sources and plan your budget and expenses with a new approach. A free government booklet, "Retirement," available from the Social Security Administration at 800–772–1213, will advise you on the rules of this new lifestyle.

Day 328

SACRIFICE NOW OR SUFFER LATER

Youth is wasted on the young.

—Oscar Wilde

Michelle and Marcus are twins who are as different as night and day. When they graduated from college at age 22, Michelle started a career as a computer technician and was careful to stay out of debt, begin paying off her student loans, tithe 10 percent of her income, put money into her 401(k) plan, and invest $1,000 a year for the next ten years in a mutual fund with a 10 percent total return. Marcus laughed at the idea of saving and investing and spent every dime from his career in the music business on clothes, cars, lavish vacations, and an endless string of girlfriends who wanted to eat out every night. At their parents' anniversary party, Michelle told Marcus how her $10,000 has now grown to $17,531 but she will be getting married soon and will change her investment strategy. Marcus realized that at 32, he wasn't getting any younger and decided that it's time for him to get serious about saving and investing for the future. He opened a similar savings account, putting away $1,000 a year for the next 20 years. When the twins got together for their 50th birthday celebration, Michelle and Marcus compared investment account balances. Her $10,000 had turned into $117,940. Even though he invested the same amount for twice as much time, Michael only had $63,002 in his account.

Affirmation:

I will start automatic investing and be consistent with my investment program.

Action Step:

Open an automatic wealth-builder account with American Century mutual funds, 800–345–2021, which has a $50 monthly minimum. You can find a list of its funds and returns on its Web site at http://www.americancentury.com.

Day 328

START EARLY—QUIT EARLY

While we consider where to begin, it is already too late.

—Latin Proverb

At 33, Helen Matthews's life is right where she wants it to be—she is a successful television producer with a six-figure salary. As far as retirement goes, Helen is ahead of schedule. Ten years ago, she didn't think twice and was smart enough to begin contributing the maximum amount to her 401(k) plan since she was lucky enough to be debt-free when she started the job. She has continued at the maximum contribution level each year, picking up 6 percent in matching funds from her employer. With a diversified investment plan of 50 percent in aggressive stocks, 25 percent in blue-chip stocks, 10 percent in international stocks, and 15 percent in corporate and government bonds, she has earned from 18.2 percent to 23.4 percent on her 401(k) plan investments and has accumulated more than $200,000. At these rates, and with her continuous investments, Helen will have more than $3 million when she can finally withdraw some of this retirement money at age 65. She has bought herself a two-bedroom condo, and is paying off her mortgage early. Helen also divides $500 a month among seven different dividend reinvestment plans contributing to a tax-deferred annuity. If she continues her current investment strategy, even if the stock market gives meager returns of 10 percent year, Helen will easily achieve her goal of being debt-free and having $1 million before her 50th birthday.

Action Step:

Get a copy of a free brochure called "Eight Ways to Make $1 Million With Your 401(k) Plan" from the National Association of 401(k) Investors by sending a self-addressed stamped envelope to: Patty Roberts, President, National Association of 401(k) Investors, P.O. Box 410755, Melbourne, FL 32941.

Day 329

READING THE FINE PRINT—AGAIN!!!

The least-read books in the country are not The Rise and Fall of the Byzantine Empire *or* The Repair and Maintenance of the Edsel. *Topping both are most company* Summary Plan Descriptions *describing the 401(k) plan.*

—Jim Jorgensen

The rules and regulations of your 401(k) plan may seem like great sleep-inducing material, but at the very least you should take them to bed with you, so that even if you fall asleep on them, there is a chance you will absorb the rules of how you can use these retirement options for yourself. Here's what you need to understand:

1. Plans are set up by employers, not you, therefore the menu of investment choices is weighted to benefit them.

2. Employers are not required to match your contribution to your 401(k) plan, but most add 50 cents for each dollar that you contribute. To take advantage of this "free money" and get every dollar you can, you have to make the first move by having regular deductions taken from your paycheck.

3. When you set aside money for your 401(k) plan, you don't pay taxes on those dollars in the plan until you withdraw the money in the next 20 or 30 years. That means your current taxes are reduced, based on your reduced income.

4. This is the only retirement plan that will legally allow you to put away up to $10,000 a year for your future well-being.

Action Step:

Many employers offer annual or quarterly enrollment meetings to review and discuss the company's 401(k) plan. Find out when the next one will be held and sign up for it. The week before the meeting force yourself to go through the plan description book with a Magic Marker and highlight all the statements and phrases you don't understand. Be prepared to ask what they mean. Don't be embarrassed. Everyone else in the room will probably thank you.

Day 330

RETIRE A MILLIONAIRE!

I have all the money I'll ever need as long as I die by next Thursday.

—Ronnie Schell

You never know how long you will live or how much money you will need. Sure you want to retire as soon as possible, but given a rate of 3 percent inflation, every $1,000 of expenses that you have now

will cost $ 1,314 in ten years. Unless your investments are signifi-
cantly outpacing inflation-by growing at a rate of more than 10 percent—you could run out of money before you run out of steam. You
also need to consider that the average life expectancy is getting longer
as we all take vitamins, exercise, eat better, and learn how to control
the diseases of aging like diabetes, blood pressure, and heart disease.
The average man who is in good health today at age 50 can expect to
still be here at 82. The average woman who is in good health today at
age 50 can expect to live until 90. If you don't want to outlive your
money, you must look for consistent investment returns that will
continue to grow and give you income beyond the day you get your
last paycheck. Consistently investing of $200 a month in a growth
equity mutual fund with a 12 percent return for the next 30 years
will make you a millionaire.

Three Five-Star Growth Mutual Funds
That Will Never Disappoint You

Fund	Five-Year Average Return	Phone Number
Columbia Growth	29.6 percent	800–547–1707
Dreyfus Appreciation	40.21 percent	800–645–6561
Fidelity Fund	23.42 percent	800–544–8888

Action Step:

Compare the long-term return you have gotten over the last few
years and consider switching your investments if these long-term
returns appeal to you. Visit the Web site for *Mutual Funds* magazine
online at http://www.mfmag.com for the most up-to-date, objective
evaluations of the 9,000+ mutual funds now available.

Day 331

REVERSE MORTGAGES

Reverse mortgages are traditionally viewed as the chemo-therapy of the personal finance world.

—Stephen Pollan

The biggest expense for retirees is mortgage payments, so one major financial goal should be paying off your mortgage before you get your last paycheck. There's a wonderful sigh of relief when you don't have to make that payment to the bank anymore. There's another reason to celebrate a mortgage-free retirement. If you reach 62 and don't have a sufficient monthly income to support yourself, you may qualify for another financial advantage that comes with aging: a reverse mortgage in which the money you put into your house is loaned back to you. If an extra $500 a month will help you maintain your independence, look into this option as a means of enhancing your income. Several government programs sponsored by HUD and Fannie Mae, the government mortgage company, appraise your house, determine its value, and arrange for a monthly payment to be deposited to your bank account in the same way that your Social Security check is automatically deposited for you. The amount of each monthly payment, the length of the mortgage, and other provisions will be decided based on the value of your home and the length of time you will probably need the income. Loan advances from a reverse mortgage are not treated as income for tax purposes, so a reverse mortgage will not put you in a higher tax bracket. The one sticky problem is that if your heirs want the house that carries the mortgage, they will have to assume the responsibility for paying it off after they inherit the property. Otherwise, the bank has the right to sell the house on the open market.

Action Step:

Get a free brochure called "Home-Made Money—Consumer's Guide to Home Equity Conversion," from the AARP Home Equity Information Center, 601 E Street, N.W., Washington, DC 20049. The National Center for Home Equity Conversion (NCHEC) offers a list of reverse-mortgage lenders. Send $1 and an SASE to NCHEC, 7373 14th Street West, Suite 115, Apple Valley, MN 55124. Fannie Mae, the U.S. government mortgage agency, will also provide information on the pros and cons of reverse mortgages. Call 800–732–6643 for details.

Day 332

SOCIAL SECURITY

In spite of the cost of living, it's still popular.

—Kathleen Norris

Beginning in the year 2000 you won't have to call or write to the Social Security Administration to see what it has in its files and how much (or how little!) will be coming to you when you retire. You'll automatically receive an annual statement of your Social Security retirement benefits telling you what the estimated monthly payment will be when you reach 65, based on what has accumulated so far. The shock of seeing that you'll only be getting $437 a month may be the wake-up call you need to get serious about exploring other options and putting away more of your own money in other retirement plans. If you're between 40 and 47, you fall into that "iffy" category of wage-earners who may or may not find a Social Security trust fund to collect from. The other bad news for the under-35 age group is that after 2000 the earliest date for receiving retirement income has now been moved up to age 70. This is partly because the Social Security system wants to delay paying retirement benefits as long as possible. The other reason is that most of us are living a lot longer than the government ever expected when Social Security was set up, therefore it wants to shorten the number of years that it is paying out benefits to you by having you work longer.

Action Step:

Don't wait for the government to send it if you're curious now. Write to: Social Security Administration, Department of Health and Human Services, Baltimore, MD 21235, and request a "Statement of Earnings" (Form SSA–7004) or call   800–772–1213. You can also request a Statement of Pension Benefits by logging onto the Web site at http://www.socsec.gov.

Day 333

HOW MUCH DO YOU NEED?

I have all the money I need unless I buy something.

—Jackie Mason

Sure the joke can make you chuckle, but don't overlook the truth in it if you haven't gotten serious about investing for retirement. How long will you live? Who knows, but medical statistics show that if you manage to live until 55 with no indications of serious illness, you have a fairly good chance of making it to 85 before you say your last goodbyes to your grandchildren. If you have nightmares about eating cat food and bussing tables at Burger King in your old age, that should be enough motivation to get you to start planning for the inevitable: the day you can no longer work. You want to look forward to a comfortable financial future, so don't joke about not living long enough to spend all your money. Don't forget that you have to accumulate it in order to spend it. Estimates of how much you'll need vary from $500,000 to $1 million.

Action Step:

Order a retirement planning software program from one of the mutual fund families. Those listed below, along with many other investment firms, offer inexpensive programs (priced from $15 to $18) that will show you how much you need to put away each month starting now to avoid working at Burger King or baby-sitting in your old age.

1. Fidelity, 800–526–7251 or www.fidelity.com
2. Vanguard, 800–523–8797 www.vanguard.com
3. Dreyfus, 800–782–6620 www.dreyfus.com
4. American Century, 800–345–2021 or
   http://www.americancentury.com.

Day 334

ENDURANCE

Patience allows you to keep your wealth.

—Dave Ramsey

Americans seem to be allergic to the idea of delayed gratification. We want everything done yesterday or at least instantly. Who invented instant coffee, instant breakfast, an overnight success? What you don't want is instant wealth. Saving for retirement is building wealth the slow way. If you want to retire as a millionaire, start early. Assuming an 11 percent average annual return on your investment, if you start investing $20 a week at age 20, by 65 you'll have that million. If you wait until age 30, you'll have to invest $56.33 a week to achieve the same results. Time is on your side if you use it wisely.

Age	Annual Investment	Total Invested at 65
20	$1,025	$46,125
25	$1,720	$68,800
30	$2,920	$102,200
35	$5,000	$150,000
40	$8,770	$219,250
45	$15,600	$312,000
50	$29,000	$435,000
55	$60,000	$600,000
60	$161,000	$805,000

FINAL EARNINGS = $1 MILLION

Affirmation:

I am patient and gentle with myself as I gradually work toward my financial well-being.

Action Step:

Ask your parents and grandparents about the cost of living and how it has changed in the last 20 to 30 years. That should give you some perspective on why it's important to invest for long-term growth.

Day 335

BORROWING FROM YOUR 401(K) PLAN

Never consider borrowing from your 401(k) unless you have absolutely no other choice. Even then, it is not a good idea at all since it is probably the only retirement money you will have. That's why the IRS rules deliberately make it difficult to get access to this money, although it isn't impossible. Legally, you are allowed to borrow from your 401(k) for three reasons: unexpected medical expenses, tuition for a college education, and a down payment on a first home.

Employers will set up an automatic repayment plan, deducting the payments from your paycheck, with interest. If the money is not paid back within five years, or you leave the job before the repayment plan is completed, you face a 20 percent tax penalty as well as taxes on the funds withdrawn. Although hardships are allowed and expected, careful planning will protect you from having to make this choice.

Action Step:

Sit down with your benefits counselor, a calculator, and your monthly budget to see if this is a wise idea before you take the money out. Open a money market account and start a consistent savings plan outside the 401(k) plan to cover emergencies.

Day 336

REVIEW AND REASSESS

Take another look at that Social Security chart. When were you born and when can you start collecting? If you haven't already done so, call the Social Security Administration to request your Personal Earnings Benefit Statement today.

Day 337

AARP

I never wanted to be 65 until I got to 64.

—Phyllis Diller

The American Association of Retired Persons has a talent for letting you know that you're reaching middle age and need to think about the latter half of your life. It somehow manages to find you shortly after your 50th birthday and invites you to join its membership. Since aging is unavoidable, take advantage of its resources and collective power. AARP is the largest organization that does advocacy work for senior citizens across the country. The most economical way to join is for a ten-year term, which will cost only $50. The magazine for members, *Modern Maturity*, is the best investment you can get for the money, with advice on health and financial issues, relocation to other states, and so on.

Action Step:

Call 800–424–3410 for a membership application or sign up through the Web site at http://www.aarp.org.

Day 338

SOCIAL SECURITY RETIREMENT AGE LIST

While the traditional expectation is to retire at age 65, the Social Security Administration may have a surprise for you. It has created a new schedule for paying out the benefits that may or may not still be there by the time you retire. Here's the schedule for qualifying for retirement benefits as of 1998.

Year Born	Retirement Age
1960 and later	67
1959	66 years and 10 months
1958	66 years and 8 months
1957	66 years and 6 months
1956	66 years and 4 months
1955	66 years and 2 months
1943 to 1954	66

1942	65 years and 10 months
1941	65 years and 8 months
1940	65 years and 6 months
1939	65 years and 4 months
1938	65 years and 2 months
1937 and earlier	65

Action Step:

Make a note on some long-term future calendar when these dates will be important to you in your retirement planning.

Day 339

PENSION PROTECTION

If you're one of the lucky people who is covered by an old-fashioned defined-benefit plan where your employer has been putting money away for you over the last 30 years you are truly blessed. But don't take any chances on how safe your money is. Check with the Pension Benefit Guaranty Corporation, an industry-funded insurance program, that protects your future retirement dollars up to $33,136.32 as of 1997 for a single worker who retires at age 65. Note that PBGC does not cover all company benefits that you may expect to receive, such as health, life and disability insurance. As you approach age 60, start examining your lifestyle, your income and expenses, and investigate how your pension plan will allow you to make withdrawals. If you are a widow and are concerned about your spouse's pension, contact the following agencies that can assist you with your rights and how to proceed to collect what's coming to you.

1. Pension Rights Center, 202–296–3776.
2. AARP Pension Advisory Center, 202–434–2277.

3. National Center for Retirement Benefits, 800–666–1000.
4. U.S. Department of Labor, Pension and Welfare Benefits Administration, 202–219–8771.

Action Step:

Order the free publication, *Protect Your Pension*, 800–998–7542, or get it through the Web site at http://www.dol.gov/dol/pwba.

Day 340

EXTRA RETIREMENT SAVINGS

Put money in thy purse.

—William Shakespeare

If you're lucky enough to collect Social Security when you retire, you have to be prepared for one painful truth: It will cover only about one-third of your living expenses. The current maximum payout is 42 percent of your current income if you earn $22,000 or less. If your salary is $55,000 or more, your maximum payment will be only 27 percent of your current income. No matter how much you earn or contribute to the Social Security retirement system, the maximum amount that you can collect is $65,400 each year. After you swallow this truth, the next step is to decide how you plan to make up the difference. If you're starting late, you should put as much money as you possibly can into your 401(k) plan or whatever program is available to you through your employer. If that won't be enough, it's time to consider some other retirement savings options.

Annuities are tax-deferred savings and investment products offered by insurance companies. They come in four basic flavors:

1. Fixed. Like a certificate of deposit with an interest rate that changes each year and is locked in until the following year. No taxes are paid on the earnings until you withdraw them.
2. Variable. Investing in bonds and equity mutual funds under the guise of the insurance company with no promises or guarantees regarding earnings, which are still tax-deferred until withdrawn. Variable annuities carry heavy annual maintenance fees, commissions, and mortality charges, along with surrender fees that make you stay locked into the plan for five to seven years.
3. Immediate. Drop in a lump sum, calculate a life expectancy date, and they will start sending you a regular monthly income within six weeks. You pay taxes on the amount that is withdrawn, not the accumulated earnings that are still growing in the plan.
4. Single-premium. Make one large payment, leave it there indefinitely, and don't touch it until you want to or until you're 80, when most insurance companies will insist that you start spending some of the tax-deferred dollars.

Action Step:

Look at your projected retirement needs and add this additional investment option if (1) you're starting late, and (2) you won't need to touch this cash for at least ten years. The surrender charges and penalties can wipe out any earnings that you accumulate in a shorter time period. Order a copy of *Annuity and Life Insurance Shopper* ($14) from 800–872–6684. This quarterly publication evaluates the health, safety, structure, and benefits of over 1,800 different types of annuities from fixed and variable to deferred and immediate, offered by over 60 insurance companies.

Day 341

ROTH IRAS

Roth IRAs are a new retirement savings option that has been created for "late starters" in the retirement investing game, which covers most Americans. As of 1998, you can add an additional $2,000 a year to a new kind of retirement account; the only difference is you do not get a tax deduction off your current income for the investment. The best thing about Roth IRAs is that if you leave the money in the account for more than five years, you can withdraw your principal and your earnings *tax-free*—that's not a typo! This is the best gift Congress has ever offered so before they wake up and change their minds, take advantage of this lucrative loophole for your long-term benefit. For young home buyers, the other advantage is that you can put away the $2,000 a year and withdraw tax-free up to $10,000 after five years to use as a down payment on a house. Any good growth mutual fund is an excellent place to invest this money.

Action Step:

Any bank or brokerage firm will happily send you an application and a brochure that will help you to decide where to invest that $2,000.

Day 342

ROLLOVERS AND DISTRIBUTIONS

Leaving a job where you have a 401(k) plan requires another decision about retirement money: Should you leave your money in the plan and let the company continue to manage it, or move it to a self-directed account at a bank or brokerage firm? If you don't deal with this issue carefully, you can end up with a tax penalty. Choosing to take responsibility for your retirement money instead of leaving it with your employer is also a wise way to diversify your investment assets. Most 401(k) plans have very limited investment choices that you have no control over, but changing jobs gives you the opportunity to move your 401(k) to a mutual fund family or set up a self-directed IRA using no-load mutual funds, or to a discount brokerage firm like Discover, Charles Schwab, Waterhouse, or Quick and Reilly. You can also talk to investment consultants at your bank, but keep in mind that they will probably recommend mutual funds investments that eat up 4–5 percent of your investment dollars in commissions. Since 1993, the rules on transferring tax-deferred accounts have changed. You must now make a "trustee-to-trustee" transfer that does not allow you to get your hands on the cash for 60 days as they did in the past. If the check is made out to you, the IRS assumes that you have cashed it and used it. Have your employer send the check directly to whatever new retirement account you choose to open.

Action Step:

Safeco Mutual funds at 800–426–6730 and T. Rowe Price at 800–541–8460 both offer excellent brochures explaining the steps and procedures for rolling over an IRA, 401(k) plan, or pension distribution.

Day 343

MONEY MILESTONES

Money is better than poverty—if only for financial reasons.

—Woody Allen

The older you get, the less you care to remember birthdays as they accumulate, but there are several ages that you should mark on the calendar when planning for retirement.

50   If your spouse is deceased, you, as the survivor, can begin collect-
        ing his or her Social Security retirement benefits if you are dis-
        abled. If you are not disabled, you must remain single and wait
        until you reach age 60 to start collecting.

55   You may take penalty-free withdrawals from employer-sponsored
        retirement plans such as a 401(k), 403(b), or 457 plans if you no
        longer work at the sponsoring company.

59½   You can begin withdrawing money from any and all retirement
        investments including IRAs, tax-deferred annuities, 401(k) and
        similar plans without worrying about the 10 percent tax penalty.
        Speak to your accountant about a payout schedule and to learn
        what your taxes will be on your minimum withdrawal.

60   Surviving spouses who aren't disabled and haven't remarried can
        begin receiving 71.5 percent of the retirement benefits that would
        have gone to their deceased spouse.

62   You can begin collecting Social Security, but you will forfeit as
        much as 20 percent of the amount you would have received if you
        had waited until you reached age 65. This is also the minimum age
        to apply for a reverse annuity mortgage.

65   If you reach 65 before 2000, you can collect full retirement bene-
        fits. Medicare eligibility starts on the first day of the month you
        reach age 65.

65–69   If you continue working after you start receiving Social Security,
        the maximum you can earn before paying taxes is $14,500. This
        penalty vanishes at age 70.

70½   You must take income from all your tax-deferrred retirement plans
        by April 1 of the year after you reach 70½ whether you need the
        money or not.

Action Step:

Mark each of these ages and dates on a calendar for future reference. Visit *Agenet* on the Web at http://www.agenet.com to keep up-
to-date on financial and legal news affecting retired senior citizens.

Day 344

NEW RETIREMENT LIFESTYLES

*Many otherwise intelligent adults save for retirement the same
way they studied for exams: Wait until the last moment and cram.*

—Carolina Edwards

At 71, Maurice B. has buried his wife, Rachel, and decided that
their three-story, four-bedroom house was finally too much for him
to maintain on his own. Although Maurice still enjoys a round of
golf once a week and attends the health club to go swimming a couple of times a week, the isolation of living alone has led to depression.
With his diabetes and arthritis, he has found it hard and expensive to
continue to live alone. His two sons, now married with children, no
longer live in the same city and are not able to provide a comfortable
living space for him. Nor does Maurice want to be a burden to them,
financially or socially. He has decided to sell his home and live in an
assisted living community. Assisted living is a new choice that many
senior citizens are considering. It provides private space for residen-
tial housing, with supportive services such as meals, laundry, and
housekeeping, as well as minimal health care monitoring. Because
they are living longer and have lower incomes, and need some attention and maintenance, many elderly have been forced to change how
they spend their later years, particularly if they are in good health
and don't need to be in nursing homes. Most assisted living commu-
nities offer a variety of options, from independent support services
to assisted nursing care, based on individual need. These living
arrangements, however, must be paid for out of the individual's private income. They do not qualify for federal funding.

Action Step:

Contact Senior Living Alternatives at 800–350–0770 or visit the
Web site at http://www.senioralternatives.com for in-depth information about how you might explore this new retirement lifestyle.

Day 345

THE MEDICARE MAZE

Three months before you reach 65, you qualify for Medicare coverage, which is offered in two parts, and you must fill out an application for both.

Medicare Part A covers hospital insurance or skilled nursing care in a hospice, lab tests, X-rays, prescription drugs, and all related medical supplies and appliances. Monthly premiums as of September 1998 are $221, but you don't have to pay them. The U.S. government Medicare Trust includes this as part of your Social Security benefit.

Medicare Part B covers doctors' fees and services, outpatient care, clinical lab tests, X-rays, and medical supplies that are part of your treatment which cannot be self-administered. Part B is optional and can be applied for later, but there is a 10 percent surcharge added for each 12-month period that you could have been enrolled but were not. Monthly premiums for Part B as of September 1998 are $43.80 and must be paid by you.

Action Step:

If your Medicare provider has not responded to your queries or if you suspect fraud, abuse, or mismanagement of your Medicare services, call the Health Care Financing Administration at 800–638–6833 for advice and assistance. When you request your application for Medicare you should also get a free copy of *The Medicare Handbook* from the U.S. Department of Health and Human Services, 6325 Security Boulevard, Baltimore, MD 21207–5187.

Day 346

SELF-EMPLOYMENT BENEFITS

He who waits for a dead man's shoes is in danger of going barefoot.

—Danish Saying

If you have a small business that you run on a part-time basis, such as selling Amway, Avon, or Mary Kay, you are a self-employed person. You are responsible for recording and deducting expenses and paying taxes on the new difference. Use that money to contribute to a supplementary retirement plan and reduce those taxes.

1. IRAs. If you earn at least $2,000 in self-employed income you can put up to $2,000 into an equity mutual fund and leave it there until you reach 59½.
2. SEP-IRAs. You can donate up to 13.0435 percent of your net earnings or $24,000, after deducting all expenses on Schedule C of your income taxes.
3. Simple IRAs. A new simplified pension plan for small businesses that allow you to put away up to $6,000 a year. If you have any employees they must be given the chance to make the same contribution to the plan.
4. Keogh Plan. This is a more complex plan but it allows you to put away 20 percent or up to $30,000 of self-employment income.

Action Step:

Any bank, brokerage firm, or mutual fund company will provide several excellent brochures that explain your choices. Investment counselors at one of the Dreyfus (800–645–6561), Vanguard (800–962–5161), or Fidelity (800–544–3069) walk-in offices will advise you. The Armchair Millionaire, an investment Web site from Charles Schwab, offers several pages that help you to evaluate which retirement plan works for you. Check out http://www.armchairmillionaire.com.

Day 347

COBRA

If you retire before 65 you still have health benefits under this law, the Consolidated Omnibus Budget Reconciliation Act, which was passed in 1986. It requires any employer with more than 20 employees to continue your health benefits for up to 18 months after you retire—with one catch. You must pay for it yourself. The cost can range from $150 to $250 a month for a single person and $350 to $500 a month for a family plus 2 percent administrative fees since you are now unemployed.

Action Step:

Ask your employer about the individual cost of health insurance so you won't be surprised and can fit it into your retirement budget.

Day 348

LUMP SUM OR MONTHLY PAYOUT

You're about to punch that time clock for the last time, get your gold watch, buy your RV, and head off into the sunset, but first you have to decide what to do with that lump sum they plan to give you after the retirement party. Since you know this day is coming, congratulate yourself on having achieved as much as you have and now having the freedom and the time to pursue so many other interests that matter to you, whether it's more time with the family, a second business, time to travel, that woodworking or gardening hobby you've wanted to develop—if you have saved and invested as you wanted to do you can do these things in comfort.

Action Step:

Meet with a CPA, an attorney, and an investment adviser who can help you maintain what you have accumulated, continue to allow it to grow with caution and look forward to the next 30 years without having to think about working!

Day 349

CONTEMPLATION OF MORTALITY

Death does not discriminate. All cultures have traditions and rituals surrounding death that are older than time. In Ghana, the Akan people dance, sing, and celebrate the life of the deceased with a five-day feast. The body is washed and dressed by the surviving spouse and close family members. The casket, which has been ordered, designed, and paid for long before the event, is an elaborately carved work of art that is exhibited for all to admire as a symbol of respect for the worldly achievements of the departed one. In Israel, the deceased is not embalmed and, according the strictest traditions, is buried in the simplest casket within 24 hours of death.

The desire for death with dignity transcends gender, race, culture, and financial status. At some point in life it's best to make a statement of how you would like your final passage out of this life to be arranged. Straightforward handling of the legal and financial issues surrounding death and the transfer of assets will make your funeral and the dispersal of your estate less agonizing for your survivors.

Day 350

PLANNING THE END OF YOUR LIFE

As more than 70 million baby boomers approach retirement, the health issues related to aging are beginning to attract more attention. Medical technology has improved to the point of being able to keep a comatose patient alive almost indefinitely regardless of the quality of life. Unless you have previously specified in writing how you would like this kind of situation to be handled, the hospital is legally required to make every effort to keep you alive. The ongoing medical services could drain away valuable financial resources needed to sustain your survivors. Creating a living will is a gracious, loving gift that you extend to your loved ones. It is also a way to be sensitive to their emotional concerns for your care as your health declines. The *Five Wishes* document addresses some painful but necessary questions about the end of your life. It allows you to designate:

1. Who will be responsible for making your health decisions if you are comatose and unable to respond.
2. What kind of medical treatment you want and do not want administered, including how long you want to be kept on a feeding tube if you're brain dead.
3. How comfortable you want to be, including how much medication you want for pain, and if you want to be allowed to leave the hospital to spend your last days at home.
4. How you want people to treat you. Medical professionals may avoid discussing all the details of your condition directly with you unless you specify that you want to be told.
5. What you want your family to know about your condition and when you want them to be notified.

Action Step:

Contact Five Wishes at 215 South Monroe Street, Suite 620, Tallahassee, FL 32302 for a copy of a form that designates how you want health issues handled if you become terminally ill. You can also download a copy of it from the Web site at http://www.agingwith-dignity.org or call 888–594–7437.

Day 351

LIFE'S PAPER TRAIL

Nobody who has wealth to distribute ever omits himself.

—Leon Trotsky

For eight years Oliver Harris worked as a systems analyst for a large mid-Atlantic computer company, earning a comfortable $82,000 plus benefits. His reputation as a good technical troubleshooter was well-earned, given the overtime hours he put in. His 401(k) plan savings were small since he had borrowed 50 percent of the funds in it to make a down payment on his condo, which was worth about $180,000. He also owned a vacation time-share condo in Puerto Rico, valued at $79,500, which he visited twice a year. Oliver drove to work in a 1996 Honda and treated himself every payday to flowers from a flower shop two blocks from his apartment. When he got an extra bonus check or added income from working overtime, he purchased paintings and sculpture by up-and-coming young Caribbean artists. For Mother's Day each year he showered his mother with two dozen roses, and when she retired from her job as a secretary in the Minneapolis school system where she had worked for more than 30 years he treated her to a Caribbean cruise. His greatest weakness and biggest hobby was collecting signed first edition art books. These facts were pulled together from Oliver's careful records by the administrator of Oliver's estate when his will was finally probated three years after his sudden death in an automobile accident.

We leave behind a paper trail in the receipts, invoices, and canceled checks that document the financial choices and habits we develop over a lifetime. Do your family a wonderful favor: get your records in order. Good records are also essential to keeping track of your dollars and documenting your assets in case you are audited by the IRS or want to get a mortgage.

Action Step:

Set up a filing system for vital papers, such as your will, income tax statements, insurance policies, pension and Social Security records, credit card bills, canceled checks and receipts, and medical records in a location that is easily accessible for you and your family. Call Nolo Software at 800–992–NOLO for a copy of its Personal Recordkeeper ($29.95), which will guide you through establishing computerized financial records.

Day 352

SAFE DEPOSIT BOXES

Your bank is the best place to safely store irreplaceable records. The cost of a safe deposit box will depend on the size of the box and the size of your bank balance. If you have several accounts with a particular bank, you may be entitled to this benefit at no cost, otherwise you can count on spending from $12 to $100 a year to protect your documents. Your box is the place for original copies of:

1. Birth and death certificates, adoption papers, marriage licenses, divorce papers.

2. Real estate deeds, business ownership documents, and satisfied mortgages.
3. Copies of wills, living trust agreements.
4. Citizenship papers, military discharge documents, and naturalization records.
5. Stock certificates, savings bonds, investment records, and automobile titles.
6. Family heirlooms, such as jewelry, photographs, and mementos.
7. Insurance policies—life and homeowner's.
8. Photographic or video records of special items in your home, such as antiques, paintings, furs, and jewelry.
9. Coin and stamp collections.
10. Appraisals of collectors' items that you own.

Action Step:

Call your bank and find out what the fees are for maintaining safe deposit boxes and their availability at your branch.

Day 353

FINDING ESTATE PLANNING ADVISORS

To accept good advice is but to increase one's own ability.

—Johann Wolfgang von Goethe

The laws, regulations, and taxes related to passing on your assets to the next generation can change from year to year and vary from state to state, so you should seek out someone who is a specialist in estate issues. Federal regulations require that if you have total assets of $650,000 or more, your heirs will owe taxes on whatever part of the estate exceeds that amount. Federal estate taxes begin at 37 percent on $650,000 and can go as high as 55 percent on $3 million. Don't approach such a vital issue alone. Experienced professionals are worth every penny that you will pay them for their right advice in this area. Fees for a good financial adviser or CPA can range from an hourly rate of $150 to $300. A comprehensive, written analysis can take several months and will cost anywhere from $3,000 to $6,000. This may sound pricey, but think about the time and taxes your family will save in the long run.

Here are the top three nationally know professional organizations for CPAs. They can refer you to a local financial advisor who can assist you.

1. National Association of Personal Financial Advisors, 888–FEE–ONLY.
2. Institute of Certified Financial Planners, 888–237–6275.
3. American Institute of Certified Public Accountants, 888–999–9256.

You can also ask your local chapter of the American Bar Association for a referral.

Action Step:

After you have made a net worth statement and compiled a list of questions, make the call to one of these organizations for some professional help. Ask your accountant or a bank officer for a referral to an estate planning professional who is not an insurance agent in your area. Some tips on selecting an adviser are available from the Better Business Bureau at 703–276–0100 and at http://www.bbb.org.

Day 354

PEACEFUL RESOLUTION

There are several ways in which to apportion the family income, all of them unsatisfactory.

—Robert Benchley

All historical evidence indicates that you don't get out of this life alive. Since hearses don't have U-Hauls behind them, you have to make some arrangements for how you want your survivors to handle what you leave behind. The house, the pearl necklace, and the book collection, as well as the stocks, bonds, and insurance policies, have to be doled out and accounted for in writing before your earthly business is finished. That way, your heirs can avoid the fights, arguments, misunderstandings, and hurt feelings that are likely to take place once you are gone if you don't specify that you want Cousin Hazel to have your fur coat and your nephew Lewis to have your collection of Vietnam peace rally posters. Too many lawyers, courts, and state tax authorities fill their coffers because of the reluctance shown by the deceased when they were above ground to confront these issues and make decisions about how to allocate assets. Thinking about dying won't bring it on, but it will make it easier for you and your spouse to be in control while you still have a choice.

Action Step:

Contact WillWorks at 888–838–2497 to get information about its online will-writing service. It's $49.95 for a single person, or $79.95 for two wills for a couple. Its Internet site at http://www.willworks.com offers a simple five-page questionnaire that will guide you through the process of writing a will.

Day 355

LIVING WILLS

Medical science has now made it possible for us to live at least 30 years beyond retirement and treat us for illnesses long after our mental faculties have diminished. If you do not want to be kept alive and on a life-support system you must put it in writing. Your family members should be aware of your decision, and your doctor and the hospital where you have medical records should be made aware of your choice. This decision could mean the difference between salvaging the family fortune for your survivors or draining the family coffers for your medical care. The choice is in your hands—before you become ill.

Action Step:

Contact Choice in Dying at 200 Varick Street, New York, NY 10014, 212–366–5540, to get copies of its booklet on how living wills should be written. It will also supply you with a sample form and inform you if living wills are legal in your state.

Day 356

GIVING AWAY YOUR POWER

A power of attorney is a legal document that gives another person the right to act on your behalf in some legal or financial capacity. If you're going to Europe on an extended vacation, relocating because of your job, and your house still needs to be sold, you can give power of attorney to a relative to sign and close the deal for you. If you become ill and incapacitated, this document allows a relative or designated friend to handle your affairs. This should be a temporary arrangement, meaning that the power of attorney will expire as of some preset date so the person won't have access to your bank account on an indefinite basis. There are two forms:

1. General power of attorney. This give another party the right to act on your behalf in some business or financial matter when you are unavailable but it becomes invalid if you become ill or incapacitated.
2. Durable power of attorney. This covers illness, accidents, and any form of representation as long as you live. It allows your accountant or attorney to sign checks, buy and sell property and securities, and manage your business affairs for you, which could lead to abusing the privilege. You can find sample copies in a legal stationery store for about $2 per copy or have an attorney create a special document for you, but the cost can be $200 to $500.

Action Step:

Take a look at the various forms that you will need by visiting the Web site at http://www.easylegalforms.com or calling 888–891–1578 to get copies of the brochure.

Day 357

PREPLANNING FUNERALS

Though one of the hardest topics to discuss in many families, planning funerals is an extremely important issue to talk about before a crisis occurs. Funeral expenses can be as varied as any other financial concern based on your preferences. A $600 cremation can be followed by a modest memorial service, or an extravagant service with flowers and limousines, and an ornate casket and headstones can cost in excess of $12,000. Your survivors could be too grief-stricken and stressed out to make a clear-headed decision, so laying out the details before the event can be a sensitive gesture on your part to help keep costs under control as well as to ease the burden for your family. Keep your funeral planning list in some obvious and convenient place and tell your relatives where it is. If you include this information in your will and put it away in your safe deposit box, it could be too late before anyone notices it.

Action Step:

Call 800–955–3337 about Pre-Need Funeral Planning Software ($39.95) or check out the Web site at http://www.funeral-software.com to evaluate your funeral planning needs.

Day 358

HEALTH MATTERS

Decide who will be your health power of attorney. This person should be able to make decisions for you in case you are comatose and cannot respond to the information and participate in the decision making for your own care. Someone in the family or a close friend/lover/companion should have a copy of your medical history. Set up a file of all your recent medical treatments and the various prescriptions you are taking and put it in some obvious place and give it to a family member.

Action Step:

Spend a Saturday organizing your financial documents and put them in a file box with clear labels attached to them. If you need help call Financial Advantage at 800–695–3453 for a copy of its Financial Planning Kit. It includes a 48-page handbook explaining how to set up files with suggested labels and dividers.

Day 359

ELDER CARE COUNSELING

The only things you can count on are an old dog, an old wife and ready money.

—Ben Franklin

The laws that govern your life when you reach age 65 are so complex that a whole new specialty has been created in the legal profession called elder care law. Attorneys in this field can advise you on the proper way to manage your funds in retirement, how to set up trusts and estates, and the appropriate form of living will that your state has approved. Elder law consultants are usually attorneys who specialize in the legal and financial issues of the elderly. Find a firm that can advise you and help. The fees for these attorneys are typically $150 an hour, but they usually offer a 30-minute "getting to know you" consultation at no cost. Make sure they have references to offer and make you feel comfortable with them.

Action Step:

Ask a friend or relative who is an attorney for a referral or call your local bar association to find out if there is a firm in your area that can assist you with your questions. Take advantage of at least one free appointment but prepare your questions before you arrive in the office. The National Academy of Elder Law Attorneys at 520–881–4005, http://www.naela.com, can refer you to one of its members in your area.

LONG-TERM CARE INSURANCE

Nothing in life is to be feared. It is only to be understood.

—Marie Curie

No one looks forward to the aging process, but one painful truth we must accept is that sooner or later our bodies will become infirm and we will probably need assistance to manage the most menial daily tasks. Nearly 32 percent of senior citizens need long-term health care as they age, varying from convalescent care to modified medical assistance and supervision. Daily rates for nursing homes vary from $90 a day to $225 a day, and these costs are not fully covered by Medicare. If you're in good health at age 55, with no family history of serious illnesses, you will probably live to be 90, but there's no guarantee of what your physical condition will be. Medicare does not cover long-term care in nursing homes or home-based nursing care. If you anticipate needing health care assistance, you want to be prepared for the $35,000 to $90,000 annual cost of such care. If you don't want to bankrupt yourself and your family in order to be taken care of, you should investigate long-term care insurance. Look for a policy that:

1. Pays a benefit of at least $110 a day.
2. Provides a minimum of three years of coverage, although four years is preferred.
3. Has a short waiting period of less than 90 days.
4. Offers payments that will automatically keep pace with inflation.
5. Has premiums that will remains stable as you age.
6. Covers home-based care and custodial care as well as nursing home care.
7. Has a waiver of premium once you become ill and confined to a home.

Use your membership in AARP to get unbiased advice and useful information on how to evaluate these policies.

Premiums are based on your age and the state in which you live. At 60, a couple will pay about $4,800 a year. If you wait until 75, the premiums can skyrocket to $15,000 a year. Most companies stop selling policies to anyone over 80.

Action Step:

Get a free copy of *The Consumer's Guide to Long-Term Care Insurance* from the Health Insurance Association of America, 555 13th Street, N.W., Suite 600 East, Washington, DC 20004. You can call 202–824–1600.

Day 361

CHOOSING AN EXECUTOR

Few rich men own their property. Their property owns them.

—Robert Ingersoll

The most important person in the estate planning process is the executor. This person must represent your wishes and follow through on tidying up your personal affairs after you're gone. It's time-consuming and paper-intensive so you must choose carefully and discuss this responsibility with the person before you surprise him or her at the reading of the will. The best choice is someone who lives nearby, has some knowledge of your financial affairs, knows where your records are kept, and has the integrity to get the job done promptly. Fees can add up and tax bills can mount from delayed filings and mismanagement of assets and paperwork. Executors are usually paid 5 percent of the total amount of the estate, which is modest when you realize how much work has to be done. The major duties of the executor are:

1. Pay all your final bills including the undertaker, the hospital, the mortgage, and complete other paperwork.
2. Assemble a list of assets such as bank and brokerage accounts, insurance policies, and retirement plans, including debts owed the deceased and final paychecks.
3. Notify Social Security and all government agencies of your demise.
4. Work with your accountant to file your final tax return.
5. Distribute any remaining assets to your heirs as designated in your will.

Action Step:

Talk to your family members and decide if you want a relative or an attorney or accountant to be your executor. You may also appoint coexecutors to assure that the work gets done properly and on schedule.

Day 362

EASY WAYS TO AVOID PROBATE

First, kill all the lawyers!

—William Shakespeare

Probate is an expensive, time-consuming process that may not be necessary if you carefully plan your affairs. Here are a few moves you can make that avoid going to court:

1. Register your brokerage/investment accounts in beneficiary form. That way your heirs have no rights to your money while you're alive but will inherit your stocks and bonds without probate after you pass on.

2. Specify beneficiaries on your IRA and 401(k) plans. Whatever is left in the account will be transferred to them without getting tied up in court.

3. Set up "POD"—payable on death—accounts at your bank. If you notify the bank of the designated beneficiaries, your heirs will be able to collect the funds only when they present a death certificate.

4. Hold property in joint ownership. Assets such as cars and houses can be passed on to a spouse or a child by designating that the ownership be filed with the letters JTWROS, which means "joint tenancy with right of survivorship."

5. Small estates frequently can avoid the probate process, depending on the total value of the deceased's assets. Heirs must file a copy of the will, a copy of the death certificate, and a short affidavit verifying the right to inherit. After court approval—which can take two days or two weeks, depending on the jurisdiction—the financial institutions that receive these documents will release the designated money or property. Laws vary from state to state and each state defines its own version of what is a "small estate" ($500 in Mississippi, $10,000 in New York, and $200,000 in Nevada).

Action Step:

Find out how your bank and brokerage accounts can be transferred to your heirs after your death, and what forms are used. Check with an attorney or financial adviser who handles small estates to find out what the threshold for avoiding probate is in your state. *Probate: A Practical Guide for Settling an Estate* is published by HALT, an organization created to limit the need for lawyers. Membership is $15. Write to: HALT, 1319 F Street, N.W. Washington, DC 20005.

Day 363

JULIUS ROSENWALD

Born in Springfield, Illinois, in 1862, Julius Rosenwald worked in the clothing business in New York before setting up his own retail store at age 21. His next step was to build his own manufacturing plant in Chicago so he could make his own clothing. Not a particularly remarkable story until Rosenwald started to deliver goods to Richard Sears of the new direct mail business that eventually became Sears Roebuck & Co. Sears became known for honesty and plain talk rather than slick sales pitches. What you saw advertised was what you got, and you paid the price in full in cash. (COD could be negotiated, but for the cheapest bargains it was cash on the barrelhead, a proposition that appealed to hardworking farmers and skeptical small townsfolk.) Rosenwald had excellent credit so he borrowed money and bought a one-fourth interest in Sears for $37,500. He so impressed Sears with his managerial skills that Sears made him vice president of the company in 1895. In 1907, their separate visions of how to run the business clashed. Sears wanted to spend more for advertising but Rosenwald thought it prudent to cut expenses during economic instability. Sears retired as president in 1908, although he remained chairman of the board. When he died in 1914 Rosenwald became president, until his own death in 1932. Some of the practices he instituted were money-back guarantees, "send-no-money" advertising, employee profit-sharing plans, and stock options. When he died, Rosenwald's wealth was estimated at $80 million dollars; $63 million went to philanthropic causes. He established the Museum of Science and Industry in Chicago, built over 50 YMCAs across the country, and donated thousands of dollars to building schools for black children in the rural South through the Rosenwald fund.

Day 364

LIVING TRUSTS

Money is like an arm or a leg—use it or lose it.

—Henry Ford

This estate planning technique, also known as an inter vivos or family trust, has become quite popular in the last two decades as another means of avoiding probate and keeping your financial matters private. Living trusts are not "do it yourself" legal matters. The fee for an attorney to set up a trust can range from as little as $650 to $5,000 for the paperwork. You should also have a will done as a mechanism to move all new assets or unaccounted-for assets into the trust upon your demise. A trust can be revocable or irrevocable, meaning that once the assets are transferred into an irrevocable trust it cannot be broken except by declaring yourself mentally ill when you set it up. A complex problem with trusts is that you personally do not own your assets anymore. You can appoint yourself as trustee of the trust but you should also have another person as co-trustee for legal purposes. The trust is a useless waste of time if you initiate the paperwork but don't change the titles and ownership papers that transfer the assets such as your house, rental real estate, cars, investment accounts, and so on into the trust. Think twice about doing it and study the pros and cons with a good attorney before you do this.

Action Step:

"Estate Planning Through Trusts" is a free booklet that is available from Neuberger & Berman Trust Company, 605 Third Avenue, New York, NY 10158, 212–47–9100. Nolo Press also has an excellent self-help book, *Plan Your Estate with a Living Trust* ($19.95) available through its Web site at http://www.nolopress.com.

Day 365

TESTAMENTARY TRUSTS

Put not your trust in money, but put your money in trust.

—Oliver Wendell Holmes

Testamentary trusts are an excellent alternative to using a living trust. They become legal only when you finally close your eyes for the last time, but the terms and guidelines for how you want it to operate have to be created in your will. The terms of the trust are kept private, therefore your wishes are shielded from public eyes. It can also be an irrevocable document.

Testamentary trusts can also be used to isolate special funds out of your estate for a special purpose such as college costs for minor children or a disabled child. If you are in a second marriage and want to preserve property for children from a first marriage you can specify that in a testamentary trust, but try not to go too far and control things from the grave. Consult with an attorney and an accountant to understand the tax implications of these decisions.

Action Step:

Call your local bar association for referral to an attorney who specializes in trusts and estate matters. Look for a copy of *The Complete Book of Trusts* (John Wiley, $24.95) by Martin Shenkman to get answers on how a trust can work for you.

Final Thoughts

My ultimate goal in writing this book was to make it simple, comfortable, and easy for you to understand that money does not have to be frightening, overwhelming, or difficult to understand. If you have followed the steps that have been laid out for you here you have gained an elementary but competent understanding of how money operates in your life, what choices you have in the money management game, and a good idea of how you can begin to take charge of your financial future. If you haven't followed the steps each day, that's okay, too. You may start over, go back through the days and review what you've learned, or at least be ready to graduate to more complex books and publications to enlighten you in the wealth-building process.

If you want to share your thoughts, ideas or questions with me after going through a year of using this book, you can reach me at:

P.O. Box 400450

Pratt Station

Brooklyn, NY 11240-0450

Web site: http://www.brookestephens.com

E-mail address: StephensB@aol.com

INDEX

2/5/78